Misrecognitions

Misrecognitions

Gillian Rose and the Task
of Political Theology

Edited by
Joshua B. Davis

CASCADE Books • Eugene, Oregon

MISRECOGNITIONS
Gillian Rose and the Task of Political Theology

Copyright © 2018 Wipf and Stock Publishers. All rights reserved. Except for brief quotations in critical publications or reviews, no part of this book may be reproduced in any manner without prior written permission from the publisher. Write: Permissions, Wipf and Stock Publishers, 199 W. 8th Ave., Suite 3, Eugene, OR 97401.

Cascade Books
An Imprint of Wipf and Stock Publishers
199 W. 8th Ave., Suite 3
Eugene, OR 97401

www.wipfandstock.com

PAPERBACK ISBN: 978-1-5326-1360-9
HARDCOVER ISBN: 978-1-5326-1362-3
EBOOK ISBN: 978-1-5326-1361-6

Cataloguing-in-Publication data:

Names: Davis, Joshua (Joshua Bradley), editor.

Title: Misrecognitions : Gillian Rose and the task of political theology / Joshua B. Davis.

Description: Eugene, OR : Cascade Books, 2018 | Includes bibliographical references and index.

Identifiers: ISBN 978-1-5326-1360-9 (paperback) | ISBN 978-1-5326-1362-3 (hardcover) | ISBN 978-1-5326-1361-6 (ebook)

Subjects: LCSH: Rose, Gillian. | Political theology. | Philosophy.

Classification: B1649.R74 M57 2018 (paperback) | B1649.R74 M57 (ebook)

Manufactured in the U.S.A.   11/01/18

For

Jeremiah Gabriel Davis

Jeremiah 31:33

Contents

Introduction: By Way of the Valley of Roses | 1
 —*Joshua B. Davis*

Part 1—The Struggle for Recognition: The City, the Middle, the Political

Chapter 1
Beginning in the Middle: The Third City and the Politics of Membership | 29
 —*Anna Rowlands*

Chapter 2
Toward a Rosean Political Theology of Recognition | 47
 —*Andrew Brower Latz*

Chapter 3
Rose *contra* Girard: Kenotic Comedy and Social Theory (Or, Žižek as a Reader of Rose) | 67
 —*Marcus Pound*

Chapter 4
"The Tree Is Really Rooted in the Sky": Beside Difficulty in Gillian Rose's Political Theory | 87
 —*Kate Schick*

Part 2—Thinking the Absolute: Law, Education, Theology

Chapter 5
Mis(re)cognition of God and Man: The Educational Philosophy and Politics of Gillian Rose | 109
 —*Rebekah Howes*

Chapter 6
Between Hegel and Wittgenstein: Reflections in the Wake of Gillian Rose and Rowan Williams | 126
   —*Gavin Hyman*

Chapter 7
One Absolute Substance | 143
   —*Joseph W. H. Lough*

Chapter 8
"A Frenzy of Self-Deceit": Commodity Fetishism, Labor, and Rose's Critical Marxism | 175
   —*Joshua B. Davis*

Chapter 9
Law All the Way Down: Gillian Rose and Robert Cover as Jewish Philosophers | 202
   —*Vincent Lloyd*

Index | 227

Introduction

By Way of the Valley of Roses

JOSHUA B. DAVIS

... There are achievements
that carry failure on their back, blindness
not as in Brueghel, but unfathomably
far-seeing.[1]

—GEOFFREY HILL

We've got to bring the soul and the city back together somehow and stop separating them off intellectually and culturally. I think that, in the wake of the perceived demise of Marxism and of Heidegger's Nazism, everybody's looking for an ethics. But in fact they should be looking for a political theology. We need to think about God and the polis and not about this anodyne "love ethic."

— GILLIAN ROSE[2]

Gillian Rose is equivocal—like the middle she commended to us. She is not ambiguous and in no way coy. She is vulnerable and difficult. Before her death to ovarian cancer at the age of forty-eight in 1995, Rose

1. Hill, "In Memorium: Gillian Rose."
2. Lloyd, ed., "Interview with Gillian Rose," 7–8.

wrote a sizable body of work that is as fierce in its beauty as it is strange in its passions. The cornerstone of her project is an idiosyncratic and, some might say, dubious reading of Hegel, but it is a reading that is often most instructive at the point that her voice overwhelms Hegel's. She attempted to reestablish critical theory on that reading of Hegel, and developed out of it a unique analysis of modern society and philosophy, which made jurisprudence the central focus. She challenged the fundamental tenants of social theory, structuralism, and postmodern philosophy championed by her contemporaries, and she did so with a vision whose main themes were established early, even as they expanded in scope and changed in subtle ways. Nevertheless, despite her boldness, candor, and consistency, there is an unusual variance in interpretation among Rose's readers.

For some Rose is the erstwhile Marxist, a child of the Frankfurt School, who boldly set out to forge a path beyond their impasses. For others, Rose is a relentless political realist, forcing us to submit our utopian and revolutionary illusions to the compromised struggles of everyday political life. For others, Rose is the paragon of a politics of recognition, the attempt to found a broad and pragmatic cosmopolitan liberalism on the phenomenological critique and embrace of our limitations. For others, she is one of the great Jewish philosophers of the twentieth century, and rightfully takes her place among the other women thinkers of Jewish history—Rahel Varnhagen, Hannah Arendt, and Rosa Luxemburg, whom she names explicitly. For yet others, Rose is a religious thinker, a Jewish philosopher, a nascent Christian theologian, and perhaps some kind of mystic.

Perhaps this variation in interpretation is due, at least in part, to Rose's relentless compelling of her readers to interrogate their immediate assumptions about the world, themselves, and others. Indeed, Rose wants to situate the critique of illusion at the center of social life, a task made all the more imperative, according to her, by the fact that modern social life is riven by the contradictions of bourgeois law. "My relation to myself," she says in perhaps her most lapidary formulation, "is mediated by what I recognize or refuse to recognize in your relation to yourself."[3] This well captures what is at stake on the matter of equivocation. What matters in how I understand myself is not the truth that I succeed in communicating either to myself or another, but that I understand myself on the basis of what I recognize or misrecognize in how *you understand yourself*. Social relations are complex, dynamic interchanges that proliferate exponentially through these reciprocal variations of recognitions and misrecognitions. We never secure communication, meaning, or knowledge of ourselves or another, but this is not

---

3. Rose, *Mourning Becomes the Law*, 74.

a sad—although it may require mourning—but happy fault, a *felix culpa*. This movement of understanding, failing to understand, and yet continuing to speak and understand is a relation, whether to the world, ourselves, or another. Rose is not captivated by what we cannot grasp in the relation, but by the fact that communication and knowing always take place in a relation.

So, Rose is equivocal, but this is as much about us, her readers, as it is about her. Of course, this fact is no truer of Rose than any other writer, but she is relentless in exposing us to the experience of that fact. One may read and reread one of Rose's works, even just a paragraph, and experience the difficulty, the struggle to comprehend, the dynamic movement of meaning as it happens in what we recognize or fail to recognize in our relation to her. This is certainly true of her early works, which she tells us are written in the "severe style," and which trod through the esoteric worlds of German Idealism and critical theory. But it is no less so with her late, autobiographical writings, which are colloquial and meditative. Rose gives us the experience of the work, the struggle that is involved in all hearing, knowing, seeing, loving.

Unlike the major postmodern theorists who were her contemporaries, Rose was adamant that truth and meaning are real and not simply arbitrary. What interested her was not the absence or instability of truth, but the fact that unpredictability and even failure are essential aspects of all truth worthy of the name. For Rose, every act of communication or meaningful understanding entails a fundamental risk—of failure, falsehood, misunderstanding, devastation, loss. These acts have no sure place from which to begin or end, but all meaning, love, joy, and justice in the world is real because it was risked. Rose is enthralled, enraged, invested by this strange reality that even our failures bond us, communicating and meaning sometimes much more than what we take for our successes. The meaning, the truth, that happens between us, the world, and others—a meaning of which we are often unaware—this is law, for Rose, and it cannot be obviated.

Readers of this collection of essays on Rose and political theology will surely be struck by the differences of interpretation and emphasis in her work. Each of these authors is indebted to Rose's reading of Hegel, contributions to critical theory, and social philosophy, and believes that her work is of considerable significance for political theology. They depart from one another, sometimes in considerable ways, in how they understand the development of Rose's work, how to interpret some of her key themes, and what their implications are for political theology. The result can, in some instances, make for sharp divergences not just regarding the details of Rose's body of work, but of its overall trajectory. Nevertheless, several key concepts in Rose's writing recur throughout these essays, and these are concepts that are of special importance for her work's relationship to political theology. These concepts are engaged, sometimes explicitly, sometimes implicitly, by each of the authors in the collection. A brief rehearsal of them, then, will be helpful for the reader.

Political Theology

Some clarification about the use of the term *political theology* and what it means in the collection are in order. *Political theology* is itself equivocal. It has one quite specific meaning within the discipline of academic theology, a different but often overlapping meaning within religious studies and critical theory, and a still further meaning that is specific to Rose's *The Broken Middle*. First, within theological studies, the term refers to a series of German theologians, like Johann Baptist Metz, Dorothee Sölle, and Jürgen Moltmann, who at the close of the 1960s and beginning of the 1970s drew on the resources of critical theory to think through the reasons for German Christians' failure to resist Nazism. Political theology, in this sense, represented an attempt to develop the social and political implications of Christian faith in direct relation to social, material, and historical life. It was a development within European Christianity, however, and one that wanted in particular to critique its bourgeois form. These distinctive qualities distinguished it from liberation theology, which was also intent on developing the political implications of Christian theology, but which arose from among oppressed and minority communities in colonial and postcolonial contexts.[4]

Second, in recent years, another meaning of political theology has gained prominence in continental philosophy and theory due to the increased attention that the German jurist and philosopher Carl Schmitt's book *Political Theology* has received in recent years.[5] Thinkers like Jacob Taubes, Giorgio Agamben, Slavoj Žižek, and Chantal Mouffe have each developed in their own distinctive ways the particular meaning that Schmitt attributed to the term.[6] Schmitt's use of the term predates its use in European Christian theology, and he used it as a way of talking about his assertion that the categories of modern political theory are secularized theological concepts. Schmitt's understanding of political theology is quite close to one of Rose's central concerns: the speculative identity of the state and church (which I will discuss in a separate category below). In this regard, Rose's

---

4. See the discussion in Livingston et al., *Modern Christian Thought*, chap. 9.

5. Schmitt, *Political Theology*; and Schmitt, *Political Theology II*.

6. For example: Taubes, *The Political Theology of Paul*; Agamben, *The Kingdom and the Glory*; Mouffe, ed., *The Challenge of Carl Schmitt*; Žižek, *The Puppet and the Dwarf*.

INTRODUCTION   5

work is relevant to discussions of political theory that engage Schmitt's thesis, and especially as that thesis is developed by a thinker like Agamben, whose reflections aim to reveal the intimate imbrication of politics, theology, and philosophy. Today, political theology may refer to one or both of these ideas.

However, in the third place, Rose does use the term *political theology* in *The Broken Middle* as a general reference to a trend that she wants to reject. The examples of that trend are Johann Baptist Metz (whom she refers to, further confusing the terminology, as a *liberation* theologian), Emmanuel Levinas, Mark C. Taylor, and John Milbank. What she rejects in these forms of political theology is the tendency to invoke theological concepts to "mend" the broken middle between law and ethics. In the introduction to *The Broken Middle*, for example, she notes that political theology, in this sense, enters the discourse at the precise moment that comprehension of the middle's brokenness is disavowed. Political theology, in other words, is a ruse that confounds our condition. And yet, adding an even further layer of complexity, Rose recognized that it is, in fact, political theology that is needed to understand and address our condition. She stated in a late interview with Vincent Lloyd that, while everyone thinks what we need—after Nazism and the "supposed" demise of Marxism—is an ethics, "in fact, they should be looking for a political theology."[7] We can infer, based on Rose's growing interest at the time in theology, and Christianity in particular, that the best interpretation of this statement will include elements from all three of these uses of the term, and the reader will find all three represented in these pages.[8]

Finally, readers ought to bear in mind that Rose's work is not merely theoretical, but the whole of her body of work took shape in the shadow of Britain's conservative government's project of dismantling the social democracy and inauguration of what we today call neoliberalism.[9] She published her first book four years into Thatcher's service as prime minister, and died five years into John Major's. These years saw the collapse of state socialism[10] in the Soviet Union and Germany, and a massive pressure to commodify all aspects of social life, the rise of globalization, and the financialization

---

7. Lloyd, ed., "Interview with Gillian Rose," 210.

8. See Lloyd's introduction to his interview with Rose in ibid. As Lloyd points out, political theology means, for Rose, something that is metaphysical, ethical, and political at once.

9. See Harvey, *A Brief History of Neoliberalism*.

10. She notes this context as significant for her reflection in the introduction to *The Broken Middle*, and continued to speak about the *supposed* demise of Marxism.

of capital.[11] Rose makes the suggestive remark in the introduction to *The Broken Middle* (1993) that, in the wake of the collapse of state socialism, we are in a position to return our attention to the much more pressing issue of the intimate connection between liberalism and fascism.[12] Such a statement serves to remind us that Rose's project was born within the Frankfurt School, with its concern to analyze the subtle ways that fascism is reproduced within modern social and cultural life, as well as its intention of recuperating and reinventing the relevance of Marxism after the rise of state (as opposed to industrial) capitalism, in the wake of World War I. Rose's analyses are as much a response to the social conditions dawning at the end of the 1970s as the Frankfurt School was a response to the postwar world. Those same conditions that began in the 1970s are very much with us in the present, after the financial crisis of 2008, the dire threat of global warming, the increased rise of nationalist and racist politics, the Brexit vote in the UK, and the presidency of Donald Trump. Any reading of Rose that seeks to develop the consequences of her work for political theology will think through the consequences of her work in the light of how those conditions have unfolded in the twenty years since her death.

A Critical Marxism

Another issue is the status of Rose's project of critical Marxism in relation to her body of work as a whole. Rose makes programmatic statements at the end of *Hegel contra Sociology* that what she is doing is working out a "critical Marxism," one that can avoid the problems she finds in Marx and Marx*ism*, and that would not reinscribe the revolution into the bourgeois order it resists.[13] She means a project of social transformation that moved beyond the contradictions of bourgeois law and freedom, and in a way that was not susceptible (as traditional Marxism and state Socialism were) to reproducing that same form and its contradictions.

Several Marxist critics of Rose's critical Marxism have arisen since it was first proposed, the most salient being Peter Osborne[14] and Tony Gorman.[15] The common objection that Osborne and Gorman make, despite several differences in details, is that Rose's adoption of a phenomenological

11. See Mason, *Postcapitalism: A Guide to our Future*, 3–30.
12. Rose, *Broken Middle*, xi.
13. *Hegel contra Sociology*, 232–35.
14. Osborne, "Hegelian Phenomenology and the Critique of Reason and Society"; and Osborne, "Gillian Rose and Marxism."
15. Gorman, "Gillian Rose and the Project of a Critical Marxism."

method, her dependence on a critique of consciousness, may be sufficient for the analysis of the bourgeois relations but it cannot transform them. As Gorman put it, Rose's method does not grasp the "difference between the comprehension of the social in phenomenological reflection and its theorization by the critique of political economy."[16] As a result, Rose is compelled to give only a negative determination of what lies beyond the contradictions of bourgeois law and freedom, lest her proposal be reincorporated back into what she opposes. She does not give any account, according to Gorman, of the way that social life beyond capitalism is already present within bourgeois relations now. This problem arises because of Rose's privileging of subjective consciousness, which an objective, materialist analysis can obviate, so claim Osborne and Gorman.

A crucial aspect of this critique is the claim that, beginning from the publication of *The Broken Middle* (1992), which was published eight years after *Dialectic of Nihilism* (1984), Rose shifted her emphasis away from the project of objective social critique and toward "inwardness and an ethic of singularity."[17] This development is viewed as further evidence of the fundamental flaw in her Marxist project, and is interpreted to mean that the project was "shelved."[18] This question of the status of that project is of special relevance to political theology because Rose takes up direct engagement with political theology in *The Broken Middle* and because, for the next four years, Rose turned to theology more and more. What is more, many of those who work at the intersection of Rose's work and religion/theology seem to presume that this reading is correct in its conclusion that Rose abandoned that earlier project. Rowan Williams, for example, who defended Rose against Osborne's critique, does not attempt to show that Rose's later project is a critical Marxism, but seeks only to show that her later work does have political significance, while rehearsing Rose's own negative evaluations of Marx and Marxism. The outcome appears to be a general affirmation of multicultural liberalism and social democracy, an interpretation that Williams's own politics supports.[19] In general, the question of Rose's relationship to Marx remains underdeveloped among her religious and theological interpreters.

16. Ibid., 36n40, quoted in Osborne, "Gillian Rose and Marxism," 60.
17. Gorman, "Gillian Rose and the Project of a Critical Marxism," 25.
18. Osborne, "Gillian Rose and Marxism," 59.
19. Williams's reading of Rose is available in two essays. Williams, "Between Politics and Philosophy"; and Williams, "The Sadness of the King." A good example of the political results of this read is two editorials of his: Williams, "Leader: The Government Needs to Know How Afraid People Are"; and Williams, "Mass Democracy Has Failed."

It is fair to say that on this question, too, Rose is equivocal. What is at stake in her relationship to Marx is, in fact, a question that bears directly on the theological dimension of Rose and political theology. That is, it is really about whether the brokenness of the middle is a metaphysical reality, a transhistorical and constitutive aspect of consciousness and social life, or whether it is a contingent reality, a specific social and historical determination of consciousness and social life. Some authors address the issue directly, while others develop an interpretation that merely assumes a position on the matter. The metaphysical status of the middle is central to interpreting Rose's project, given the importance she ascribed to retrieving the mutual implication of metaphysics, ethics, and politics. How this question is answered, then, has far-reaching consequences for the way we read Rose. The nature of Rose's political project changes in substantial ways according to the answer one gives to the question. So readers will want to be attuned to what position the authors in this collection take on the question, especially where it is unstated. Can Rose's later work, for example, be interpreted in a way that is consistent with the project of critical Marxism, or does she develop a position that is much more consistent with liberal realism and pragmatism, which is John Milbank's allegation when he concludes that Rose adhered to the "end of history" narrative?[20] Put another way, is the broken middle the standpoint for all critical thought, as Williams's emphasis on its being "between metaphysics and politics" (continued in his most recent essay on Rose) suggests, or is the broken middle the object of critique, a social condition that is to be overcome? This is perhaps the most important issue of interpretation in Rose, and one for which there appears to be conflicting evidence.

Speculative Thought, Recognition, and Law

The revival of Hegel's idea of speculative reason is at the nerve center of Rose's project. Speculative thought is, one might say, a tactical response to the fundamental condition of reason as it is shaped by modern, liberal, capitalist social life. That condition takes a number of different conceptual forms, all of which are binary oppositions: universal/particular, theory/practice, necessity/freedom, state/church, law/ethics, etc. These binary pairs are instances, according to Rose, of the most basic contradiction in modern experience, which is that between objective, universal social life (law) and particular, subjective social life (morality). The "middle," which mediates the relation between these two poles is fractured—they do not have a

20. Milbank, "On the Paraethical: Gillian Rose and Political Nihilism," 76.

positive, mutual relation, and so they cannot be reconciled. Instead, this middle is, as Rose says, broken. It mediates only their perpetual opposition and contradiction.

Speculative reason, according to Rose, is not Hegel's way of achieving conceptual—that is, abstract—reconciliation of the contradictions between law and morality that shape our everyday experience. Rather, it is a kind of tactical use of reason that disrupts the illusions that our abstract concepts create, illusions that suppress our experience of everyday contradictions. Speculative reason makes these contradictions palpable to us, often for the first time, and with this awareness we can think through and confront their effect on us. Rose commends speculative reason in response to what she sees as the replete abstractness of reason's function in modern, liberal, capitalist social life. Our reason is abstract, she argues, because it is ensnared by its own attempts to think about the social reality that shapes it. Whenever reason attempts to conceptualize its social world, it resolves or mends the contradictions that rive it, hiding them from us. Our concepts of the social world are abstract, not because they are generalized, but because they deceive us about the reality we are seeking to understand. As a result, the normal condition of reasoning within the broken middle is a ruse where our attempts to understand the world only perpetuate our misrecognitions. With no concrete way of living the mutuality of law and ethics, with our social relations founded on their conflict, every concept of their unity will be an illusion. When reason mends the middle, in other words, it only deepens our alienation.

Rose's most illuminating statement of the stakes of this condition are set out in her lapidary distinction between the two cities, "old Athens" and "new Jerusalem."[21] Old Athens is the ancient ideal of the rational city of traditional forms of authority. Old Athens is the city in which the law is paramount, but that law lacks any critical concept that can justify its authority as more than arbitrary and abstract.[22] This is the reason that Antigone's conflict with Creon is tragic, because without a critical justification of ethical action, the law comes into irreconcilable conflict with itself. As Rose puts it, "Antigone stakes her life as the individuated pathos of substantial [law] life in collision with itself [ethics]: she presents part of its truth and she acknowledges the part of that truth *which exceeds her.*"[23]

Modernity arises, however, in response to the absence of this critical concept. Modern cities are the New Jerusalem, founded on the insistence

21. Rose, *Mourning Becomes the Law*, 15–39.
22. Ibid., 18–22.
23. Ibid., 72–73.

that all authority (*Gesetz*) be legitimated through the free, self-determined activity—positing (*setzen*)—of the ethical agent. Thus, Rose remarks (following the comments on Antigone above): "By contrast, modern law is that of legal status, where those with subjective rights and subjective ends deceive themselves and the other that they act for the universal when they care only for their own interests."[24] The subjective rights of the self-legislating ethical agent is not universal at all, but is simply the attempt to grant bourgeois law transcendental status.[25] Where Old Athens had no critical justification for law, the New Jerusalem has no empirical authority apart from the critical concept. Old Athens is blind, but New Jerusalem is hollow. Rose writes, with the modern city "we hope to solve the political problem; we hope for the New Jerusalem; we hope for a collective life without inner or outer boundaries, without obstacles or occlusions, within and between souls and within and between cities, without the perennial work which constantly legitimates and delegitimates the transformation of power into authority of different kinds."[26] This impulse to live without boundaries, obstacles, or occlusions means that the foundations of the modern city are abstract. Whether Old Athens or New Jerusalem, the contradiction between practice and theory, freedom and necessity, particular and universal remains. The middle remains broken.

Rose recognizes that there are two ways of addressing this contradiction. The first, which she opposes and identifies as the cornerstone of all modern social theory, is what she calls "neo-Kantianism."[27] The details of her discussion of neo-Kantianism, which are complex, need not be recounted for this introduction, but it will suffice to note that Rose argues that the whole of the social theory tradition, from Simmel to Habermas, can be reduced to an attempt to deploy the neo-Kantian tradition to address the impasse created by the unsuccessful mediation of law and ethics, Old Athens and New Jerusalem. Rose locates the problem with the neo-Kantian paradigm in its assumption that there must be identity between a proposition's subject and its predicate. Even Adorno, who wanted to repudiate this kind of identity thinking as totalitarian, remained enthralled to it, argues Rose, because his negative disruption of identity is still, at root, deploying the very contradictions that animate identity thinking.

The other way of addressing this contradiction is speculative thinking, which Rose commends from her reading of Hegel. As she defines it,

24. Ibid., 73.
25. Ibid., 26–31.
26. Ibid., 16.
27. *Hegel contra Sociology*, 1–50.

speculative thought "means that the identity which is affirmed [in a proposition] between subject and predicate is seen equally to affirm a lack of identity between the subject and predicate."[28] Speculative thinking is much more than a dialectical negation of identity, in the mode of Adorno, because it attains to a positive knowledge of the actuality of the terms it analyzes. Speculative thinking recognizes a separation (non-identity, difference) between the terms that is simultaneous to a connection (identity, union). It grasps the two terms of the proposition as in some way subsisting in a mutual implication and separation. Rose summarized her position in a gnomic rejoinder to Levinas's neo-Kantian preoccupation with the other's unknowability: "This is experience—the struggle to recognize: to know, and still to misknow, and yet to grow."[29]

Rose uses the term *diremption* often to discuss the nature of the separations—universal/particular, ideal/real, necessity/freedom, validity/value—that mark modern consciousness and social life, as speculative reason conceives them. Diremption is a way of talking about the relation of two poles in both their separation and connection. It is also a way of talking about the mediation of these two poles, a mediation that produces and reproduces their separation, rather than reconciliation. Rose acknowledges that, although Kant maintained a connection with empirical reality that his later followers lost, the pattern of thought that he inaugurated separated the self from its world. What post-Kantian philosophy has been unable to recognize, as a result, is that this way of conceiving of the self and its relation to the world is simply a projection of the existing social relations of bourgeois freedom and selfhood onto a transhistorical definition of human consciousness. Rose goes to great lengths in *Dialectic of Nihilism* to show that these assumptions permeate the structuralist, historicist, and postmodern theories that intend to reject bourgeois categories. In this sense, Rose uses *diremption* to underscore the role of speculative thought, but also to identify the perversity, in the Lacanian sense, of modern and postmodern philosophies. Diremption names the primal connection that persists between these concepts despite their separation.

Yet, diremption names another dimension of this separation. While the modern mediation of subject/object or law/ethics thinks their relation in an irrational way, Rose does not mean by this that we once possessed a rational mediation that we have lost. Rose calls this circumstance of law and ethics "modernity's ancient predicament."[30] It is an ancient problem because

28. Ibid., 52.
29. Rose, *Broken Middle*, 264.
30. Ibid., xii.

it has been with us since Antigone, for whom law subsisted only as intuition, lacking a corresponding conceptual justification. But it is modern because the same diremption of law and ethics continues in the present in the inverted form of the pure concept, mere positing, mere ethics—the imposition of an arbitrary *ought* (*Sollen*). Where Antigone lacked the required ethical concept, we lack the required intuitive law. In each case, the condition is one in which the separation of intuition and concept, of law and ethics, is broken, and any mending of that brokenness will be abstract—that is, false, illusory, ideological. We have no recourse to a pure origin (*arche*) or goal (*telos*). We must begin in the middle, as Rose says, risking the equivocation of the ethical, and the struggle of authorship.[31]

This emphasis on authorship highlights the sense in which the mediation of the middle is a task, a vocation, a habitus to acquire, realize, or achieve. And whatever the mediation of the middle means, whatever conclusion one draws about the status of its brokenness, Rose does not allow for any mediation that occludes that task, the risk, the relation. This is the paradox. If we think that we can overcome the middle's *brokenness* with the right mediating concept, then we are producing an illusion and deepening our predicament, but if the brokenness is perpetual (as it is with Dionysian revelry, for example) and mediation is simply impossible, then we have not conceived the *middle's* brokenness. In large measure, Rose's objection to Levinas's, Mark C. Taylor's, and John Milbank's projects is to an objection to their desire not just to evade mending the middle but also to forego the vocation of mediation as a task and a relation.[32] As she notes, in the same way that in *Dialectic of Nihilism* Rose sought to show that poststructuralist nihilism (Nietzschean) is completed only in the reproduction of (bourgeois) law, so she intends to demonstrate in *The Broken Middle* that the opposition to law in postmodernism is completed only in a political theology, in a "new ecclesiology" that "mend[s] the diremption of law and ethics."[33] Nihilism repeats the law it opposes and antinomianism becomes ecclesiology (political theology) because of their common refusal to "comprehend" the social and material conditions that are the occasion for their thinking. And Rose continues, insisting that it is not that such comprehension "completes or closes" the need for mediation, but rather it "returns diremption to where it cannot be overcome in exclusive thought or in partial action."[34] "Exclusive thought" here is the equivalent of abstract thought in her earlier work. It names the

31. Ibid., 245–307.
32. Ibid.
33. Ibid., xv.
34. Ibid.

tendency of bourgeois social life to produce a form of thought that "mends the gap" in ideality, but reproduces that gap in reality. "Partial action" refers here to another form of this tendency to abstractness, but arising in this case from the idea that a limited, pragmatic act can mediate the brokenness by imposing an ought (*Sollen*). All of this is fairly straightforward in the interpretation of Rose, but what is often missed is the qualification that follows the em dash: ". . . returns diremption to where it cannot be overcome in exclusive thought or in partial action—*as long as its political history persists*."[35] In this simple statement, Rose seems to suggest that this diremption is not a transhistorical dimension of consciousness, not quite the transcendental self-dispossessing form for all knowing that we see affirmed in Williams's interpretation or rejected in Osborne's, but is instead a distorted and contingent social condition that we have misrecognized.

What is recognition and misrecognition, for Rose? In one respect, recognition is not something that is complete, finished, fixed. It is integral to mediation and, as such, is a task, an ethical task. But it is also a habitus, a disposition to be cultivated and that can be done better or worse. It is a way of acting, thinking, living that can and must be learned. One is tempted to use a language that Rose does not use, and speak of recognition as a certain virtue, a capacity for acting in accordance with the excellence of humanity. One may come to practice recognition, perhaps, in much the same way that one practices courage or prudence or love. And in the same way that one does not cease needing to act courageously, prudently, or lovingly, nor does one overcome the task of recognition. Nonetheless, we must be educated, learn how to recognize, by passing through our misrecognitions, and still come to know.

In all of these ways, speculative thought, mediation, the struggle to recognize—these are all a triune affair. They are not binary or dualistic. We come to know ourselves, others, and the world through a process of formation in which consciousness "learns its investment in denying the actuality of itself and the other as always already engaged in some structure of recognition or misrecognition, in some triune (triple) relation to its own otherness and the self-relating of the other . . . . The law is the falling towards or away from mutual recognition, the triune relationship, the middle, formed or deformed by reciprocal self-relations."[36] This is a vital clarification for understanding the relationship between speculative thinking, recognition theory, and law in Rose's thought. Law itself has a kind of metaphysical, essential status, and is a reality that lies behind the illusions of social exis-

35. Emphasis mine.
36. Rose, *Mourning Becomes the Law*, 75.

tence that may distort it.³⁷ The actuality of law is full mutual recognition, not perpetual misrecognition. But the law appears to us, as we become conscious of it in phenomenological analysis of our modern social formations, as a reality that is dirempted by "subjective rights separated from the law of the modern state."³⁸ On this point about the diremption of subjective rights from state law, we come to a second aspect of Rose's analysis that is vital for her work's relation to political theology—that is, the speculative identity of the church and state.

State and Church, God and Knowledge

There are three points in *Hegel contra Sociology* in which Rose draws upon Hegel's speculative proposition about the fundamental relation between religion/church and the state. Each of these formulations elaborates upon the implications of speculative thinking for theology and religion. The first is in the epigraph to the second chapter, entitled "Politics in the Severe Style," which is a direct quotation from Hegel: "In general religion and the foundation of the state is [sic] one and the same thing; they are identical in and for themselves."³⁹

The second statement is Rose's own gloss on the meaning of this provocative statement. After acknowledging that the proposition is peculiar on several grounds—that it can be shown to be false in empirical history, that it is a prescriptive statement that can be affirmed or rejected, or that it could only be true in tautological terms—she insists that objections to the idea that religion and the foundation of the state are one and the same base their protests on the assumption that Hegel's claim is an "identity" proposition, one that "affirm[s] an identity between a fixed subject and contingent accidents."⁴⁰ Instead, Rose insists, Hegel's statement is a speculative proposition, and in fact the "identity of religion and the state is the *fundamental* speculative proposition in Hegel's thought."⁴¹ Because Rose maintains that this claim is fundamental to Hegel's project, it is also central to Rose's own appropriation of speculative reason, and is at work in every other aspect of her thought, from her analysis of the diremption of law and ethics to the triune formation of recognition and misrecognition.

---

37. See Vincent Lloyd's essay in this collection.
38. Rose, *Mourning Becomes the Law*, 75.
39. Hegel quoted in Rose, *Hegel contra Sociology*, 51.
40. Ibid., 51–52.
41. Ibid., 53, emphasis mind.

But Rose further clarifies what she takes this speculative proposition to mean: "[T]he *speculative experience of the lack of identity* between religion and the state is the basic object of Hegel's exposition."[42] The subject of the proposition is never a fixed, transhistorical essence, which receives its historical determinations through its predications. Instead, both the subject and predicate—here, religion and the state—"acquire their meaning in a series of relations to each other," such that "[o]nly when the lack of identity between the subject and predicate has been experienced, can their identity be grasped."[43] The term *grasped* here means conceived or understood in a conceptual sense. There is no predetermined relation between the two terms, but rather the proposition is a "result to be achieved."[44] What is affirmed in the proposition is a reality that now "fails to correspond" to the experience of the subject or the predicate. Both the subject and the predicate acquire their meanings as we think through how we experience the two terms now and what kind of relation the proposition sees as obtaining between them. It is the lack of correspondence to our experience that is decisive.

In the case of this particular speculative proposition, Hegel intends for "natural" consciousness, or our immediate experience of both religion and the state, to be brought into critical analysis, where their mutual implication can first be recognized. Rose wants us to see that religion itself "presuppose[s] an overall economic and political organization which may not be immediately intelligible."[45] And on that basis, this proposition can reveal that ethical life itself in the modern world is dirempted between state (law) and religion (morality). The proposition elicits the experience of their lack of identity, such that we can see, perhaps for the first time, that religion is determined by politics and economics in ways that are concealed by our immediate experience of religion, and that politics is religious in a foundational way that goes unrecognized. And yet, even as our critical analysis leads us to see these mutual implications of politics and religion, the proposition also shows us the reality of their fragmentation. We see, in other words, that religious morality (church) is sustained now through its determination by a political and economic domain (state) from which it mistakenly understands itself to be separate. It is not that the church (or religious morality in general) thinks that it has no relation to the state (or politics and economics in general), but rather religion conceives itself as a mediation that reconciles objective ethical life (God/law) and subjective

42. Hegel quoted in ibid.
43. Ibid., 52.
44. Ibid.
45. Ibid., 54.

ethical life (ethics). The trouble is that religion does not reconcile these two in material history. Religion can only claim it reconciles them on the condition that it does so in a transhistorical, ideal realm that is separate from our actual social relations (state).[46] As a result, in just the moment that religion imagines itself as free of history, that is the moment that religion is most fully determined by its historical, material, and social conditions. Lacking any concept of those conditions, it cannot comprehend itself and misrecognizes its own truth. But the situation is no better from the standpoint of the state. Because the law and ethics are dirempted, the state subsists by imposing its law in separation from religion. Where religion unifies law and ethics in the ideal, the state seeks its unity within the real, which means that it must impose its abstract authority on the social world by domination, suppression, "rul[ing] without any respect for people's conscience or beliefs."[47]

Church and state, then, each respond to the failure of mediation by deploying different strategies for achieving an abstract union of law and ethics. The church imagines a unity apart from the social world, while the state seeks to achieve unity by imposing an abstract ideal upon the social order. Religion and the state, thus, struggle with one another for ascendency, but the same social conditions that reproduce their separation simultaneously discloses interconnection. As Rose puts it, "both religion and the state in this condition of misrecognition refer to real recognition, and thus they can, in principle, guarantee and secure each other."[48]

It is at this point that we come to Rose's third articulation of the speculative relation of religion and the state. That point is the nature of what it means to think, to know, God or the absolute under these social conditions. This point, too, is marked by a quotation from Hegel: "The idea which a man has of God corresponds with that which he has of himself, of his freedom."[49] Rose maintains that everything about the social significance of Hegel's philosophy hinges on our ability to "think the absolute."[50] If the absolute—the unity of ideal/real, theory/practice, necessity/freedom—is not knowable for us, or is simply not a reality, then neither can we be free: we are doomed to be dominated by abstract illusion. It is important to realize, however, that all religions have, contrary to their self-understanding, made God unthinkable, because religion has functioned as the representational

---

46. Ibid., 83.
47. Ibid.
48. Ibid.
49. Hegel quoted in ibid., 92.
50. See ibid., 98.

index of human unfreedom.[51] "A nation which has a false or bad conception of God," Rose quotes Hegel, "has also a bad state, bad government, bad laws."[52] Thus, another implication of the speculative identity of religion and the state is that we come to recognize our "*experience* of a bad religion and a bad state, where the state and religion are in opposition, not identical."[53] The diremption of religion and the state infiltrates and deforms our concept and experience of the absolute. The state assumes the role of the absolute, within politics, dominating and suppressing moral difference from itself; its absoluteness is something it must achieve. But, on the other hand, when religion has no awareness of its determination by the political, which in modernity is the state, then "God" mediates a union that excludes the social, political, and economic.[54]

One question then remains: How are we to think about the increased role of religion and theology that we see in Rose's work from *The Broken Middle* to the end of her life? One thing that we must say is that Peter Osborne's attempt to account for Rose's turn to religion and theology in terms of "relational pragmatics," that her focus on the topic is "because [they are] excluded or remained unrecognized" in social theory, can be seen to be a severe mischaracterization, given the analysis of religion Rose gives even as early as *Hegel contra Sociology*.[55] It is also, at the very least, dubious to conclude, as Osborne does, that Rose's commitment to thinking through the co-implication of religion and the state "distance[d] the general project, decisively, from its initial 'critical Marxist' formulation, to the point of incompatibility."[56] For Rose makes clear in *Hegel contra Sociology* that the exposition of the speculative identity of religion and the state redounds to the social conditions of bourgeois social relations in a direct way, such that the very articulation of human unfreedom is bound to the diremption of politics and religion. There is, without doubt, a sense in which Rose follows Hegel, at this time, in suggesting that religion is a misrepresentation of the absolute that would recede from human life within social relations of full mutual recognition, but that is only true inasmuch as "religion" under those conditions would have a (theological) concept of its political determination, by which humanity lived and knew its true freedom.[57] To frame

51. Ibid.
52. Ibid.
53. HCS, 99.
54. See ibid., 99.
55. Osborne, "Gillian Rose and Marxism," 56.
56. Ibid.
57. A suggestive correlate here may be found in Barth's discussion of original sin as sloth and his claim that humanity was created to realize its freedom. See *CD* IV/1.

the matter as though this is not as much a "religious" social relation as a "political" one is to have abandoned speculative thinking altogether and reproduced the diremption of the bourgeois standpoint. It appears, then, that Rose's later works do not show any significant departure from her early analysis of religion and theology in *Hegel contra Sociology*, and at least in this regard, are consistent with her critical Marxism. What is adumbrated in that early work, though, is an anticipation of a religious form that attained a conceptual recognition of both its political determination *and* of itself as the concrete actuality of political freedom. Under the conditions of diremption, however, such religious activity must take shape not just as awareness of political determination but also as the disruption of the state's effort to dominate society with its abstract ideal—a religious form, that is, with revolutionary actuality, which is un-reformable by the conditions of bourgeois social life.[58]

It is as if there is an even more severe inversion of Harnack's and Feuerbach's maxim about the form and content of faith, the formulation that Žižek recently has sought to redeploy.[59] As that claim is often made, the conceptual content of religion can be comprehended and fulfilled in a political form that leaves the religious behind. But the relationship of form and content takes on a very different relationship when they are conceived speculatively. From this standpoint, the form and content of human social life, and the actualization of human freedom, is at once religious and political in universal form and particular content. Perhaps this is the best way to interpret Rose's remark that what we need, rather than an ethics, is a political theology.[60] In this sense, a political theology would amount to the concept (theology) through which the mutual implication of politics and religion is comprehended as the actuality of human freedom.

～

The essays in this volume are divided into two sections. Those sections reflect the two dirempted poles of practice and theory, which are at the center of Rose's analysis of modern social relations and consciousness.

Anna Rowlands situates her reading of Rose in the shadow of the Brexit vote in the UK and the election of Donald Trump in the US. Given the rise and deployment of nationalist sentiments in these two events, which set the terms of political struggle between those who, on the one hand, insist on prioritizing the particular, provincial interests of the nation, and those who,

---

58. *Hegel contra Sociology*, 229–35
59. Žižek, *The Fragile Absolute*.
60. See note 7 above. Lloyd, ed., "Interview with Gillian Rose," 210.

on the other hand, insist on the priority of universal, cosmopolitan goods of the global collaboration, Rowlands brings Rose's commanding critique of the "old Athens" and the "new Jerusalem" to bear on the assumptions by the "politics of populism, membership, and migration" at work in each of these positions. Rowlands analyzes Rose's rich meditations on the "third city"—and the fourth (Auschwitz)—to describe the "ambitions and failures of our contemporary social, political, and ecclesial life." Rowlands traces Rose's often oblique treatments of the "third city," which occur across the whole of her work, even in relation to her own dying body, at the end of her life. She points out that what both of these responses to the "material life of the city in an age of Trump and Brexit" leave unthought is the extent to which they arise out of and contain one another, in a repressed form. What Rose reminds these two positions, Rowlands argues, is that they are not separated from one another as two poles of a binary relation, but are entangled in one another, "contesting the same territory in ways that both resembled and differ from one another." The response to this, Rowlands maintains with Rowan Williams, is the speculative task of pursuing a form of social relations that has no need of a final mending, but which can affirm the irreducibility of the middle as the locus of our relation, our mutuality.

Andrew Brower Latz's essay focuses on the significance of Rose's contribution to recognition theory, and the role of intersubjectivity in particular, which has gained prominence in the last twenty years. Latz acknowledges that Rose's remarks on recognition were suggestive and written late, but argues that her specific inflection of the theory, within the framework of the influence of the Frankfurt School, is a vital contribution both to the theory itself and to the development of religion and theology within it. Latz commends Rose's Hegelian inflection of recognition theory for its awareness of the role religion plays in nurturing recognition within society, and in ways that are both more attentive to how individuals perform recognition and that neither presuppose conflict nor deny it. He offers a salutary illustration from the fiction of Marilynne Robinson of the kind of Rosean religious recognition theory that is capable of meeting Rose's determination that theory must reach beyond a mere ethics to attain a political theology.

Marcus Pound wants a middle that is less fraught with anxiety and more filled with delight. Pound interrogates Rose's contention that negotiating the illusions inherent to our broken social mediation is a comedic, not a tragic affair. Pound agrees with Rose's critique of Girard, that he lacks "humour and irony," and Pound's own reading highlights the neo-Kantianism that permeates his theory. Pound applies his own reading of Hegel on comedy and tragedy to Rose's account of the comedic in Hegel, as well as Girard's own definition of tragedy and comedy. Pound maintains that Rose's appeal to the comedic in Hegel is undercut by her emphasis on the tragic, and he offers his own rereading of Girard, supplemented by Žižek, as an alternative to Rose, in order to complete Rose's account of the middle as comedic, rather than tragic.

Kate Schick offers a different assessment than Pound of the comedic in Rose's work. Schick notes that Rose delighted in her reputation for being "difficult," and praised the aporetic journey, which abandons paths that are certain, conclusions that are foregone, and identities that are stable. Schick maintains that Rose's work is indeed difficult but it is also joyful, yet its joyful aspects are often obscured by the difficulty of what she is affirming, namely, a "different orientation to knowing and acting." Rose is affirming the value of life lived in vulnerability and exposure to the possibility of loss, suffering, and alienation, but it is only in our continual exposure to that risk, Schick maintains, that we can experience the surprises of "love, beauty, and grace." This difficult path is the "speculative negotiation of the middle" in which we labor to understand how what we consider opposites are, in fact, mutually implicated, both forming and informing one another. This way of thinking, Schick maintains, is a political practice that refuses despair and utopianism in favor of the dogged struggles of the everyday. Conceiving of reason and practice as arising from within this fundamental vulnerability—a vulnerability with no guarantees against the tragic—Schick contends, is itself our openness to the possibility of joy, as Rose's two memoirs, written as she was dying from ovarian cancer, testify.

Rebekah Howes emphasizes the educative (formation, *Bildung*) dimension of Rose's work. Howes maintains that both the Marxist and liberal (in the main) religious interpreters "suppress what is most at stake in comprehending the broken middle of state and religion," according to Rose. It is only an educational logic, Howes maintains, that can understand the peculiar nature of the modern configuration of God and humanity, religion and the state. Howes interrogates Rose's reading of Hegel's difficult premise that "religion and the foundation of the state is [sic] one and the same thing."[61] Howes notes that central to Rose's work is the notion that modern consciousness is defined by bourgeois freedom, which is founded on the idea of thought's separation from the absolute and reproduces that separation in its activity—both theoretical and practical. This means that our philosophical and theoretical as well as political and economic activity are determined by contradictions that we inhabit between our idea of freedom and our idea of God, or the diremption between the state and religion. Because we are determined by these historical, political, and social situations,

---

61. Hegel quoted in Rose, *Hegel contra Sociology*, 49.

"we are dependent," Howes maintains, "on illusion and on our relation to illusion." The importance of this point is that "the absolute in Rose is both the comedy of recognition and misrecognition in its various 'misadventures' and the comic and tragic life of reason making the experience of contradiction substantial."

Gavin Hyman emphasizes that Rose's interest in recuperating Hegel is not at all a conservative reaction to the Marxism of critical theory, but is an attempt to commend a form of thought that is more radical even than Marx. Hyman addresses two of Rose's admirer-critics, Peter Osborne and Rowan Williams, and charts a subtle path between their two quite different readings of the political viability of Rose's vision and the place of theology in it. Hyman argues that Rose's embrace of Hegelian phenomenology as a supplement to the social theory tradition requires a much more robust, positive account of absolute ethical life than Rose can give, one that can guide political judgments and activity. Hyman invokes Wittgenstein for this positive vision, a narrative or language-game, which itself would not be reducible to an abstract positing, but would instead be an authoritative form of life that facilitates meaningful social and political action and speech. Hyman points to Rowan Williams's reading of Rose as providing an important theological supplement that functions in just this Wittgensteinian way, provided that this supplement was not construed as a "holy middle" that obviated the brokenness of the relation of law and ethics. Hyman concludes by acknowledging the equivocal conclusion his analysis generates. There is no clear adjudication of whether this theological (narrative) supplement is, in fact, prior to the middle's brokenness, such that the broken middle itself arises out of it, or whether the broken middle is itself prior and simply plays out in a number of different domains at once, the theological being just one among them. Hyman concludes that the task of political theology lies in this equivocal space.

Joseph Lough's contribution is unique in the collection, since he is writing as both a Marxist economist and a Christian. Lough challenges Rose's reading of Hegel, arguing that Hegel's one absolute substance is not the thinkable but unknowable object Rose takes it to be, but is instead the "misrecognized instance of the capitalist social formation" and that the sublime, which Hegel insists must be grasped within that one substance, is a "misrecognized instance of the . . . value form of the commodity." Lough also takes issue with Rose's reading of Marx, arguing that her dubious charge that Marx was Fichtean applies only to his work prior to the failed revolutions of 1848/49, and that after this time Marx develops a more faithful, even speculative reading of Hegel, that locates the one absolute substance "socially and historically." Lough charts an economic history that, in many ways, offers the objective, material supplement that Peter Osborne and Tony Gorman lament the absence of in Rose's later work. That history goes beyond Rose, though, in identifying the social and historical determinations of abstract modern consciousness and the diremption of law and ethics not simply with bourgeois law and freedom but also with "the empty, abstract, yet sublime value generated when productive human activity came to be measured in equal units of abstract time." This social and historical rereading of Marx and Hegel allows Lough to protest Rose's tendency, evident also in her theological admirers, to treat the brokenness of the middle as a transcendental phenomenological structure. Lough protests this claim on both historical and theological grounds, arguing that the experience of the separation of God and the world is a modern, social, and economic actuality, a contingent effect of capital itself, as the one absolute substance.

Joshua Davis's essay shares Lough's reading of Marx and much of his evaluation of Rose. Davis uses this rereading of Marx to argue against the tendency among Rose's readers, both Marxist and religious, to presume that Rose abandoned the project of critical Marxism in her later work in favor or an "inward" and "ethical" turn. Though her Marxist readers are critical of this development, it is largely shared by her theological and religious interpreters, too, who generally neglect the continued influence of commodity fetishism in the idea of the broken middle. Davis argues that in order to read Rose well, this Marxist element must be retained across her whole body of work, giving it greater social and historical significance than her Marxist critics are inclined to allow, but also much more material significance than her religious readers recognize. Davis concludes by noting that the rereading of Marx that he has proposed allows the absolute to be known as the reality of capital, and therefore identified as idolatrous. Such recognition gives Rose's work both political and theological significance in direct proportion to its Marxist dimension.

Vincent Lloyd isolates the jurisprudential core of Rose's project and the important role her Jewish identity plays in that project. Lloyd identifies the close connection that Rose saw between critical theory and Christian theology in that both recognize that our immediate experience of the world conceals its more fundamental, even beautiful truth, and that her project ought to be understood as having a close relation to another Jewish philosopher of law, Robert Cover. Lloyd argues that both Rose and Cover are dissatisfied with the standard discussions about the relationship between law and morality, and resist any interpretation of law that sees it as one aspect of culture among others. Instead, both thinkers view law as "foundational," and even call it "essential." Law is, in other words, what lies hidden behind the natural experience of the world, but this law is not a more primal reality (for example, Heidegger's *Being* or Deleuze's *virtual*) but is the very activity of contestation and debate about normative social claims. In fact, it is this truth about the contestation of normative claims that is obscured by natural experience. Lloyd is keen to emphasize that this way of viewing law is not a theory of law—not a second-order theorizing of a law that is otherwise concrete, but the theorizing of law is inseparable from its actuality. Recognizing that the law's practice and theory are bound together in this way means that we can never hide from the violence of jurisprudence. We must wrestle with that violence in the law, without any assurance of purity from it, in the struggle for justice, and there is no possibility of justice when we occlude the reality of that violence. The most important implication of this interconnection between law's actuality and its theory is that violence is never hidden. By reading these two thinkers side by side, Lloyd argues we can correct many of the deficiencies in both projects, in particular Cover's focus on the law's publicness and Rose's emphasis on its status as a philosophical or written activity. For Cover, law's publicness is what reveals its violence and makes possible its contestation.

∼

Rose ended her essay "Athens and Jerusalem: A Tale of Three Cities" by associating herself with three other Jewish women writers, Rahel Varnhagen (eighteenth century), Rosa Luxemburg (nineteenth and twentieth century), and Hannah Arendt (twentieth century).[62] Each of these extraordinary women are examples of the kind of "critical rationality and political action" that she commends to us. They are, she says, persons whose lives embody that "activity beyond activity," which is marked by ceaseless risk, and that kind of inaugurated, as opposed to aberrated, mourning that Emmanuel Levinas's *passivity beyond passivity* cannot conceive. These women were certainly flawed and may have failed in many ways, but Rose notes each "exposed the inequality and insufficiency of the universal political community of her day, but without retreating to any phantasy of the local or exclusive community. . . ." She admires them because they "staked the risks of identity without any security of identity."[63]

These three women's lives advert to Rose's third city. As women—Jewish women—and as thinkers, writers, and political agents, they testified to that human political community that suffers the illusions of neither old Athens nor new Jerusalem. Their lives were lived within the broken middle, as testimonies to the false pretensions and failures of the political communities

---

62. She recounts these womens' stories in *The Broken Middle*.
63. Rose, *Mourning Becomes the Law*, 39.

of their time. Yet what is most important to Rose is that they did not simply critique their communities, but they ventured their own lives, desires, loves, and identities in service to transform the social and political life of their times. As such, their lives embodied the possibilities of truth, justice, and full mutual recognition that their communities could not know or imagine. Rose says, "they suffered, struggled, acted and died at the boundary wall" of that political life of full mutual recognition.[64] This boundary wall was not just the social and ideological errors that foreclosed on the reality of this third city, but it was the actual boundary wall that all three of these women had to traverse to enter the city of Berlin, a crossing that was transformative for each of them. Rose tells us that she imagines them all crossing that boundary at the Rosenthaler gate, which only Varnhagen would have actually used, each of them "returning to mourn and to be mourned at . . . one of the three legal entry-points into the city for Jews in the eighteenth century."[65] Rose then tells us that *Rosenthal* is her family name, which her family adopted to enter the German political community, a name they later shortened, a name that means "valley of roses."

Rose is right to locate herself among these three women, right to identify her suffering, struggling, acting, and death with that place of moving into and out of the city. Each of the following essays aspires to speak of such a life of risk for the sake of justice, love, and transformation as no mere ethics, politics, or jurisprudence—but as something hallowed, consecrated, and perhaps even (not just despite, but because of her objection) holy.

Bibliography

Agamben, Giorgio. *The Kingdom and the Glory: For a Theological Genealogy of Economy and Government*. Translated by Lorenzo Chiesa and Matteo Mandarini. Stanford: Stanford University Press, 2011.

Barth, Karl. *Church Dogmatics*. Vol. IV/1, *The Doctrine of Reconciliation*. Edited by Geoffrey Bromiley. Translated by Thomas F. Torrance. Edinburgh: T & T Clark, 2004.

Gorman, Tony. "Gillian Rose and the Project of a Critical Marxism." *Radical Philosophy* 105 (2003) 25–36.

Harvey, David. *A Brief History of Neoliberalism*. Oxford: Oxford University Press, 2007.

Hill, Geoffrey. "In Memorium: Gillian Rose." *Poetry* (2006) 187–91.

Livingston, James, et al. *Modern Christian Thought: The Twentieth Century*. Minneapolis: Fortress, 2006.

Lloyd, Vincent, ed. "Interview with Gillian Rose." *Theory, Culture and Society* 25 (2008) 7–8.

64. Ibid.
65. Ibid.

Mason, Paul. *Postcapitalism: A Guide to our Future*. New York: Farrer, Strauss, and Giroux, 2015.

Milbank, John. "On the Paraethical: Gillian Rose and Political Nihilism." *Telos* 173 (2015) 69–86.

Chantal Mouffe, ed. *The Challenge of Carl Schmitt*. New York: Verso, 1999.

Osborne, Peter. "Gillian Rose and Marxism." *Telos* 173 (2015) 55–67.

———. "Hegelian Phenomenology and the Critique of Reason and Society." *Radical Philosophy* 32 (1980) 8–15.

Rose, Gillian. *The Broken Middle: Out of Our Ancient Society*. Cambridge, MA: Blackwell, 1992.

———. *Hegel contra Sociology*. Radical Thinkers. Brooklyn: Verso, 2009.

———. *Mourning Becomes the Law: Philosophy and Representation*. Cambridge: Cambridge University Press, 1996.

Schmitt, Carl. *Political Theology: Four Chapters on the Concept of Sovereignty*. Translated by George Schwab. Chicago: University of Chicago Press, 2006.

———. *Political Theology II: The Myth of the Closure of Any Political Theology*. Translated by Michael Hoelzl and Graham Ward. Malden, MA: Polity, 2008.

Taubes, Jacob. *The Political Theology of Paul*. Translated by Dana Hollander. Stanford, CA: Stanford University Press, 2004.

Williams, Rowan. "Between Politics and Philosophy: Reflections in the Wake of Gillian Rose." *Modern Theology* 11, no. 1 (1995) 3–22.

———. "Leader: The Government Needs to Know How Afraid People Are." *New Statesman*, June 9, 2011. Accessed August 13, 2017. http://www.newstatesman.com/uk-politics/2011/06/long-term-government-democracy.

———. "Mass Democracy Has Failed—It's Time to Seek a Humane Alternative." *New Statesman*, November 20, 2016. Accessed August 13, 2017. http://www.newstatesman.com/world/2016/11/mass-democracy-has-failed-its-time-seek-humane-alternative.

———. "The Sadness of the King: Gillian Rose, Hegel, and the Pathos of Reason." *Telos* 173 (2015) 21–36.

Žižek, Slavoj. *The Puppet and the Dwarf: The Perverse Core of Christianity*. Boston: MIT Press, 2003.

Part 1

The Struggle for Recognition
The City, the Middle, the Political

Chapter 1

Beginning in the Middle
The Third City and the Politics of Membership

Anna Rowlands

Before we reorientate our theology, let us reconsider the relation between the city and philosophy. Neither politics nor reason unifies or "totalizes": they arise out of diremption, out of the diversity of peoples who come together under the aporetic law of the city, and who know that their law is different from the law of other cities—what Rousseau called "power" and we now call "nation." Philosophy also issues out of this diremption and its provisional overcoming in the culture of an era. Without "disowning that edifice" philosophy steps away to inspect its limitations, especially when the diremptions fixated in the edifice have lost their living connections. We should be renewing our thinking on the invention and production of edifices—cities—apparently civilized within, dominion without—not sublimating those equivocations into holy cities. For the modern city intensifies these perennial diremptions in its inner oppositions between morality and legality, society and state, and the outer opposition, so often now inner, between sovereignty and what Rousseau called "power" and we call "nations and nationalism."[1]

---

1. Rose, *Judaism and Modernity*, 50.

Thus Gillian Rose moves to conclude her chapter on the "Shadow of Spirit" in *Judaism and Modernity*.[2] The challenge embodied in this extract, to responsibly reconfigure the discourse and praxis of the city for our times, is a central concern across Rose's work and it is a concern that has risen once again to political prominence in the course of the last year. Much postliberal political debate following the Brexit vote in the UK and the election of Donald Trump in the US has attempted to take up this task of reconfiguring the discourse of the city through positing a fundamental political divide or agonistic alienation between adherents to two largely opposed worldviews. Those who seek the national interest over the global interest, the particular over the universal sit in supposed tension with those who seek a cosmopolitan commitment beyond and within the boundaries of nation-states, prioritizing the universal over the particular. Mapping this landscape, British postliberal thinker David Goodhart argues that the basic and most meaningful political distinction now lies between "Anywheres" and "Somewheres." "Somewheres"—seemingly representatives of an older Romantic and Counter-Revolutionary tradition—value place, group attachment, stability, skill, kinship, and locality: the particular in all its dimensions. By contrast "Anywheres"—representatives of a cosmopolitan globalism and those who possess greater power in market, culture, and state—are urban, socially liberal, and highly educated and value mobility, autonomy, openness, and fluidity. The former are described as communitarians or "decent populists," the latter are assumed to be progressive liberals. According to this account older cleavages of class, race, and gender become less significant in the face of an increasingly apparent cultural division between those espousing liberal progressive and socially conservative worldviews—although both categories are presented as iterative constructions. In defense of this proposition Goodhart draws intellectual succor from recent polling evidence: when presented with the statement, "Britain has changed in recent times beyond recognition, it sometimes feels like a foreign country and this makes me feel uncomfortable," 62 percent of respondents agreed with the statement and only 30 percent disagreed. He interprets this data as a reliable sign of the rise of a new ("decent") populism as a variation on older forms of populism: this new populism retains the conventional populist preference for authoritarianism, nativism, and suspicion of elites but now manifests a settled acceptance of sexuality and racial diversity. He also interprets such populism as merely a shade different in tone to mainstream centrist views—hence, in Goodhart's view, the ease with which a disaffected populace has shifted from center left or right to various forms of populism.

2. See Caygill, Preface to *Paradiso*, by Rose.

Germinating from her earliest work, *The Melancholy Science* and coming to powerful fruition in her final collection of philosophical essays, *Mourning Becomes the Law*, Rose takes on her own challenge to reconfigure the discourse of the city beyond the false dualisms of what she names Old Athens and New Jerusalem. At the heart of this account is a suspicion of a constant cycle of regeneration of exclusive, oppositional, and disguised forms of communitarianism. In the first chapter of *Mourning Becomes the Law* Rose lays out a complex, multifaceted account of a third—and indeed a fourth—city that exist beyond the dualisms attendant upon the cities of Athens and Jerusalem. This chapter explores the thought that Rose's prescient account of the third city offers us a perspective held in thought and directed toward practice that enables a different and necessary analysis of the central ambitions and failures of our contemporary social, political, and ecclesial life.

Four Cities

Rose's motif of the third city is an expression of her ambition to refound philosophy as a form of aporetic metaphysics and of her enacting that commitment as a critique of representation in the context of the rise of new forms of liberalism and communitarianism in the 1980s and 90s.[3] Her assessment of these resurgent political forms contains an analysis that anticipates brilliantly—even eerily—today's febrile debates about the assertion and critique of identity politics, the (re)emergence of narratives of nation and (argued-to-be-suppressed) cultural particularity, the politics of violence and inequality, the irruption of suppressed theopolitical forms (where the theopolitical indicates something beyond the secular construct "religion") into the life of the city. She catches the early fluttering of these nascent late modern political life forms and "fails towards" naming some of their dynamics. In this vein, Kate Schick has noted the prescience of Rose's analysis for recent debates about cosmopolitanism and cultural difference. Drawing on Rose, Schick suggests that a cosmopolitan sensibility that "sets its face against boundaries" and proposes—in the light of suffering and loss—abstract universal rights rooted in the mere fact of being human, fails to see its own Other. This Other, sidelined in pursuit of equality, reasserts herself in the name of the particular. Schick suggests that Rose enables us to continue to see the imbalance in the main liberal and postmodern philosophies on

---

3. See Rose, Introduction to *Mourning Becomes the Law*, 12–13, where Rose lays out her vision of an aporetic metaphysics that engages with threefold forms of representation.

offer for critique and representation of this reality: themselves representing in thought an imbalance in attending to the relation of universal and particular. Schick suggests that Rose finds a different way to explore these dilemmas by starting not with the universal or the particular but with the broken middle between the two terms. This chapter seeks to build upon such work, exploring the theopolitical motif of "the third city" as it appears in Rose's work and putting it to work in a limited concluding manner in the context of current European and North American debates about the rise of populism and the politics of membership.

The notion of "the third city" is a gradual evolution in Rose's thought and consequently the definition of the contours of "the third city" has to be pieced together from across the whole body of her work.[4] The idea of "the third city" appears in its most disguised form in *Love's Work*, mapped onto her suffering and dying body. She compares the first city of rational modern medicine, which emerges as a failing but necessary technology, to the false hope of the second city, alternative medicines with their "religious hope," and arrives finally at "the third city," which embodies the fragile and vulnerable power of an eros that knows loss, failure, being failed, and yet "stays in the fray." "The third city" functions in the gap *between* the discourse of Old Athens and New Jerusalem in hermeneutical territory common to both. But this shared hermeneutical territory does not take the form of a linear third term, which succeeds, or comes after, the decaying edifices of Athens and Jerusalem: the survivor that conquers or vanquishes both. "The third city" exists as the gap—and the relation—between Athens and Jerusalem. Here we must take care: Rose is not employing a postmodern deconstructive technique and excavating the gap, the in-between, thus dissolving the opposition between Athens and Jerusalem. The gap Rose wishes us to attend to is the gap that emerges between theory and practice, which exist for her as "torn halves that do not add up," and in the analogical relation between the soul, the city, and the sacred. The gap is not a break in meaning, a false apophaticism rendered as lack or absence, but rather the gap exists as *aporia*, a constitutive, intelligible, and substantive part of the relation *between*: a critical part in the composition of the "inter-est" between persons, to express this in Arendtian terms. Rose argues that the suppression of this gap can be seen at work in deterministic renderings of metaphysics (political and theological), but it can also be seen at work in forms of contemporary ethics that collapse or refuse the complex relation of particular and universal, and the "equivocation of the middle." Thus Rose's account begins "in the middle" and works with the tension between the three cities (or four cities,

---

4. See also earlier work on Jerusalem and Athens in *The Broken Middle*, 277–95.

including Auschwitz), their inherent mutual constitution, their contrasts and oppositions, their respective inscriptions of desire. What is important to grasp is that Rose wants us to understand that these are competing and colliding cities whose material *perichoresis*—and falling away from each other—forms the possibility and actuality of contemporary ethical life: *Sittlichkeit* in Rose's borrowed Hegelian terms.

Rose's clearest and most sophisticated exposition of the life of "the third city" is to be found in her inaugural lecture as Professor of Social and Political Thought at Warwick delivered on 15 February 1993, which later became the opening chapter of *Mourning Becomes the Law*. Reawakening the classical analogy between the soul, the city, and the sacred, she spoke analogically of the relation between four colliding cities. The first city is Old Athens, representing reason, traditional authority, "the city of rational politics."[5] This is now a demonized city functioning in all its parodied negativity as the legitimator of its polar (but always connected) opposite: the New Jerusalem. The second city is thus an idealized utopian city predicated upon love, mutuality, dissolved power—it represents both a realized eschatology, and thus a falsely perfected ecclesiology. The present stature of this city derives from the new ethics and pure theologies developed in dialogue with postmodernism.[6] Rose offers a controversial critique of the genealogy of New Ethics, noting its formative links to renewed Jewish post-Holocaust social thought, which she argues presents Judaism as "the sublime other of modernity."[7] This alleged misrecognition of modern Judaism by itself exercises Rose greatly and is one of the most challenging and uncomfortable aspects of her polemic.[8] In the context of Christian theology this reading of New Jerusalem is also used as searing critique of Mark C. Taylor's a/theology and John Milbank's neo-Orthodox "nomadic city" in *Theology and Social Theory*.

From the second city we move unexpectedly to the fourth city. For Rose the recent regeneration of the second city, New Jerusalem, owes much to the dreadful reality of the fourth city, Auschwitz.[9] Auschwitz is characterized as

5. Rose, *Mourning Becomes the Law*, 20.

6. See the play between Athens and New Jerusalem, *Mourning Becomes the Law*, 21–26.

7. See discussion of New Ethics in *Mourning Becomes the Law*, 26–30. This develops earlier work on Levinas, Rozensweig, and Fackenheim, *The Broken Middle*, 247–307; on Midrash and Political Authority in *Mourning Becomes the Law*, 77–100, esp. 88–89 and 96–100. See also full text of *Judaism and Modernity*.

8. See the essay by Kavka, "Saying Kaddish for Gillian Rose," 104–29.

9. See overlapping discussion of the second, third, and fourth cities, *Mourning Becomes the Law*, 26–31 and 31–35. See earlier discussion of Auschwitz in context of false

a city not because of the internal workings of the death camp as a pseudo-community with basic human structures of exchange and ritual, but rather with reference to Nazi plans studied only latterly by architectural historian Robert Jan van Pelt detailing plans for a complex city of dwellings, trade, and social community:

> Auschwitz was to become the administrative center of the Germanification of eastern Upper Silesia, in the Nazi version of the medieval German ambition to civilize the Slav lands by colonizing the territories between the River Oder and the River Bug.[10]

Here Rose reinforces her choice to offer a material account of the city, defining the city "historically, according to the rule of law" rather than "transhistorically, according to listed functions."[11] Rose's definition in accordance with the presence of the rule of law thus throws the focus of understanding upon the contingent social historical factors that determined patterns of power and legitimacy: upon the practical and ideological construct of the city.

This troubling account of Old Athens, New Jerusalem, and Auschwitz becomes the gateway that leads us toward recognizing the middle term: "the third city." In his review of *Mourning Becomes the Law* philosopher and journalist Daniel Johnson defines "the third city" narrowly as: "[t]he invisible, internalised third city . . . that of capitalism, private property and modern legality."[12] A closer textual examination of Rose's work reveals a more multifaceted, evocative, and opaque definition. Certainly, in accordance with her earlier retrieval of a critical Marxism, Rose considers the roots of modern contradiction to stem from the distorted social status of private property and its death grip on the philosophical imagination. However, a more developed definition of the third city might run as follows. Firstly, the most general definition that can be given to "the third city" is that it represents our perennial condition: the repeated dilemma of the internal relation of law and ethics and externally of religion and the state. Secondly, developing earlier Hegelian themes of misrecognition and failure, the motif of "the third city" seems also to stand for that which is most occluded in the consciousness of the present; that which as individuals and as collective subjects we are least aware of in terms of our formation and action. "The third city" thus represents in part the Hegelian misrecognition of actuality but also, and not unconnected, the Kierkegaardian "silence of the paradox."

---

holy middles in *The Broken Middle*; later in *Mourning Becomes the Law*, 78, 86, 96.

10. *Mourning Becomes the Law*, 31.
11. *Mourning Becomes the Law*, 33.
12. Johnson, "Mourning, the Consolation of a Philosopher."

So, in order to hold meaningfully to this non-emblematic and opaque city we might talk of its fragmentary and contradictory faces.

The first of these faces, I suggest, echoes Johnson's critical Marxist emphasis—and finds its most systematic articulation in Rose's *Hegel contra Sociology*. This "face" of "the third city" represents: "The city that separates each individual into a private, autonomous, competitive person, a bounded ego, [with] . . . a phantasy life of community, a life of unbounded mutuality, a life without separation and its inevitable anxieties? A phantasy life which effectively destroys the remnant of political life?"[13]

Rose, driven by a strong critical Marxism, understands both critique and commodification to be bound up equally with religion and the modern state and its systems of exchange. This fundamental economic stance developed in her earlier work remains present in her analysis of the third city. The fantasy life of the product drains energy from the truer exchange relation, which is rooted in the political negotiation of goods (in all senses of the word). And yet the series of question marks that complete each sentence are important here. They represent the slim possibility of the irruption of the ethical, even within this configuration. Rose seems to advocate that we will find modernity and "secular reason" primarily in social institutions. As both citizens this is the common territory where our discourse (secular and religious) is "subverted and implicated." Expressed theopolitically, this is the site of our own (incarnational) "worlding."

To comprehend something further and distinctive about the second "face" of "the third city" requires us to emphasize Rose's exposition of the triadic relation between universal, singular, and particular. She calls our attention to the singular, the third term, which appears as the middle: the ethical. In this vein she issues this warning, drawing from the language of Jeremiah: "To oppose anarchic, individual love or good to civil or public ill is to deny the third which gives meaning to both—this is the other meaning of *the third city*—the just city and just act, the just man and the just woman."[14]

This central notion of "the third city," which seems to come increasingly into focus for Rose as she works through a representation of her own illness and death, is deeply evocative. This appeal to the language of Jeremiah is not concerned with pure, innocent, or holy acts of witness so much as with the possibility of intelligible and necessarily risky action that gives justice—felt to be absent—presence. Her writing returns constantly to the figure whose just act manifests itself on the boundary of the city or beyond

13. Ibid.
14. Rose, "Athens and Jerusalem," 26.

its walls. This is mournable justice, whose absence is given presence through the actions of the just man or woman, for the redemption of the city. Rose offers both before and after her inaugural lecture a number of reflections on figures that appear in this guise as the singular, those who embody this relational and broken "failing towards" wholeness that she associated with "the third city." The figures of Rosa Luxembourg, Hannah Arendt, and Rahel Varnhagen represent exactly this appearing as the main actors in the drama of *The Broken Middle*. With reference to this in her subsequent inaugural lecture she notes: "In her own way each of these women exposed the inequality and insufficiency of the universal political community of her day, but without retreating to any phantasy of the local or exclusive community: each staked the risks of identity without any security of identity. Each suffered, struggled, acted and died at the boundary wall of *the third city*."[15]

In her final collection of essays, published posthumously, the figures of Antigone and the wife of Phocion (Plutarch and Poussin) appear as further representations of the singular.

Rose's third "face" of "the third city" takes us back to the territory of Auschwitz and requires us to understand the metaphysical grounds of her work and her equivocal acceptance of the possibilities of Enlightenment modernity. Rose worked to demonstrate the latent resources that exist within modernity for speculative, metaphysical thinking, which is able, in the words of Andrew Shanks, to "cope with corporate trauma."[16] The device of "the third city" thus emerges in Rose's work as a way to insist on the (re)generation of a philosophy that is capable of thinking what appears unthinkable. Thus Rose dissolves the fourth city disarmingly into the third, arguing that rational historical analysis with an emphasis on political community "understands the plans [for Auschwitz] as arising out of, and as falling back into, the ambitions and the tensions, the utopianism and violence, the reason and the muddle, which is the outcome of the struggle between the politics and the anti-politics of the city. This is *the third city*—the city in which we all live and with which we are too familiar."[17]

In noting the relationship between the third and fourth cities it becomes clear that the capacity for reason to engage productively with intelligible action and thereby to be able to think corporate trauma, requires a political movement that opens a space beyond dogmatic assertion for the

15. Rose, *Mourning Becomes the Law*, 39.

16. See Shanks, *God and Modernity*, for an account of the assumed failure of second modernity to cope with corporate trauma; in his view this failure is a key impetus toward the development of postmodern discourse. Extending Rose's reflections on trauma, see Schick, *Gillian Rose*, 57–80.

17. Rose, *Mourning Becomes the Law*, 34.

failure, repentance, and mourning of practice within the city.[18] Rose witnesses to the possibility of a conscious engagement with the work of mourning, which the failure of our individual and communal lives necessitates: the failure that "arises out of misrecognition of desire," a misrecognition of "my and your self-relation mediated by the self relation of the other." Simon Barrington-Ward, who received Rose into the church in the final hours of her life, argues that we might call this process something like "the repentance of reason."[19] We find this notion hidden between the lines in Rose's presentation of the third city and broken middle in her short essay on the *Comedy of Hegel* and simply and mystically in the startling epigram "Keep your mind in hell and despair not." This spiritual refrain acts as our inauguration into Rose's autobiography, *Love's Work*, and is also the final note entered into her notebooks hours before death. The possibility of *Sittlichkeit* (ethical life) rooted in the divine rests upon the *habitus* of such a repentant reason. It is the acceptance of the substantiality of repentant reason that marks the potential for practices of right relation. It is the refusal of the work of repentant reason that has such devastating effects: perpetuating the myth or "unsubstantiality" of autonomy and self-mastery.

Theopolitics and the Third City

The broad relevance of Rose's work to theology was outlined by Rowan Williams, writing in *Modern Theology* in 1995.[20] Williams warns of the danger posed by a facile appropriation of Rose's work into theology. He argues that it is Rose's neo-Hegelian understanding of "education" and "formation"

18. Here again we see that a Secular Theology working through the motif of "the third city" does not "other" that which is nihilistic (despite the polemic of *The Dialectic of Nihilism*) as Radical Orthodox theologians appear to do; this remains the internal struggle of any live city and as such the ugly, the chaotic and the nihilistic warrants representation in our theologies.

19. See Barrington-Ward, "'Forgiven, Forgiving.'" While some are troubled by what is inferred by Barrington Ward's *repentance of reason* Rose herself, in *Paradiso*, talks of inhibited reason, which must be enlarged and transformed in the domain of *praxis*. This echoes earlier work in *Hegel contra Sociology* (see 71–79 in particular). Interestingly, echoes of such a *praxeology* are clearly present in the conversations she has with the chaplain of the Walsgrave, David Robinson, prior to her Baptism, concerning the theological quality of pastoral ministry. See final blue scrapbook located in University of Warwick Archive where Rose comments on her conversations with Robinson.

20. Williams, "Between Politics and Metaphysics." This article is a careful reading of Rose's text *The Broken Middle*. While offering a startling and brilliant reading of Rose's work, Williams's essay does not include reflection on themes developed in *Love's Work*, *Mourning Becomes the Law*, or *Paradiso*, in which we see some development in Rose's treatment of theological themes.

that offers most to theology's self-comprehension. It is in insisting upon a more adequately self-critical theology that demands of theology an account of the very grounds of being self-critical that Rose becomes a hopeful if uncomfortable conversation partner for theology. As such her work rejects the possibility of a "sentimental" faith that "refuses to labour at its own substance." For Williams: "Rose's fundamental Hegelian insight is . . . that it is the understanding of the basic character of deformed consciousness as the myth of the subject in possession that grounds not simply a 'negative dialectic' but a clear speculative recognition of the inevitable need for negotiation of goods."[21]

So Rose turns the contemporary mono-critique of the speculative on its head, reinvesting the speculative in the very territory it is alleged to shun: *eros*, loss, difficulty, comedy, and scarcity; in other words, reinvesting the speculative in the ground of *praxis*. For Williams and Rose speculative reflection on both theological and philosophical experience enables the possibility of change within secular and ecclesial politics beyond the pragmatic re-arrangement of existing power relations: it embodies a double countercultural movement that continually expands an elastic notion of *praxis*. For this to be possible both Williams and Rose argue for a reading of secular and ecclesial politics always in relation to each other, embodying a continual and complex relation of (non-)identity between religion and the state.[22] What is shared as foundational *praxis* between religion and the state is an *economy of exchange* rooted in a perpetual movement of imagining how things might be otherwise, *negotiation*, *dispossession*, and *legislation*.[23]

Williams reads Rose as concerned with three key questions: How do we entertain the particular in its strangeness? How do we reconceive our goal and interest in what is "other"? How do we find a politics beyond the superficial rearrangement of current power relations? Each of Williams's questions finds its symmetry in the three major themes of *The Broken Middle*. Where do we begin? How do we make sense of the equivocation of the ethical? What is the meaning of the agon of authorship? Williams argues that Rose's account is rooted in an understanding that difficulty and

---

21. Williams, "Between Politics and Metaphysics," 17.

22. See *Hegel contra Sociology*, 48–91, for discussion of the relation of religion and the state in terms of a critical exposition of Hegel's *Phenomenology* and *Philosophy of Right*, and further to this discussion of the suspension of the political in relation to Arendt and Luxemburg in *The Broken Middle*, 153–246.

23. On a poetics of law that develops her work on misrecognition and identity between religion and politics constructively in terms of a rereading of Hegel's *Phenomenology* (itself, I would argue, a disguised reflection on Kierkegaardian repentance), see chapter 3, *Mourning Becomes the Law*, 63–76 esp., in summary, 74–76.

aporia are born from scarcity and that conflict arises from the distribution and exchange of goods. In this light politics is negotiation and negotiation is politics. Revision is always possible, but the critical question is the degree to which such revision is ever any more than a loose redistribution of power. Already present here are the dynamics of desire, its formation and deformation, satisfaction and frustration. This is partly how Rose takes us beyond a narrow view of sociality as no more than competition for resources, toward a more expansive account of a moral and aesthetic understanding of the (non-idealized) communal. This is the site of material agency and immanent otherness—open to intelligible thought and to labor understood as *reasonable work* (in various senses).

Williams argues that Rose is constructing a speculative account that inherits firstly the Platonic task of constructing a city in discourse, which attempts to reflect on the conditions for judgement found in material instances of the city's life. In turn this implies a *praxis* of judgement as communal and political, moral and aesthetic. The possibility of the metaphysical is found in the life of the city as it is constructed and reconstructed, as its political and aesthetic life is ventured, broken, and reconfigured. Rose interprets politics as coming into being not "when you act on behalf of your own damaged good, but when you act, without guarantees, for the good of all—this is to take *the risk* of the *universal* interest."[24] Unlike the tendency to crudely polarize particular and universal interests in current political debate, Rose insists on the necessity of beginning in the middle between these terms, invoking both, excavating their relation, noting the inevitable tension and gap that constitutes part of their relation.[25] The life of the city is built upon a profoundly speculative process and it is broken in its middle by the relation of religion and the state, theory and practice, law and love.[26] Rose sets her face against any form of political philosophy or theology that imagines it can fundamentally mend this middle or even narrate or "relocate" reality and the status of what can be known of this middle as a single "knower."[27] Precarious and equivocal action toward a good beyond simple self-assertion, and in so doing "failing towards" the life of the universal, becomes the stuff of Rose's political theory: conceiving "individual and communal formation as fallible and precarious, but risk-able." What we can know and what we can do remain inalienably—and yet problematically—communal

---

24. *Mourning Becomes the Law*, 62.

25. See Goodhart's tendency to polarize particular and universal interests in creating his categories of Anywheres and Somewheres in *The Road to Somewhere*.

26. See Plato's *Republic* and *Phaedrus*.

27. *Mourning Becomes the Law*, 13.

for Rose. This is the site of aporetic metaphysics. This is also, I think, what makes Rose's work particularly challenging and helpful for two sets of (quite different and yet not unconnected) debates with which I am concerned: the (perennial modern) question of the formation of bounded political communities and the determination of their membership the debate about the coherence of a Christian political theology.

For the political theologian caught between the polarities of liberal and neo-communitarian forms of political theology and wishing to interpret the (partly) analogous dynamics discernible in the contemporary public debates about cosmopolitanism, communitarianism, and political belonging, Rose offers the possibility of an account that avoids both a naïve appeal to the communal or any notion of a social life that returns us to little more than the competition of self-possessing, self-asserting individuals. Rose presents the city understood as *a set of material practices:* diverse people negotiating common laws. These practices form a pattern that is never simply informal, which might be said to call always beyond the casual and the atomistic— but also, just as crucially, beyond the naively communal. Attention to these practices betrays the presence of the metaphysical in all its complexity, immediacy, and accessibility. And this is where Rose's Hegelian inheritance makes most sense and has most to offer to contemporary political theology; it is (to repeat) the adoption of the Hegelian task of understanding the "basic character of deformed consciousness as the myth of the subject in possession that grounds not simply a negative dialectic but a clear speculative recognition of the inevitable need for negotiation of goods."[28] This is the challenge of ethical life in the third city, a process that so easily collapses into clarion calls for pure cities of Athens or Jerusalem.

This central analytical commitment is also what makes Rose's work particularly apposite for addressing current debates about the politics of populism, membership, and migration—the surface of which we will only scratch here. In her inaugural lecture, Rose mapped her newly outlined four cities onto the politics of the 1980s and 1990s, arguing that the political landscape was being reshaped by new forms of libertarianism and neo-communitarianism representing forms of Old Athens and New Jerusalem political thought respectively. It is striking reading this material again after twenty years that Rose uses the term "new communitarian" not to refer—as we (political theologians) might now expect—to postliberal communitarians bearing the influence of Alasdair MacIntryre, among others, but rather to name those who stake their claim to the political in the name of identity: ethnic, religious, sexual, gender, and so forth.

---

28. Williams, "Between Politics and Metaphysics," 17.

While, twenty years on, contemporary political postliberals tend to view "identity politics"—the debate over "safe spaces" being a highly charged case in point—and the "politics of diversity" as an excessive and self-destructive form of rationalizing progressivist cultural liberalism, Rose's analysis sets a framework for reading such politics as representing in fact a strong vein of New Jerusalem thinking. Thus she views what others quickly castigate or praise as liberalism (depending on standpoint) as also a variation on a communitarian and even theopolitical theme. She has in mind any political and civic practices that appear to imply the opposition of "community to the social and political totality."[29] Her critique is also a form of judgment: in both "new communitarianism" that roots community in the politics of identity and in some emerging forms of postliberal communitarianism (political and theological in guise) Rose sees an unfortunate "hope of evading the risks of political community," a refusal to remain "with the anxiety and ambivalence" of exercising power and seeking knowledge.[30] Rose is not to be read against communitarianism but she remains critical of the mainstream—more obvious and more disguised—forms of communitarianism she sees as irrupting into the late modern political and ecclesial space.

In so doing Rose's work suggests to us now surprising commonalities between seemingly antagonistic movements, thus challenging the more facile analytical polarity of identity politics and what has become, after her, mainstream forms of political postliberalism. To be clear: her work would not deny hostility and antagonism between such movements—to replace a historical and material account of the city with its ideal typical features—rendering them (us) as in some sense the same. Rather, Rose can be read as proposing an early naming of the relation of identity and non-identity between these morphing political and intellectual movements of our time. What Rose's account of the four cities, read in the context of her earlier economic analysis, does is to invite us to read each movement as positing some form of ideal community, enabling us to ask the revealing question: "What do we hope for from our ideal community?" And we might add, "Who constitutes our community?" and "Who decides where the boundary wall is situated?" In response, she offers both grounds for a refreshing analysis of the visions and illusions of contemporary political movements but also a constructive metaphysical and political response: the work of mourning and the risk of staking oneself again for the sake of the universal, knowing that this will involve *aporia*.

---

29. *Mourning Becomes the Law*, 19.
30. Ibid., 16. Note again her critique of political theology in Taylor and Milbank.

For these reasons, and returning to where we began, it is interesting to imagine what a Rosean response to Goodhart's analysis of postliberalism and populism might look like. At a glance there is much in Goodhart's account that might resonate with Rose's reading of the four cities: Goodhart names the Other of progressive liberalism and he does so in ways that note both radical and indigestible difference in worldviews while also noting that these differences should not be over interpreted, they represent shades of difference and emerge in complex and even contradictory forms—the presence of religious groups who are socially conservative but also contain high numbers of recent immigrants express both Somewhere sentiments in value terms, but are also perceived as Other by many with whom they might share these values. In doing so he partially names one face of Rose's third city. Nonetheless Goodhart's analysis might also, I think, be read as evading the deeper and more demanding tasks of the ethical life of the third city: he seems to propose but ultimately evades and suppresses the metaphysical. The material life of the city in an age of Trump and Brexit betrays the metaphysical structure of our experience—the search for and suppression of the good, the gap between the universal and particular, the complex relation of soul, city, and sacred, and thus presents philosophy with its founding diremptions. Goodhart veers away from the risk of handling the complexities of this more demanding and agonistic political task, arguably he avoids the heart of the broken middle.

To put some flesh on these bones, what Goodhart fails to spot is that upon careful philosophical examination the worldviews he names as "Anywhere" and "Somewhere," liberal cosmopolitan and populist communitarian, each contains their suppressed Other, and furthermore each shares two common flaws: a repetition of the economic logic of the self in possession as the ground of political reflection, and an invocation of the presence of a community of the good without the formal deployment of an explicit discourse of the good. On a Rosean reading, I suggest, "progressive liberals" are more communitarian than their communitarian opponents such as Goodhart seem able to recognize, and the self-professed communitarians emerge as more deeply and problematically liberal. Each contains within themselves their suppressed Other. To make this concrete for a moment, the discourse about "safe spaces" is arguably a fairly good example of what Rose would have understood as a New Jerusalem form of thinking: neocommunitarian in its appeal to an ideal speech community of mutual exchange and ethical immediacy shorn of the difficulty of negotiating power and violence. Nonetheless in so far as advocates of safe spaces also suppose the self-possessing individual as the ground of action, they remain thoroughly liberal constructs. While superficially appearing to name the agon of power and knowledge they dissolve the possibility of either being truly known. That politics might be thought to emerge from such spaces would, for Rose, betray the risk and the violence necessary in negotiating the ethical life of the third city.

However, Rose's work also counsels us to note the suppressed Other within contemporary self-professed communitarianism. Contemporary populism is not without its appeals to—or policing of—identity, nor without its desire to construct spaces that resolve the tension of negotiating the life of different people as the basis of the law and its renewal: thus we might say that the suppressed Other of identity politics irrupts as the broken middle of populism. Now some care should be taken not to reproduce the very thing that Rose is so often criticized for: polemic textual readings. Goodhart does acknowledge—in an insightful breakthrough line—that in the politics of 2016/17 there is a whiff of identity politics within the populist/communitarian camp, and briefly wonders about this. Noting an "identity paradox at the heart of a Somewhere power" Goodhart argues that "power was emphatically expressed in Britain and the US in 2016 through the stirring of a semi-conscious majority identity politics yet conventional identity politics is the enemy of social solidarity and the communitarian aspirations of the Somewhere worldview." Goodhart resolves this tension elsewhere in the text through his proposition—without very clear grounds—that new populism in Britain and the US is not in fact generally nativist, racist, or ethnocentric but rather assumes in effect (to rephrase Goodhart in older medieval moral terms) that whoever is *in* the territory is *of* the territory and is seen by most people as a political member, regardless of origin. But Goodhart does not pause to think about these tensions concerning the life of the city much further, or to sustain this line of thought toward the really interesting conclusions it might yield. This face of the third city he does not see.

What Goodhart's account half sees but cannot keep in view is the competing forms of communitarianism and liberalism at work within contemporary political cleavages. He fails to see that, in Rosean terms, they represent not entities or peoples separated by a chasm but "competing and colliding cities," contesting the same territory in ways that both resemble and differ from one another. Rarely in such presentations are cosmopolitans understood in communitarian terms: either in self-presentation or at the hands of their analyzing "other." The conceptual frameworks deployed by each movement tend to deny that possibility. And in so doing, it is possible that these movements also fail to provide us with the necessary structural, analytical, and political tools to attend to the principle challenges concerning political membership they profess to address.

There are further theopolitical suppressions that mark Goodhart's account. Religious communities represent a paradox that Goodhart can't quite stay with and doesn't seem to have a unifying language through which to handle their representation. Religious communities and individuals irrupt into the text as complexifiers: they are both singular and communal representatives of social conservatism and tend toward valuing the particular, but they are also (as often migrant communities in significant part) beneficiaries of the "Anywhere" worldview—tied economically and culturally to the elites. Nonetheless, Goodhart has also noted—without developing the thought or connecting it up to his other religious concerns—that religion might also have been part of the production of the very universalist bias he sees as the root of the contemporary political problem: here his concerns are about a form of Catholic social ethics that impels a priority for a common good that is imagined as transgressive of national imperative or priority. As such religious communities and theological complexities are both evoked and occluded in these accounts.

This failure to work through the competing and colliding cities evident in current political culture reveals itself most clearly in Goodhart's final chapter in which he proposes a "new settlement." He argues that a better politics is rooted in a tension or balance held between "Anywheres" and "Somewheres"—we need a bit of both, but the dominance of neither. In one sense this might be the basis for a promising conclusion: the Other is not so other after all, mutual receptivity might be necessary. In the event, the constructive account offered does not deliver on its possibilities. While Goodhart has raised to voice the suppressed goods articulated by the "Somewheres" (kinship, place, skill, and so forth), politics emerges less as a process in which goods are negotiated and the self is both under formation and reformation and more as a process in which interests are brokered and balanced and denigrated self-interest is given voice. The rebalancing of interests in favor of the suppressed social conservatism of Somewheres would, Goodhart argues, calm anxieties about security and borders and restore the reciprocal bonds of mutual welfare. Beyond the task of rebalancing interests Goodhart notes commonalities that can create bridges (his choice of architectural imagery) between "Anywheres" and "Somewheres"—where some sameness can be found. Would Rose not tell us that this vision—despite its promise—feels eerily like the multilayered repetition of the myth of the self-in-possession, that it feeds without rendering meaningful the perennial anxieties of our collective life? Somehow Goodhart does not venture enough and does not risk enough.

If the predominant modes of political life on offer to us face the same risk—that they both dissolve the difficulty of self-other relations, of the complex relation of particular, universal, and singular into forms of idealized identities—that they are communitarian without any real account of power, violence, or ethical difficulty of invoking the communal and endlessly suspend the necessary work of mourning and risk taking, then the political becomes facile. In Rose's account the political happens not when we defend or assert wounded or lost interests but when, from the grounds of the particular, we risk articulating and acting—and failing—according to the demands and possibility of the universal. For Rose, we begin in the middle; for Goodhart, we rename or reclaim the middle as the majority and thus we resolve our agony. In so doing it is unclear how the figure that Rose names so well as the Singular—the just woman, just man who gives mournable justice its presence—who acts in ways that are inalienably particular in the name of the universal has presence, is represented as the hope and possibility of the political present and future.

Rowan Williams points out that the theological question at the heart of Rose's work emerges from her "insistence on a sociality never 'mended' in a final way." This is not "the facile and tempting question of law's relation to grace, but the harder one of how the very experience of learning and of negotiation can be read as something to do with God."[31] This is partly to place theology in a border terrain between politics and metaphysics (hence the title of Williams's piece), where "between-ness" implies a dynamic position in hermeneutical territory common to both rather than a pure space separated from both, or a space of confinement. Williams's meditation on the function of law in Rose, as love and violence made manifest, effaces any possibility of such tactical segregation. This spatial in-between does imply however, a constant pattern of negotiation and of self-dispossession. This is a moment in the laying bare of the contemplative structure of transformative practice.

The political location of metaphysical discourse is not the reduction of metaphysics to functional subordination within an alien setting, but something more like the laying bare of a contemplative or nonfunctional dimension to the political, the element of "seeing" that is contained in any idea of intelligible action in a world of diverse agents.[32]

Williams is among the subtlest interpreters of Rose's work and finds there a sense that what speculative philosophy yields through reflection on "natural" consciousness and its workings is not a use-value but meaning that precedes and exceeds necessity. This is not a *methodology* for (theological) critique but an intense reflection on its possibility. We might say it is

31. Williams, "Between Politics and Metaphysics," 9.
32. Ibid., 6.

critical scholarship as *poiesis*, which is nonetheless a seeing and a fabrication of a kind. Primarily this *possibility* is found between each other.

Bibliography

Barrington-Ward, Simon. "'Forgiven, Forgiving,' 'Failing Towards . . .'—The Goal and the Journey." Unpublished paper presented at The Social Theory Centre, University of Warwick, December 2000.

Caygill, Howard. Preface to *Paradiso*, by Gillian Rose, 7–8. London: Meynard, 1999.

Goodhart, David. *The Road to Somewhere: The Populist Revolt and the Future of Politics*. London: Hurst, 2017.

Johnson, Daniel. "Mourning, the Consolation of a Philosopher." *The Times*, December 21, 1996, 16.

Kavka, Martin. "Saying Kaddish for Gillian Rose." In *Secular Theology*, 104–29. London: Routledge, 2001.

Plato. *Phaedrus*. Translated by Robin Waterfield. Oxford: Oxford University Press, 2002.

———. *Republic*. Translated by Robin Waterfield. Oxford: Oxford University Press, 1998.

Rose, Gillian. "Athens and Jerusalem: A Tale of Three Cities." In *Mourning Becomes the Law*, 15–40. Cambridge: Cambridge University Press, 1996.

———. *The Broken Middle*. Oxford: Blackwell, 1992.

———. *The Dialectic of Nihilism*. Oxford: Blackwell, 1984.

———. *Hegel contra Sociology*. London: Athlone, 1981.

———. *Hegel contra Sociology*. London: Athlone, 1995.

———. *Judaism and Modernity*. Oxford: Blackwell, 1993.

———. *Love's Work*. London: Chatto & Windus, 1995.

———. *Mourning Becomes the Law*. Cambridge: Cambridge University Press, 1996.

———. *Paradiso*. London: Meynard, 1999.

Schick, Kate. *Gillian Rose: A Good Enough Justice*. Edinburgh: Edinburgh University Press, 2012.

Shanks, Andrew. *God and Modernity: A New and Better Way to Do Theology*. London: Routledge, 2000.

Williams, Rowan. "Between Politics and Metaphysics: Reflections in the Wake of Gillian Rose." *Modern Theology* 11, no. 1 (1995) 3–22.

Chapter 2

Toward a Rosean Political Theology of Recognition

Andrew Brower Latz

For the last twenty years "recognition" has been an important concept linking questions about how individual identity is formed with those about ethics and justice. Theories of recognition, picking up from early nineteenth-century German Idealism, argue that only through mutual and intersubjective recognition of one another can healthy individuals be formed and a just society created; and that people are harmed by misrecognition. For example, minorities' self-esteem and self-perception are damaged in racist societies, even when individuals from those minorities know they are being unjustly misrecognized. A methodological strength of recognition theories is their ability to blend sociological description with normative considerations, such that the theory of justice produced is closely tied to concrete social analysis and its philosophical components are historically moored.

To date, however, there has been surprisingly little theological engagement with recognition theory given its major status and fruitfulness in social philosophy as a contemporary theory of justice.[1] At the same time, recognition theory suffers from three deficiencies: it has focused too heavily on a conflict-based model of recognition; it has paid insufficient attention

---

1. See now, however, Saarinen, *Recognition and Religion*.

to how individuals perform recognition; and it has suppressed its historical religious sources. This leaves recognition theory unable to properly account for how the desired state of society-wide mutual recognition could come about; lacking guidance as to how individuals can fulfil the moral demand to recognize others; and unable to perceive and theorize those instances of recognition that do not proceed by way of socially competitive conflict. I aim to show that a theological and Rosean account of recognition can address these issues.

Rose made some suggestive but undeveloped comments about recognition. In what follows I will first summarize some of the main contours of recognition theory and then look at the work of Kate Schick and Liz Disley, both of whom have developed aspects of Rose's thought as it relates to recognition theory. In the third section I set Rose's remarks about recognition within two features of her thought: self-limiting reason and the relationship between recognition and appropriation. "Appropriation" is the act of making something one's own, coming to terms with it, working through it. Finally, by examining an instance from Marilynne Robinson's fiction, I present a cooperative form of recognition, which involves Rosean appropriation and is explicitly theological. Cooperative recognition, I suggest, occurs when two individuals both try to recognize one another. Rather than the struggle of a group to wrest recognition from a reluctant society, cooperative recognition is the struggle of the self with the self to recognize the other fully, which is mirrored by the other trying to recognize the first person. If this cooperative model of recognition is co-primordial with or even primordial to conflict-based recognition—and there are good grounds to think so—then we are some way toward addressing the three problems with recognition theory. A fundamentally cooperative version of recognition can balance the overemphasis on recognition via conflict; the fictional example gives a thick description of how subjects perform recognition; and the theological nature of this version of cooperative recognition is intrinsic to its performance.

Religion and theology can then be seen to make substantive contributions to recognition theory as well as learning from recognition theory. As Rose put it, "everybody's looking for an ethics. But in fact, they should be looking for a political theology,"[2] and the "resources" for reflecting on "the soul, the city and the sacred . . . may be found . . . in the theology which has been more thoroughly suppressed."[3] A political theology of recognition,

---

2. "Interview with Gillian Rose," ed. Lloyd. First Broadcast October 28th and November 4th 1995 on *Dialogue*, RTÉ Radio 1; full audio version available at: www.rte.ie/radio1/podcast/podcast_dialogue.xml, accessed 13th April 2012.

3. Rose, *Mourning Becomes the Law*, 9–10.

which takes its cue from Rose's Hegelian Frankfurt social theory, is therefore worth considering.

I Recognition Theory

Recognition theory conceives both justice and identity formation as the giving and receiving of recognition.[4] It claims subjects can only develop self-consciousness as autonomous agents if they are recognized as such by others. The existence of the other person is a "summons" to the self. The self cannot become self-conscious by a pure mental act but only through the practical call of another. At the same time, the subject must take the one recognizing him or her as competent and authoritative to do so. Hence recognition is a normative concept and in most cases its ideal form is reciprocal. The theory provides an intersubjective model of autonomy, reason and, freedom, grounded in recognition.

If recognition is withheld from people it damages their self-esteem, their ability to value themselves and relate to others. The novelist James Baldwin gives a moving account of this in "My Dungeon Shook," his open letter to his nephew about the experience of being African American in the 60s in the USA. Even though African Americans knew they were being wrongly perceived by their society, they could not stop that perception from damaging their self-perception. He wrote to his nephew, "[Y]our grandfather ... was defeated long before he died because, at the bottom of his heart, he really believed what white people said about him."[5]

We can see from Baldwin's example that recognition theory is able to capture the social and psychological elements of justice better than a narrower focus on rights. It can identify "social pathologies."[6] As a result it has been used to articulate the grievances of sexism, racism, and homophobia, and the struggles of new social movements for recognition within society. But the theory should not be conflated with identity politics. On the contrary, it has a universalizing moment insofar as recognition is actually the ground of rights: rights are the legal institutionalization of the recognition citizens give one another as free persons in a modern political state.[7]

Recognition is usually considered to exist in three forms: love and the provision of needs within the family; esteem for one's achievements within

---

4. See Honneth, *The Struggle for Recognition*; and Taylor, "The Politics of Recognition," 25–73.
5. Baldwin, *The Fire Next Time*, 13.
6. Honneth, *Freedom's Right*, e.g., 86–94, 113–20.
7. Bernstein, "Right, Revolution and Community," 91–119.

civil society; and rights as a way to secure respect for individual autonomy and freedom within the state.[8] The three levels increase in scope and comprehensiveness, but at the same time lose concreteness. The worst form of disrespect is at the level of bodily needs, desires, and integrity. The next worst is to disregard the most comprehensive level, that of moral accountability and dignity. Finally, the least bad form of disrespect is not to recognize another's contributions to civil society and its projects. (This follows not the order of comprehensiveness and abstractness of forms of recognition but their historical development.) Now, "the transition from one sphere of recognition to another is always caused by a struggle to gain respect for a subject's self-comprehension as it grows in stages. The demand to be recognized in ever more dimensions of one's own person leads to a kind of intersubjective conflict whose resolution can only consist in the establishment of a further sphere of recognition."[9] Thus social conflict is not merely a struggle for brute power or self-interest but, at least sometimes, derives from "moral impulses."[10]

Most work on the theory has predominantly treated recognition as a struggle between opposed groups who want to deny one another recognition. This is based on an interpretation of the model of the master-slave dialectic in Hegel's *Phenomenology of Spirit* made influential through Kojève and Sartre. "The starting point of the process of recognition is" *loss* of self or other,[11] either the other is eliminated or compelled to recognise the self; or the other is only a place wherein the self is reflected (and so the other is erased in a different way). It is the contradictory nature of this sort of relationship, in which the other is both recognized and not recognized, which makes the relationship prone to dialectical reversal. In fact, for Hegel himself, the asymmetrical and conflict-ridden form of recognition is "self-subverting,"[12] which is why the mutual form of recognition is the only stable one and therefore a normative goal in ethics and politics. Theorists tend to note this without giving it sufficient weight. Hence Honneth can say, "the movement of recognition that forms the basis of an ethical relationship between subjects consists in a process of alternating stages of both reconciliation and conflict";[13] and, "all human coexistence presupposes a kind of basic mutual affirmation between subjects, since otherwise no form of

8. Again, see Honneth, *Struggle*.
9. Honneth, *Disrespect*, 132–33.
10. Honneth, *Struggle*, 5.
11. Williams, *Hegel's Ethics of Recognition*, 56.
12. Ibid.
13. Honneth, *Struggle*, 17.

being-together whatsoever could ever come into existence."[14] Yet for various understandable reasons, he focuses on struggle and conflict rather than the stages of reconciliation.

A second reason to consider the reconciled stages of recognition comes from the empirical support for the theory. Evidence suggests recognition is prior to cognition: a baby first experiences its caregivers as meaning- and love-conferring before it develops rationality.[15] What's more, the recognition between mother and infant is not the master-slave struggle to dominate, but mutually affirming. Although it is mutually affirming it is not symmetrical. This is important for suggesting there can be legitimate and important forms of recognition that are not symmetrically reciprocal,[16] something else underemphasized in the literature.

Recognition theory opens the possibility of theoretical attention to the contribution of religious groups because it orients the theory of justice toward civil society. Much work on recognition theory, however, downplays both the theology in Hegel and the role of religion in society. Consider two examples. Hegel, again in the *Phenomenology of Spirit*, but much later than the master-slave dialectic, asks how people who confront one another with opposing moral convictions are able to live together in society. His answer is not tolerance but forgiveness, a theological notion. His whole section on morality ends with forgiveness, and then transitions into religion. Yet most of the work on recognition simply ignores his argumentative flow.[17] Secondly, the three common sources of energy and motivation in struggles for recognition given in the literature are: affirmation gained in childhood from one's family; recognition between participants within social movements; and the idea that a just, future society would recognize the persons struggling to achieve recognition. But this ignores the energy and motivation people gain from their religion, both from the examples of others, and from the belief that God loves them—recognizes them—and requires them to do morally good and just acts. Yet religion has played a prominent part in struggles for recognition throughout history. To take just one example, the leaders of the US civil rights movement were disproportionately from the African Methodist Episcopal church.[18]

---

14. Ibid., 43.

15. See, e.g., Benjamin, *The Bonds of Love*, which makes use of attachment theory. Cf. Yeatman, "A *Two*-Person Conception of Freedom."

16. Cf. Hoelzl, "Recognizing the Sacrificial Victim."

17. Similarly, many within the Frankfurt School tradition like to stress the break between modernity and premodernity, but Hegel wanted to mediate between the two. Hegel's approach allows more breathing space for religious traditions.

18. Dickerson, "Wesleyan Social Holiness, African Methodism, and the U. S. Civil

As powerful and important as recognition theory is, then, its focus on conflict and its side-lining of religion have led to a failure to appreciate properly the significance of more cooperative forms of recognition and religion as a source for fostering those. Rose's work provides some resources for moving past these problems.

II Rosean Recognition

Kate Schick and Liz Disley have both made use of Rose in order to improve recognition theory. Schick shows how Rose's thought is able to help move recognition theory beyond a narrow focus on technical problem solving. Disley suggests some ways in which the theological elements of German Idealism are important in producing forms of what she calls "positive recognition," namely, forgiveness and love. She finds aspects of Rose's broken middle helpful in elaborating these forms of recognition.

Schick argues that recognition theory has tended to take a "hyperrationalist" form. Hyperrationalist recognition has become a tool, applied outwardly to solve social problems by "adding more" recognition. It has become "largely captured by moral rationalism, which casts recognition as a powerful tool that might be deployed in the service of justice. It is primarily outward looking, advocating more respect and understanding of others, the bestowal of equal rights, and the removal of barriers to participation."[19] Hyperrationalist recognition theory has actually regressed into individualism, losing some of its initial stress on intersubjectivity, and taken on a positivist, problem-solving intellectual mood. The fundamental nature of agents' interdependence and vulnerability has been lost, as has the sense of the difficulty of coming to know, the repeated re-cognition involved in recognition. "[H]yperrationalist recognition theory has lost the dynamism and agonism of early Hegelian recognition scholarship, which emphasizes a difficult journey towards comprehension. Instead, it has become an instrument of liberal problem-solving theory that can be wielded to 'solve' social and political ills."[20] The inward moment of subjectivity has sunk from view.[21] By contrast, Rosean recognition urges the subject to discover the

Rights Movement."

19. Schick, "Re-cognizing Recognition," 91.

20. Ibid., 88.

21. A notable exception to the tendency to ignore the self-transformation required by recognition is Foster, "An Adornian Theory of Recognition?" Yet Foster pins his hopes on engagement with high art as the best way for individuals to be open to such transformation. Important as art is for many, it is by no means the whole picture; and of course high art is only accessible to a small proportion of people, as Adorno was

ways in which s/he is complicit in misrecognition and injustice, even whilst having good intentions. It highlights the vulnerability of the subject in the process of recognition and the need to relinquish "deeply held desires for security and self-certainty."[22] It is, as such, "profoundly countercultural."[23]

Disley suggests Hegel's account of recognition involves love and forgiveness as central paradigms, and that both are best theorized using elements from the theological tradition, whence Hegel took them originally in his early work. These two forms of recognition do not embroil subjects in the struggle to the death of the more prominent master-slave dialectic, hence Disley calls them "positive" forms of recognition. In love (at least in its ideal form), the subject gladly unites with the other, embracing the intersubjectivity and interdependence involved. To forgive is to be an active subject, yet also to perceive oneself as passive because one is the object of a wrong. "Indeed, it is the very transformation from the status of 'passive' object to 'active' subject which is seen as part of the healing nature of forgiveness for the victim of an offence."[24] Hegel "sees forgiveness as a process that concludes with some kind of 'judicial' (not necessarily in the formal, legal sense) ceasing or refraining from sanctions."[25]

Disley argues for greater appreciation of the place of theology in German Idealism and social philosophy more generally. "It is a central claim of this work that theology is a great neglected element in current work on recognition and social ontology . . . recognition has to be understood together with forgiveness and *metanoia* [repentance] in a way that fundamentally involves the theological."[26] Recognition involves *metanoia*, then, changing the self, not merely one's mind. She thinks this is well captured by Rose's broken middle as a place of "constant change and anxiety," since recognition in its various forms is never finished.[27] The broken middle entails that taking a position always involves error, and therefore "violence," even within love.[28] She sums it up thus: "Imperfect and in some way incomplete (Rose's broken middle), the self in its relation with the Other is ever-changing and being remade (*metanoia*, Hegelian . . . *Aufhebung*) and is influenced by the Other and the wider community to such an extent that we cannot speak of full

---

pointing out already in the forties.

22. Schick, "Re-cognizing Recognition," 104.
23. Ibid., 105.
24. Disley, *Hegel, Love and Forgiveness*, 116
25. Ibid., 128.
26. Ibid., 12.
27. Ibid., 16.
28. Rose's term of art "violence" is somewhat confusing. It sometimes simply means "error," as in this case, though with the added thought that errors can cause real damage.

autonomy, though there is a clear space for ethical responsibility . . . . This ethical self is not ontologically pre-defined, but forms itself in the encounter or confrontation with the Other, who calls the self to ethical action."[29]

Both Schick and Disley take us a long way toward the kind of recognition theory Rose's work makes possible. In the remainder of this chapter I will add to this account of Rosean recognition and then offer a theological exemplification thereof.

III Appropriation and Recognition

Two tenets provide the most important context for Rose's remarks on recognition: self-limiting reason and the relationship between recognition and appropriation. I will show that for Rose appropriation is intrinsic to recognition, which goes some way toward explaining how recognition can be performed.

A central issue within German Idealism was reason's autonomy, its independence from external authority. Hegel, in Rose's view, accorded reason a nuanced but not absolute autonomy. Reason was based in and reliant on a shape of spirit, its ethical life, its institutions, and so on. Yet reason, via the individual, was able to take some distance from itself and the shape of spirit on which it depended, and thereby gain a certain freedom with respect to what determines it. This achievement is never perfect, such that reason and the subject are always partly free and unfree. Rather than setting these boundaries of reason or the subject once for all, they should be investigated as they change. For Rose too reason is grounded not only in itself but also on physical particulars and moments that exceed reason's grasp, such that no perfectly complete or autonomously grounded reason exists.[30] The result is, as Rose put it, "the reassessment of reason, gradually rediscovering its own moveable boundaries as it explores the boundaries of the soul, the city and the sacred"[31]; and "a rationalism which constantly explores its own limits without fixing them . . . renegotiate[ing] knowledge and responsibility under their historically and politically changing conditions."[32]

Rose would come to express this version of self-limiting reason as "aporetic" rather than "deterministic" philosophy. Like her *Doktorvater*, Leszek Kołakowski, Rose thought, "We may admit that no traditional metaphysical questions are soluble and still deny that this is a reason to dismiss them or

---

29. Ibid., 70–71.
30. Rose, *Judaism and Modernity*, ix–10.
31. Rose, *Mourning Becomes the Law*, 11–12.
32. Rose, *Judaism and Modernity*, 17.

declare them meaningless.... There is no absolute beginning in thinking .... Inevitably, we start and end in the middle of our itinerary."[33] And "we never start from the beginning.... Philosophies voice the aspirations and the choices of civilizations [which] are never perfectly coherent."[34] Hence, "we believe that contradictions which actually exist may well be overcome so that a synthesis is established between them; but we also believe, in accordance with the entire experience of history, that a contradiction which vanishes is merely replaced by a new contradiction, so that no universal synthesis is possible."[35] The always-unfinished, existential-cognitive appropriation of a preceding reality forever beyond complete comprehension has parallels to theology. Although various members of the Frankfurt School held to the doctrine of self-limiting reason, notably Adorno, Rose is unusual in drawing the inference that it opens up again the way to metaphysics and theology.[36]

Rose insisted, likewise against the dominant Frankfurt School view, on retaining Hegel's ideas of "recognition and appropriation (*anerkennen* and *aneignen*) ... [as] fundamental to Hegel's notion of a system."[37] "Appropriation" is the act of making something one's own, coming to terms with it, working through it. As such it has been largely maligned by post-structuralism and those working under its influence, on the grounds that coming to terms with something must mean domesticating it, removing its otherness, reducing it to the self or the self's preexisting categories. Appropriation therefore seems to crystallize the worrisome nature of Hegel's self-enclosed and all-encompassing system. Rose showed, on the contrary, that appropriation need not deny difference, nor trap a subject within her own terms of thought, insulating the subject from reality. On the contrary, appropriation is the way a subject opens herself or himself up to reality.[38] The reason is quite simple. Once someone (or something) has been recognized,

33. *Metaphysical Horror*, 8–11.
34. Ibid., 99.
35. Kołakowski, "In Praise of Inconsistency," 206.
36. An argument elaborated, partly by way of Rose, in Milbank, *Theology and Social Theory*, though drawing on French sources rather than Frankfurt thinkers.
37. Rose, *Hegel contra Sociology*, 45. For the dominant view, which Rose cites, see Kortian, *Metacritique*. Kortian writes that philosophy must "denounce one of the constitutive moments of Hegelian speculative experience: the moment of recognition and appropriation (*Anerkennung und Aneignung*) of the phenomenalised totality of the absolute concept in its otherness" (41).
38. For a different, though somewhat related, take on appropriation that also sees it as a necessary and helpful activity, see Jaeggi, *Alienation*. On the failure of post-structural attacks on Hegel's version of recognition, see Williams, *Hegel's Ethics of Recognition*, 364–412.

the recognition remains to be appropriated, and this applies as someone (or something) is repeatedly re-cognized. "Rose's recognition is an agonistic concept that emphasizes the ongoing process of recognition, which implies cognition followed by re-cognition or coming to know again. It works towards a more holistic comprehension of our human world, including our selves and our own implication in those norms, values and structures that marginalize and oppress. It interrogates the desires that underlie a refusal to recognize others."[39]

Appropriation involves several dimensions, all of which are important in Rose's work as a whole: time, working through, mediation, and history. Recognition and appropriation require time because recognition is not simply registering a fact but involves a change in the individual, "a new concept of the self-other relation, the self-self relation, and the self-world relation."[40] It is both intellectual and existential. Many accounts of recognition focus only on the initial moment of recognition or its end result, but thereby neglect the time it takes to work through the difficulties of recognition.

Recognition understood fully "is a process of coming to terms with, working through, what leads us to refuse recognition."[41] The labor of appropriation can be thought in terms of "working through," an important phrase for Rose[42] and driving her aberrated/inaugurated mourning distinction. Working through is a psychoanalytic term for the process in which the individual brings to consciousness and thinks through different aspects of an idea, and thereby gradually overcomes his/her initial resistance to accepting the idea. Again, this is not a narrowly intellectual exercise but involves emotions, an aesthetic sense, and may involve the body more directly too.[43] One of the recurrent themes in Rose's essays that make up *Mourning Becomes the Law* is the analogies between mourning and the activities of philosophy and politics.[44] Grief involves tasks to accomplish: accepting the reality of loss, experiencing the pain of grief, adjusting to an environment without the deceased (or lost object), and withdrawing emotional energy from the lost relationship in order to reinvest it in another relationship.[45] Rose insisted, against the endless and aberrated mourning of poststructuralism,

---

39. Schick, "Re-cognizing recognition," 96.

40. Disley, *Hegel, Love and Forgiveness*, 2.

41. Foster, "An Adornian Theory of Recognition?," 257.

42. RTÉ interview.

43. Think, for example, of responses to arguments for vegetarianism or veganism. Perhaps the largest difficulty for most people is not the intellectual arguments but the change in diet and lifestyle required once one accepts the arguments.

44. Rose, *Mourning Becomes the Law*, 122.

45. I take these from Worden, *Grief Counseling and Grief Therapy*, 11–17.

that philosophy's mourning—about the tragedies of history, the failures of Marxism, the failures of philosophy to deliver finished answers—could and should be completed in order to move on in a healthy way. Completing the work of mourning obviously does not mean forgetting what has been lost or downplaying the loss; it does involve active effort.

Working through over time involves understanding the recognized person (or object) in more and more of his/her (or its) mediations, rendering him/her more concrete and so, for Rose at least, relating him/her to some sort of totality.[46] Forms of recognition are mediated through social forms, such as gender, race and caste relations, class expectations, power formations, and the like. Any full recognition of another will try to take account of these mediations.

At the same time, one is relating oneself to the recognized other and to the totality too, and thereby discovering something about how one's self is determined, which may contribute to one's freedom from determination. Equally, appropriation involves internalizing in a deep, significant way what is recognized, and this involves a certain kind of self-relation. The self is transformed both by open receptivity to what is recognized and by active work on the self by the self. This is why Rose regards philosophy as existentially transformative: "[H]er concept of recognition invites a counter-cultural way of being that eschews the drive towards self-sufficiency and self-advantage and calls us instead to accept our radical dependency on one another."[47]

Finally, the mediations one discerns are historically shaped and can be related to historical struggles for recognition and gain their meanings from phenomenological determinate negations. The available forms of recognition vary historically. Recognition itself was neither explicitly conceptualized nor properly politically enacted until the nineteenth century. Since then it has expanded to different groups. Any attempt to further recognition would do well to learn from the history of global struggles for recognition, including religious contributions thereto. Rose's insistence on the centrality and fundamentality of mediation against any kind of ethical immediacy may leave her account of recognition less vulnerable than

---

46. A totality for Rose is a view of the social whole, something both necessary and yet impossible fully to achieve, yet nevertheless presupposed in every social analysis. As the Kortian quotation above suggests, the rejection of Hegel's concept of totality by Frankfurt thinkers was bound up with their rejection of his use of appropriation and recognition.

47. Schick, "Re-cognizing Recognition," 96–97.

Honneth's to the charge of neglecting the economic and legal deformations of consciousness.[48]

IV Cooperative Recognition

As noted above, cooperative recognition is the struggle of the self with the self to recognize the other fully, which is mirrored by the other trying to recognize the first person. Cooperative recognition occurs when two individuals try to recognize one another mutually or reciprocally. It is not a struggle to be recognized without recognizing the other nor the attempt to gain recognition from others who would withhold it.

We can read Marilynne Robinson's novel *Home* as a phenomenology of the struggle for cooperative recognition.[49] The novel shows us how, paradoxically, the cooperative model of recognition is difficult to achieve, even though both parties are working toward the same end. There is a significant dose of moral tragedy in Robinson's novels, which has two advantages for my case. It does not present religion as a facile solution, and it shows some of the difficulties encountered in achieving cooperative recognition and some of the means used to overcome them.

In *Home* Robinson tells the story of a few months at the Boughton household, set in the 50s in a fictional small town in Iowa called Gilead. Old Boughton, the father, is a retired minister. Glory, his youngest daughter, has moved in to look after her father who is now quite frail. She left her teaching job to do so and has just broken off a long engagement. The man to whom she was engaged strung her along in order to "borrow" money from her. While she is there, Jack, one of her brothers, returns home. Jack has not been home for twenty years. As a child he was constantly in trouble,

---

48. For critiques of Honneth along these lines, see Loick, "Juridification and Politics"; and Thompson, "Axel Honneth and the Neo-Idealist Turn in Critical Theory."

49. The use of novels within sociological research has been important since the beginning of the Frankfurt School. For Benjamin and Lukács, as Rose explained, "Literary criticism was not a discrete discipline but inseparable from the basic questions of epistemology and philosophical experience and, conversely, philosophical questions could not be considered apart from cultural forms" (Rose, *Melancholy Science*, 35). As Honneth noted more recently, "only rarely can we directly perceive these kinds of symptoms in empirical investigations. The analytical tools used by sociological researchers are generally too blunt to capture such diffuse moods or collective sentiments; therefore, the best approach for diagnosing such pathologies remains, just as in the time of Hegel or the young Lukács, the analysis of indirect displays of these symptoms in the aesthetic sphere; novels, films or works of art still [sic] the best source of initial insights into contemporary tendencies towards higher-order, reflexive deformations of social behaviour" (*Freedom's Right*, 87).

from mischief to nuisance pranks to small-scale criminality. While a college student, he fathered a child with a poor, illiterate young woman who lived a short distance from Gilead. He then abandoned them both and removed himself from contact with his family. It emerges that Jack has been an alcoholic for a large portion of his adult life, though has been sober for most of the last ten years. He has had a series of low-paying, low-skilled jobs. Above all, Robinson emphasizesemphasizes Jack's loneliness and separateness from others. Glory "thought she did remember that estrangement of his gaze, that look of urgent calculation of sharply attentive calm. It could only be fear, and she wanted to say, You can trust me, but that is what they had always told him, and he laughed and pretended to believe them, and wished to believe them, she was sure, and never did. Her father always said, 'That loneliness of his.'"[50] The constant fear of the family while Jack was growing up was that he would run away, that they would lose him, which they eventually did. Everyone in the Boughton immediate family is a Presbyterian, except Jack, whose relationship to theology, Christianity, and God is troubling to himself and the others. This theological context pervades the novel.

A great deal of the novel is occupied with Glory and Jack reestablishing their relationship after a twenty-year hiatus.[51] Glory wants to help Jack feel at home. She does not want to scare him away, not least because it would devastate her father, who is delighted to have his lost son returned home. She therefore takes pains not to encroach on his privacy, not to presume, not to be angry with him for hurting her father, but also to cultivate what signs of friendship he offers. Jack gradually comes to trust Glory, to rely on her, to seek her help in mending his relationship with his father, to take her advice. Much difficulty is encountered in establishing this relationship and for a long time there is the sense that its tentative achievement could be undone in a single careless, accidental, or misunderstood word or gesture. Here is an example:

> She thought about the thing Jack had seemed to ask of her, some attempt to save his soul. Dear Lord. How could that idea haunt her with a sense of obligation, when she really did not know what it meant. There are words you hear all your life, she thought. Then one day you stop to wonder. She would not bring it up again, but if he did, she should have some way to answer

---

50. Robinson, *Home*, 89.

51. There is in the novel also much about Jack's relationship to his father, and the way Glory mediates that relationship. For the sake of brevity and simplicity I have left that to one side, though a full account would obviously need to consider the mediations in detail.

him. She was not at all sure that he had been serious, that he was not teasing her. She might even have taken offense at the time, if there had seemed to be any point in it. A genteel project for a pious lady with time on her hands. How condescending. But that was what he did whenever he felt vulnerable—he found some way to sting, to make it clear that vulnerability was not all on one side. Poor man. But he was so practiced at reciting what he was also practiced at rejecting. He might have meant to draw her into some sort of argument and reject it, too, just to show her he could do it. He was uneasy. That was natural enough. And in fact he had made her embarrassed about that pleasant old habit of hers. Now she had to read the Bible in her room to avoid feeling like a hypocrite, like someone praying on a street corner. When Jack came out to the porch with his newspaper the next day and found her reading *The Dollmaker* he gave her a wistful, inquiring look, but he said nothing.[52]

We see here Glory's attempt to recognize Jack. Her efforts to recognize him require her to try to appropriate his otherness, which is in part a work on herself. In the first place, the process of recognition takes several weeks. Glory only gradually stops being angry with Jack for hurting her parents, and for abandoning his own child and its mother. She only gradually begins to trust him enough to tell him some of the story of her engagement. And this only happens as she makes the active effort to consider things from his point of view, and to think of diverse possible explanations for his behavior.

The work of cooperative recognition is an effort and labor. We can see this from Glory's constant attempts not to judge too quickly; not to offend Jack or scare him off. We can see it in the way she thinks through different explanations for his behavior rather than being offended or assuming she knows what motivates him or what he is thinking. (Glory's efforts are mirrored in Robinson's narrative perspectives: although we are privy to Glory's thoughts we are never granted access to Jack's.)

Glory's efforts happen within the historical and social context of the time, which regards alcoholism and children out of wedlock much more gravely than contemporary society. This only makes Glory's task more difficult. She was the only child left at home with her parents when Jack abandoned his own child. She saw how painful it was to them as they attempted to do something for their grandchild and were rebuffed. This personal history is part of Glory and Jack's relationship.

Since Glory is thoroughly steeped in Christianity and its theology, her constant efforts to be good to Jack, live up to her own ideals, not give in to

---

52. Ibid., 114.

her baser motives, and the like, can be seen as theological practices. This kind of slow rather than fast thinking is arguably a kind of meditation or perhaps prayer, and also a form of repentance as she changes her mind and self away from some forms of activity and toward others. Repentance is very much existentially involving, a reflection on the self as well as a turn to the other, and connects nicely to Hegel's proposal that society relies on forgiveness, not merely tolerance. Meditation fosters the kind of slow thinking and attention to others required in order fully to recognize them, to allow their otherness to transform the self. Cooperative recognition is a process of appropriation carried out by means of these two practices.[53] The self is transformed both by open receptivity to what is recognized and by active work on the self by the self.

This example from Robinson also shows how in cooperative recognition Glory does not insist on constant equal mutuality but is more concerned with doing what is right. She does not thereby downplay or lose mutual recognition as a goal, however; rather we see once again how the process leading to the end result of mutual recognition can be uneven, can involve progress and regress. Michael Hoelzl identified self-sacrifice for another as a phenomenon recognition theory has difficulty explaining.[54] Cooperative recognition by contrast has room for self-sacrifice, precisely because it affirms rather than struggles against the other.

Honneth paradigmatically divided recognition into three main spheres, as I mentioned earlier: the family, civil society, and political rights. The model of cooperative recognition we find in *Home* operates primarily but not exclusively within the familial sphere of love and direct needs. Daniel Loick has criticized Honneth and Habermas for a utopian view of recognition within the family, acting as if it is granted simply and automatically within the familial and failing to give due weight to the problems one finds within families.[55] Robinson shows how there are many difficulties within the familial sphere, even when several parties are all working toward the same end, and know they are doing so. The cooperative recognition we find there, then, is neither naïve nor utopian simply because it does not make conflict primary and central. It does not ignore conflict but places it in a different context. Nor is the model Robinson provides one between infant and parents, but between adults who have the bonds and shared history of

---

53. I do not rule out secular versions of these practices, but they would not be Glory's.
54. Hoelzl, "Recognizing the Sacrificial Victim."
55. Loick, "Juridification and Politics."

family. This is a quite different facet of familial recognition then. Cooperative recognition shows us the depths of the familial sphere of recognition.

The objection could arise: cooperative recognition is no different from Honneth's account of solidarity.[56] Solidarity is one way to translate "reciprocal intuition" (*wechselseitige Anschauung*), it is both the cognitive equal treatment of right/s (*Recht*) and the emotional attachment and care of love (a maximal definition, one would have to say). Solidarity thus allows one to respect others in their particularity; it is affective, not just cognitive. As such it is the most advanced form of recognition. Yet for Honneth, solidarity must be based on common values and goals, on "shared ideas about what constitutes a successful life within our community,"[57] a phrase Honneth glosses by referring to the division of labor enabling society to function as a whole. After all, the recognition between Glory and Jack also overlaps with the sphere of civil society, wherein people esteem others for their achievements. Part of what they must appropriate about one another is the kind of work each has done, the type of environment in which that has led them to move, and the sort of life each has led.

Yet Jack and Glory have either not achieved much socially, or their achievements are behind them and somewhat tarnished by their present misfortune. They cannot therefore esteem one another a great deal on that basis even though their recognition of one another does not ignore their work history. Yet the depth of their mutual recognition is such that it goes beyond achievements (indeed, beyond respecting one another's rights). Its depths are summoned by Glory's talk of the "soul." "She supposed it was not a mind or a self. Whatever they are. She supposed it was what the Lord saw when His regard fell upon any of us. But what can we know about that? Say we love and forgive, and enjoy the beauty of another life, however elusive it might be. Then, presumably, we have some idea of the soul we have encountered."[58] Their recognition is not, like solidarity, focused on jobs and social function, since it occurs between two unemployed adults. There is a parallel here with the early church, where slaves were granted religious equality within the *ekklesia* and even allowed to take prominent positions within it. One could even suggest that cooperative recognition, insofar as it looks beyond any socially esteemed achievements, is a way of living out the doctrine of creation *ex nihilo*: another's very being is of worth, even if they do not share one's values or goals, or if s/he lacks obvious achievements

---

56. E.g., Honneth, *Struggle*, 91.
57. Ibid.
58. Robinson, *Home*, 115–56.

or contributions to society.[59] One of the reasons it is difficult for Jack and Glory to recognize one another initially is precisely a lack of shared values: the religious person and the atheist, the good child and the tearaway, the clean living teacher and the alcoholic. Cooperative recognition is therefore not restricted to the familial sphere but even in this familial example spills out into civil society phenomena (and then of course affects the realm of the state, as we see from the political discussions in the novel). Now Honneth may respond by restricting "shared values" to fundamental cultural-political values that they probably do share, but that suggests a lack of nuance and texture in the face of Robinson's fictional world. (And, in fact, Jack is at odds with the mainstream views of his society on race and perhaps capitalism.)

A model of cooperative recognition in which social and economic achievements are not the central focus and rationale for recognition, where something like the soul is the ground of recognition, has further ramifications. According to Hegel, one of the constant, structural problems in modern societies is the tendency for economics to dominate politics. As a result, instead of society living up to its own ideal that the "absolute right is the right to have rights," we end up in a situation in which the "right to property is a right to right."[60] A person without "property, assets or work is in trouble" and will be "excluded from civil society."[61] A more widespread acknowledgment of cooperative recognition could add to the stock of those elements of society that counter this tendency. One of Hegel's philosophical themes is the idea that it makes a difference whether something is made explicit or not. It is not simply that when something is known and thereby becomes a possible object of consciousness, something at which to aim, there is more chance of realizing it; it is also that some things exist only in being known. For example, "freedom's right to presence in the world . . . is not objective until it is recognized."[62] Recognition of self and other as autonomous moral beings is a case in point; it was one of the great achievements of modernity in Hegel's view. "Reflection" is Hegel's name for this in the *Science of Logic*. In the realm of society, this means what was immediate and traditional must become posited, intentional, given a rationale. Thus, the imbalance within recognition literature on conflict and narrow, hyperrationalist versions of recognition has consequences beyond academic debate, not least because

---

59. For an argument along these lines, see Brower Latz, "Creation in the Fiction of Marilynne Robinson."
60. Williams, *Hegel's Ethics of Recognition*, 240, citing Hegel, *System of Ethical Life*.
61. Ibid., 240.
62. Ibid.

recognition theory was and is important within real political struggles (e.g., identity politics).

Yet the drawback of an explicitly theological model of recognition is obviously its limited audience. If a widespread appreciation of cooperative recognition is desirable, tying it to specific theological commitments seems a bad strategy. One response to this problem is to ask whether secular versions of meditation and repentance are possible. Put otherwise, the question may be how best to encourage slow rather than fast thinking,[63] or a better balance of left- and right-brain thinking,[64] and how to foster a culture and habits of a readiness to change direction when one is wrong.[65] It is clearly not the case that religious people have a monopoly on deep, sensitive thinking, nor on changing their behavior when necessary. Iris Murdoch had much to say about moral philosophy as exploring secular forms of religious practice. She sought "techniques for the purification and reorientation of an energy which is naturally selfish, in such a way that when moments of choice arrive we shall be sure of acting rightly."[66] She advocated the discipline of attending to reality and, as is common, associated this with art. "The appreciation of beauty in art or nature is not only (for all its difficulties) the easiest available spiritual exercise; it is also a completely adequate entry into (and not just analogy of) the good life, since it *is* the checking of selfishness in the interest of seeing the real."[67] Yet she goes further and speculates on the possibility of "a substitute for prayer" and "an analogy of the concept of sacrament, though this must be treated with great caution."[68] This of course is a large topic in itself, but it does suggest that the theological version of cooperative recognition could be to some extent successfully secularized.[69]

V Conclusion

Recognition theory has much to offer and theology has not yet sufficiently engaged with it. Theology could both learn from it and, I have tried to show,

---

63. See Kahneman, *Thinking, Fast and Slow*.

64. McGilchrist, *The Master and His Emissary*.

65. See the suggestive remarks of Fromm, *The Fear of Freedom*, 226, 233; and Gayman, "An Ethical Account of the Self Who Might Be Otherwise," 193–204.

66. Murdoch, *The Sovereignty of Good*, 54.

67. Ibid., 65.

68. Ibid., 69.

69. Much of Heidegger's early work is a secularized version of religious sources including the Bible and various figures from Christian history. See Van Buren, *The Young Heidegger*.

offer something to it. In particular, a theologically guided version of cooperative recognition can be more alert to the role of religion in fostering recognition in society and between individuals; can offer suggestions as to how recognition is carried out; and can re-balance the theory around non-conflict based forms of recognition, without denying or downplaying the importance and role of conflict and struggle. As such it is not surprising that cooperative recognition appears clearly in the theological fiction of Marilynne Robinson. Some of the benefits of the form of recognition seen there include not esteeming others solely based on their economic achievements (or luck) and the ability to cope with the often-asymmetrical nature of recognition. Rose's Hegelianism leads to a version of recognition theory much better attuned to what is going on in this case. A Rosean political theology of recognition would have much to offer.

Bibliography

Baldwin, James. *The Fire Next Time*. London: Penguin, 1963.

Benjamin, Jessica. *The Bonds of Love: Psychoanalysis, Feminism and the Problems of Domination*. London: Pantheon, 1988.

Bernstein, J. M. "Right, Revolution and Community: Marx's 'On the Jewish Question.'" In *Socialism and the Limits of Liberalism*, edited by Peter Osborne, 91–119. London: Verso, 1991.

Brower Latz, Andrew. "Creation in the Fiction of Marilynne Robinson." *Journal of Literature and Theology* 25, no. 3 (2011) 283–96.

Dickerson, Dennis C. "Wesleyan Social Holiness, African Methodism, and the U. S. Civil Rights Movement." Paper at the Manchester Wesley Research Centre, Nazarene Theological College, Manchester, England, April 1, 2014.

Disley, Liz. *Hegel, Love and Forgiveness: Positive Recognition in German Idealism*. London: Pickering & Chatto, 2015.

Foster, Roger. "An Adornian Theory of Recognition? A Critical Response to Axel Honneth's *Reification: A New Look at an Old Idea*." *International Journal of Philosophical Studies* 19, no. 2 (2011) 255–65.

Fromm, Erich. *The Fear of Freedom*. London: Routledge, 2002.

Gayman, Cynthia. "An Ethical Account of the Self Who Might Be Otherwise: Simone Weil and Judith Butler." In *The Relevance of the Radical: Simone Weil 100 Years Later*, edited by A. Rebecca Rozelle-Stone and Lucian Stone, 193–204. London: Continuum, 2010.

Hoelzl, Michael. "Recognizing the Sacrificial Victim: The Problem of Solidarity for Critical Social Theory." *Journal for Cultural and Religious Theory* 6, no. 1 (2004) 45–64.

Honneth, Axel. *Disrespect: The Normative Foundations of Critical Theory*. Translated by Joseph Ganahl. Cambridge: Polity, 2007.

———. *Freedom's Right: The Social Foundations of Democratic Life*. Translated by Joseph Ganahl. Cambridge: Polity 2014.

———. *The Struggle for Recognition: The Moral Grammar of Social Conflicts.* Translated by Joel Anderson. Cambridge, MA: MIT Press, 1995.
Jaeggi, Rahel. *Alienation.* Edited by Frederick Neuhouser. Translated by Frederick Neuhouser and Alan E. Smith. New York: Columbia University, 2014.
Kahneman, Daniel. *Thinking, Fast and Slow.* London: Penguin, 2011.
Kołakowski, Leszek. "In Praise of Inconsistency." *Dissent* 11, no. 2 (1964) 201–9.
———. *Metaphysical Horror.* Oxford: Blackwell, 1988.
Kortian, Garbis. *Metacritique: The Philosophical Arguments of Jürgen Habermas.* Translated by John Raffan. Cambridge: Cambridge University Press, 1980.
Lloyd, Vincent, ed. "Interview with Gillian Rose." *Theory, Culture and Society* 25, nos. 7–8 (2008) 203–20.
Loick, Daniel. "Juridification and Politics: From the Dilemma of Juridification to the Paradoxes of Rights." *Philosophy and Social Criticism* 40, no. 8 (2014) 757–78.
McGilchrist, Iain. *The Master and His Emissary: The Divided Brain and the Making of the Modern World.* London: Yale University, 2009.
Milbank, John. *Theology and Social Theory: Beyond Secular Reason.* 2nd ed. Oxford: Blackwell, 2006.
Murdoch, Iris. *The Sovereignty of Good.* London: Routledge & Kegan Paul, 1970.
Robinson, Marilynne. *Home.* London: Virago, 2009.
Rose, Gillian. *Hegel contra Sociology.* Radical Thinkers. London: Verso, 1995.
———. *Judaism and Modernity: Philosophical Essays.* Oxford: Blackwell, 1993.
———. *The Melancholy Science: An Introduction to the Thought of Theodor W. Adorno.* London: Macmillan, 1978.
———. *Mourning Becomes the Law: Philosophy and Representation.* Cambridge: Cambridge University Press, 1996.
Saarinen, Risto. *Recognition and Religion: A Historical and Systematic Study.* Oxford: Oxford University Press, 2016.
Schick, Kate. "Re-cognizing Recognition: Gillian Rose's 'Radical Hegel' and Vulnerable Recognition." *Telos* 173 (2015) 87–105.
Taylor, Charles. "The Politics of Recognition." In *Multiculturalism: Examining the Politics of Recognition,* edited by Amy Gutmann, 25–73. Princeton: Princeton University Press, 1994.
Thompson, Michael J. "Axel Honneth and the Neo-Idealist Turn in Critical Theory." *Philosophy and Social Criticism* 40, no. 8 (2014) 779–97.
Van Buren, John. *The Young Heidegger: Rumor of the Hidden King.* Indianapolis: Indiana University Press, 1994.
Williams, Robert R. *Hegel's Ethics of Recognition.* Berkeley: University of California, 1997.
Worden, J. William. *Grief Counseling and Grief Therapy: A Handbook for the Mental Health Practitioner.* London: Tavistock, 1983.
Yeatman, Anna. "A *Two*-Person Conception of Freedom: The Significance of Jessica Benjamin's Idea of Intersubjectivity." *Journal of Classical Sociology* 15, no. 1 (2015) 3–23.

Chapter 3

Rose *contra* Girard
Kenotic Comedy and Social Theory
(Or, Žižek as a Reader of Rose)

Marcus Pound

Introduction

For Gillian Rose, Hegel is the social theorist *par excellence*; Hegel also turns out to be one of the great comic thinkers: Hegel's social theory is comic. It is an insight that Rose carries through into her interest in Kierkegaard and informs her criticism of the social anthropologist and literary theorist René Girard whom she charges with a "lack of humour and irony."[1] Ostensibly this essay revisits Rose's critique of Girard from the perspective of Hegelian comedy. However, as I argue (in the "severe style") Rose's comic outlook is compromised by her sense of the tragic. While taking stock of Rose's criticism, I propose a Žižekian reading of Girard that avoids the severity of Rose while maintaining a fidelity to Hegel's comedic appreciation of the social task. In the first part, I outline Rose's appropriation of Hegel for the critique of social theory. I consolidate her critique by applying it to Girard's own writings on comedy and social theory to highlight the neo-Kantian element in his work. In the second part, I address Rose's comic reading of Hegel

---

1. Rose, *The Broken Middle*, 141.

and Hegel's work on comedy, with particular reference to the distinction between tragedy and comedy. I critically contrast Hegel and Girard's approaches to the forms. In the third part, I address directly Rose's criticisms of Girard from the perspective of *The Broken Middle* and the subsequent claim that Rose's ethics of the middle is tragic. I then offer an alternative reading of Girard informed by Žižek to rearticulate Rose's middle as comic.

Part I: Hegel and Social Theory

Rose understood Hegel's critique of Kant in advance of contemporary sociological method, which assumed what she called a neo-Kantian form. Kantian philosophy renders a split (diremption/divorce) between the subject and object; the transcendental deduction is an attempt to demonstrate that despite this split there are key *a priori* concepts that can be deduced as correctly applying to objects of our experience.[2] In other words, the experience of a given object must in some way conform to the categories of cognition; we can know a given object through the determinations of experience, even if we cannot know that object in itself. As Rose points out, Hegel's concern was that philosophy was subsequently restricted to the justification of objective validity by way of the application of the *a priori* forms of knowledge and taken in this fashion any given object of experience can only be understood by subordinating it to those forms. As Rose puts it, "a transcendental account reduces knowledge to 'experience,' to the synthesis of appearances. It makes the conditions of the *possibility* of experience in general likewise the conditions of the possibility of the objects of experience."[3]

Natural Law

The implications of this critique of Kant for social theory are clarified by Hegel in his essay on *Natural Law* from his early Jena period. In *Natural Law*, Hegel critiques the scientific empiricism of Hobbes, amongst other natural law theorists, who promulgated an individualist doctrine of rights. Their work is scientific to the extent they subject society to the rational method/gaze, and empirical because they claim to draw their findings from the observation of the world. Hegel draws out the circularity of the arguments involved. Natural law theorists seek to show that individuals living together had certain inalienable rights that ought to be respected and, in

---

2. Kant, *Critique of Pure Reason*, A84–130, B116–69.
3. Rose, *Hegel contra Sociology*, 4.

defending the claim, appeal to a hypothetical state of nature. The problem arises because "what in the chaos of the state of nature or in abstraction of man must remain and what must be discarded . . . . In this manner, the guiding determinate can only be, that as much must remain as is required for the exposition of what is found in the real world: the governing principle for this *a priori* is the *a posteriori*. If something in the idea of a state of law is to be justified, all that is required, for the purpose of demonstrating its own necessity . . . is to transfer into the chaos an appropriate quality."[4]

Natural law theorists assumed in advance the conclusion they set out to prove; they abstract from "everything capricious and accidental,"[5] by which Hegel means that contingent, historical, social relations and customs are subtracted from the social picture to leave only the chaos of individuals in nature, which in turn then becomes the basic truth of man. Little wonder Hegel considered the priority of individuals in a state of chaos a "fiction."[6]

In the same way, a given law can be shown to be grounded in the interests of the governing state, Hegel shows how the "fiction" that grounds natural law is taken from *bourgeois* property relations; that is, natural law derives from the want to establish universal private property relations and rights. It is not that Hegel wants to condemn private property, but to highlight how a climate that fosters a space of pure possession can take hold in a way that results in pure eudemonism.

Kant may not be associated with empirical natural law, yet as Hegel argues, Kant's practical reason offered a variant. When Kant tried to give content to the form of moral reasoning (the categorical imperative) by applying it in certain cases, he did so by posing whether the maxim to "increase my wealth by every safe means can hold good as universal if I have a *deposit* in my hands, the owner of which has died and left no record of it?"[7] For Kant, the answer is "no," because as a general rule, if someone could deny holding a deposit on the basis that they would not be found out, the practice of deposits would not survive; trust would be undermined. Hegel's point is that the example presupposes the validity of property *qua* property prior to the application of pure reason to determine lawfulness in regard of property. Hegel's criticism, like that of natural law, concerns the conceit of using *bourgeois* property as the basis for universal law.

For both Kant and the theorists of natural law, it remains the isolated and abstract individual that contractually comes together to form society,

---

4. Hegel, *Natural Law*, 56–70.
5. Ibid., 63.
6. Ibid., 114.
7. Kant, *Groundwork for the Metaphysics of Morals*, 25.

whereas for Hegel culture is a self-contained whole that must be understood in terms of its own laws and dispositions; for Hegel it is not the individual, but the state that is prior. Legality cannot be derived from universal principles, but only be exhibited in the light of the living individuality of a given nation. Therefore, to apply the transcendental method in the realm of social thought is, like natural law, to impose a false unity that obfuscates real social relations. As Rose says, "a transcendental account necessarily presupposes the actuality or existence of its object and seeks to discover the conditions of its possibility."[8]

Rose and Social Theory: The Diremption of Theoretical and Practical Reason

For Rose, the key problem of Kant's legacy is most acutely felt in the split Kant introduces between theoretical and practical reason and the place of freedom therein: legality (determinism) and morality (autonomy). Kant sets out the *a priori* conditions for moral experience, induced through the categorical imperative, the unconditional rational form for moral thought that all rational beings should follow. The imperative relies not on treating others as a means to an end but on the value placed on humanity as a whole, an imperative to determine law in the direction of the Kingdom of Ends. The problem arises because in this scheme, God is reduced to a postulate of practical reason (necessarily posited to secure the ground of the Kingdom of Ends beyond the law). Rendering God a postulate as such renders God unknowable, which in turn renders freedom unknowable and therefore impossible. As Rose says, freedom cannot be conceived by Kant because it depends upon the prior distinction between the necessity (theoretical reason/legality) and freedom (practical reason/morality). Freedom can only be conceived in a negative sense: freedom *from* necessity.[9] As Rose explains: "For Kant . . . freedom means freedom from the sensuous world, from the necessity of nature. To Hegel this notion of freedom is 'a flight from the finite.' The rigid dichotomy between the sensuous world (the finite, nature) and the supersensuous world (the infinite, freedom) prevents the comprehension of either. By degrading empirical existence in order to emphasize that the infinite is utterly different, the infinite is itself debased. For it is deprived of all characterization, and hence turned into an empty abstraction, an idol, made of mere timber."[10]

8. Rose, *Hegel contra Sociology*, 1.
9. Rose, *Hegel contra Sociology*, 55.
10. Ibid., 98.

The above quote provides a context for her repeated claim in *Hegel contra Sociology* that Hegel's philosophy has *no* social import if the absolute is banished or suppressed, if the absolute cannot be thought.[11] For Rose, the idea of all Hegel's thought is to unify theoretical and practical reason. When Hegel employs reason [*Vernunft*], he implies the identity of the subject and object, because reason is the condition of actuality. And when Hegel speaks of Absolute knowledge, he is naming a particular standpoint of reason, the standpoint from which the sets of relations that allow thought to work the way it does are shown to be the determinations that are constitutive of being.[12] For Hegel, the task of philosophy is not to set out what can and cannot be known, or in what capacity, but the articulation of the determinations of actuality. Hegel's speculative idealism, as opposed to Kant's abstract idealism, is therefore characterized by a concern for the relationship between self-consciousness and the forms of institutions that give rise to sociality. Hegel's idealism demands of philosophical thought that it not be undertaken as a purely analytical exercise in a vacuum from the constitutive communities that make thought possible in the first place.

Girard's Comic Hypothesis

At this point, I want to consolidate Rose's Hegelian critique of social theory by way of critically engaging René Girard's provocative "Comic Hypothesis." Published the same year as *Violence and the Sacred*, it provides a complementary thesis on mimesis, only from the perspective of comedy. Rose has critiqued Girard's *Violence and the Sacred* in her later work *The Broken Middle*, and so the aim of this section is to develop her critique of Girard and highlight the continuity of her early and later critical approach, while keeping the role of comedy and social theory to the fore.

Girard makes the argument for a universal anthropological theory of violence and sacrifice to which the Gospels offer an exceptional alternative. According to Girard, violence can be traced back to the mimetic character of desire. We desire not simply in our capacity as autonomous individuals (Girard's critique of Hegel), nor for the intrinsic value of an object as such, but intersubjectively. We desire things because they are already desired by another; desire is mimetic and, in the round of desire, the competition for an object or status inevitably leads to mimetic rivalry. Murderous violence is only averted through a scapegoat mechanism (a third). A sacrificial victim must be found to focus their collective envy. The death of the scapegoat

11. Ibid., 42.
12. Dudley, *Understanding German Idealism*, 146.

placates the aggression and re-establishes the social bond. However, the mechanism of the scapegoat is characteristically obscured—the basis of all mythological thinking—because the scapegoat is a substitute victim, not chosen for any intrinsic quality as such. The Gospels are the exception to the extent that they are written from the perspective of the innocent victim and hence expose the mechanism for what it is: a myth that sustains arbitrary violence.

In "A Comic Hypothesis," Girard presents mimetic theory as the unifying theory behind the classically given distinction between tragedy and comedy. As Girard says: "[C]omedy and tragedy . . . are very close to each other."[13] The essay proceeds through structural comparison of the similarities between Moliere's *Bourgeois gentleman* and Sophocles's *Oedipus Rex*, and moves to highlight the mutual catharsis in both comedy and tragedy, which Girard allies to ritual expulsion and purification. Laughter, he tells us, "must get rid of something."[14] When we laugh "we are really laughing at something which could and, in a sense, which should happen to anyone who laughs, not excluding ourselves." This, Girard argues, "clearly shows the nature of the threat, unperceived yet present, which laughter is always warding off, the still unidentified object it has to expel."[15]

Nowhere is this more evident than the tickle, the proto-joke. The laughter elicited from a tickle relies on both the real threat to one's ability to control the environment, while at the same time that threat being nil: the conditions for laughter are contradictory. This is the perilous balance. Girard offers tickling as the proto-mimetic act that can be understood as a joyous de-realization of our senses. The moment of laughter is precisely the moment one's very physiological being is scapegoated, only internally, rather than externally—rather than expel another in the round of sacrifice and violence, one expels oneself. That is to say, laughter is dependent upon expelling all air from the lungs, henceforth rendering the subject helpless, succumbing to the very condition he or she seeks to ward off. Moreover, as Aaron Schuster puts it, the tickle is "the Ur-joke, the zero-degree of comedy," and "the primordial manifestation of culture"; "tickling stands as the momentous entry-point into the universe of simulation, or to cite the Greek term, mimesis."[16] If mimesis is the basis of comedy and culture, then laughter is what prevents mimesis from descending into murderous rivalry, expelling the obscure object by turning it on oneself.

13. Girard, "Perilous Balance," 821
14. Ibid., 815.
15. Ibid., 818.
16. Schuster, "A Philosophy of Tickling."

Girard and Natural Law

At first sight, it might appear counterintuitive to claim of the above that Girard offers us a variant of natural law to the extent that he begins not with the abstract individual but from the intersubjectivity of desire. However, Girard's theory bears all the hallmarks of a form of scientific empiricism, a variant of the positivist tradition of sociology; it extrapolates from comedy the presence of more "natural" laughter to reveal the truth of the scapegoating mechanism and explain the constitution of society as a whole. For Girard, the laughter that erupts from the tickle is a kind of cosmic echo of the protosocial gesture, the original violent sacrifice. As Rose would later critically argue of Girard: "[V]iolence is here not so much 'hypothesized' as hypostatized."[17] Or, to develop Hegel's critique of Kant, mimetic rivalry is understood within the transcendental register, it functions as the *a priori* principle, the key to sacrifice. In the first instance, this renders violence unknowable as evidenced by Girard's claim that violence becomes that "beautiful totality whose beauty depends on its being inaccessible and impenetrable."[18] Because without the empirical appreciation of the historic forms of sacrifice feeding back into his understanding of violence and sacrifice in the first place, only what counts as sacrificial violence is violence. One might enquire for example as to the degree his encoding of sacrificial violence is already determined by the patriarchy of his discourse?

In the second instance, Girard's account owes something to *bourgeois* property law or rather, a John Milbank puts it, Girard maps liberal social theory into his sociological anthropology to the extent he assumes a prereligious and precultural chaos of desire. Desire, in its natural state, is nonhierarchical (in the sense that desire might be the desire for an objective good), it is desire only for that which others desire. It follows from this, that the original scene assumes one of competing equals (i.e., *bourgeois* property relations) with the inevitable violence as result of that competition. In other words, Girard's appeal to a "natural scene," like his appeal to laughter, takes its assumptions from the liberal coding of society of which violence is the principle outcome and religion (myth/laughter) is invented as a secondary phenomenon, designed to deal with the crisis of desire. Thus, as Milbank points out, Girard remains entirely within the functionalist definition of religion.[19]

---

17. Rose, *The Broken Middle*, 151.
18. Girard, *Violence and the Sacred*, 157.
19. Milbank, *Theology and Social Theory*, 394.

Part II: The Speculative Moment of Comedy

Key to Rose's reading of Hegel is the significance she attaches to Hegel's speculative reasoning [*begreifenden*]. To take an example from grammar as Hegel does, to understand a proposition "speculatively" means that "the identity which is affirmed between subject and predicate is seen equally to affirm a lack of identity between subject and predicate." In other words, in reading a given proposition, one should not assume the identity of the given subject as already contained in the predicate [Hegel's critique of natural law], but rather see it as a work, something to be "achieved."[20]

For example, read speculatively, "God exists" does not predicate the raw attribute of existence to an empty name, but as Rose says, it "implies that we, finite beings, are not free. God is a pictorial, imaginative name for something which ordinary consciousness finds impossible to conceive," that is, the relation of the finite to the infinite. Read speculatively, the claim God exists "refers to our experience that, as particular individuals, we are not immediately universal, we are not species, not God, not infinite, that we live in societies where our experience as individuals does not correspond to the experience of all . . . we are limited, but can become aware of the determinations of the limit."[21] This means that any recognition constitutive of "knowing" is also misrecognition. Likewise, to speak of the absolute speculatively is to speak of the work that must be put into thinking the social; the absolute, for Hegel, is not an entity, but a *process*, undertaken speculatively.

Throughout *Hegel contra Sociology*, Rose insists that the identity of religion and the state is the fundamental speculative proposition of Hegel's thought; or rather, the *speculative experience of the lack of identity* between religion and the state is the basic object of Hegel's exposition. As Žižek later explains, commenting directly upon Rose's restatement of Hegelian speculative identity, to read the proposition speculatively is not to assert their mutual identity (theocracy), nor to see it as a wistful aspiration. Rather, it is to recognize that, where the state is founded upon religion, religion is given expression in a perverted way, not for reasons concerning the inadequacy of state institutions, but for the insufficiency articulated in the notion of religion itself: "[T]he inadequacy of the actual state to the Christian religion *qua* its foundations corresponds to and has its ground in the inadequacy of the Christian religion itself to its own Notion."[22] In other words, the lack

---

20. Rose, *Hegel contra Sociology*, 49; Hegel, *Phenomenology of Spirit*, 38.
21. Rose, *Hegel contra Sociology* 94.
22. Žižek ,*For They Know Not What They Do*, 104.

of identity between the two is a reflection of a lack inherent in the initial notion.

Rose reads Hegel in a manner that, as the above indicates, informs Žižek. This is not the triumphalist Hegel for whom the phenomenology legitimizes "the phantasy of historical completion with the imprimatur of suprahistorical, absolute method, but focuses relentlessly on the historical production and reproduction of those illusionary contraries which other systems of scientific thought naturalise, absolutize, or deny."[23] In Rose's reading, Truth in the absolute ethical life arises, as Žižek would say, from misrecognition, the basis of comedy.[24]

The Comedy of Hegel

Read from the speculative standpoint, Hegel's *Phenomenology* unveils the series of contradictions that arise when one starts from the *a priori* separation of the subject from the conditions of its formation. The various categories Hegel develops, such as the unhappy consciousness or the beautiful soul, sketch out the historical consequences of the split that arises when the autonomy of the subject is posited as separate from the substance (totality) of ethical life and thereby afflict the substance of ethical life.[25] The *Phenomenology* on her reading is a kind of *Divina Comedia*,[26] a comedy of misrecognition: "Let me shoot from the pistol: first, *spirit* in the *Phenomenology* means the *drama of misrecognition* which ensures at every stage and transition of the work—a ceaseless comedy, according to which our aims and outcomes constantly mismatch each other, and provoke yet another revised aim, action, and discordant outcome. Secondly, *reason* is therefore *comic*, full of surprises, of unanticipated happenings, so that the comprehension is always provisional and preliminary."[27]

The *Phenomenology* is not the revocation of alienated externalization, nor a teleology of reconciliation, nor a dominating absolute knowledge. The *Phenomenology* is not a success, it is a gamble. For the perpetual occurrence of inversion and misrepresentation can only be undermined, or "brought into fluidity" by *allusion* to the law of their determination, to the causality of fate.[28]

23. Rose, *Dialectic of Nihilism*, 3.
24. Žižek, "The Truth Arises from Misrecognition: Part I," 190.
25. Abbinett, *Truth and Social Science*, 22.
26. Rose, *Mourning Becomes the Law*, 75.
27. Ibid., 72.
28. Rose, *Hegel contra Sociology*, 159.

Hegel on Comedy

If there is a criticism of Rose to be made at this point, it is by her own admission that what concerns her is "not what Hegel says about comedy as such, but *the movement of the Absolute as comedy*."[29] Hegel had already linked the role of dialectical thinking to the comic as such. His insight that the nature of thinking is dialectical and as such understanding must fall into contradiction was of capital importance to his project[30] and comic action posed the contradiction between what is absolutely true and its realization in individuals more profoundly than other aesthetic forms.[31] The implication here is that comedy is not merely an instance of dialectical play; rather, as Stephen Law has argued, Hegel sees comedy playing a key role in the development of humankind, contributing to the growth of Spirit and freedom.

In the aesthetics (to take Hegel's later works first), poetry, of which comedy is a subset, like all art, gives expression to the absolute to the extent it expresses the relation between the human (particular) and divine (universal); it is the work of negation in service of the absolute ethical life[32] and "[t]he only important thing for a work of art [within which comedy is discussed] is to present what corresponds with reason and spiritual truth."[33] Art is only truly art if it fulfills its supreme task, "when it has placed itself in the same sphere as religion and philosophy, and when it is simply one way of bringing to our minds and expressing the Divine, the deepest interests of mankind, and the most comprehensive truths of the spirit . . . . Art shares this vocation with religion and philosophy, but in a special way, namely by displaying even the highest [reality] sensuously, bringing it thereby nearer to the senses, to feeling, and to nature's mode of appearance."[34]

In the *Phenomenology*, Hegel introduces comedy under the subheading "The Spiritual Work of Art." The section dialectically sets out the way art has represented the relation of the human to divine, the particular to the universal. In epic narrative, the narrator represents the gods through speech, with the narrative medium depicting the actions of the gods (universal) as the actions of men (the particular); by way of negation, in dramatic tragedy it is the actions of the actor—as opposed to speech—that represents the gods. Yet in both cases, the relation between the two (universal/particular)

---

29. Rose, *Mourning Becomes the Law*, 64.
30. Hegel, *The Encyclopaedia Logic*, §11.
31. Hegel, *Aesthetics*, 1201.
32. Ibid., 7.
33. Ibid., 1197.
34. Ibid., 7.

is posed as a synthetic combination: the universal remains external to the individual.[35] In epic narrative, the gods' actions may well take the form of men's actions, but the universal remains unrestricted and withdrawn from the connection. In tragic drama, the split is manifest in the actor's employment of a mask: the actor *qua* acting may well represent a god, but only in the capacity of an actor.[36] In comedy, we encounter the final spiritual work of art, the negation of the negation. In comedy, "The self-consciousness of the hero must step forth from his mask."[37] In comedy, "the actual self of the actor coincides with what he impersonates";[38] comedy sits as it does for Kierkegaard, a zone of transition to revealed religion, that is, Christianity. In Christianity, God appears directly as a particular individual and therefore Christianity *is* the religion of comedy while true comedy implicitly points beyond art to religion. Read from the perspective of comedy, Hegel and Kierkegaard appear much closer together than is usually accredited.

Tragedy and Comedy

For Hegel, comedy is situated further along the road to freedom: "The actualization of freedom in the aesthetic sphere is nascent in tragedy and fully developed in comedy. The reason is that truly *tragic* action necessarily presupposes either a live conception of *individual* freedom and independence or at least an individual's determination and willingness to accept freely and on his own account the responsibility for his own act and its consequences."[39]

For Hegel, a tragic plot turns on two independently valid yet irreconcilable positions. In Hegel's reading of *Antigone*, for example, Antigone honors her brother, and thus represents the "bond of kinship, the gods of the underworld." Creon by contrast "honors Zeus alone, the dominating power over public life and social welfare." As Hegel argues, notwithstanding the validity of their purpose, they carry it out in a one-sided manner, unable not to infringe upon others.[40] However, as Hegel also maintains, there remains within the tragic drama a moment of reconciliation in as much as the dramatic representation of two irreconcilable yet valid standpoints precludes the audience from taking sides; in this way, the audience is spared the

---

35. Hegel, *Phenomenology of Spirit*, 441.
36. Ibid., 450.
37. Ibid.
38. Ibid., 452.
39. Hegel, *Aesthetics*, 1205.
40. Ibid., 1197.

one-sidedness of reflection that besets the tragic characters of the drama: contradiction is turned into reconciliation.[41]

Tragedy encapsulates the contradiction between autonomy and determination, the characters' standpoint and the wider determining events between. In tragedy, external circumstances take precedence over the subjective positions in a way that leads to misfortune. For the emergence of comedy, however, Hegel tells us, "there must have asserted itself in a still higher degree the free right of the subjective personality and its self-assured dominion."[42] In this sense, comedy is a radicalization of tragedy (both poles). Both dramatic forms rely on the contradiction between the aims of a character and the external situation, however, "in a comic action the contradiction between what is absolutely true and its realization in individuals is posed more profoundly" and therefore requires a more stringent solution. In contrast to tragedy, "what is destroyed in this [comic] solution cannot be either fundamental principle or individual character."[43] As Stephen Law succinctly puts it, "in tragedy, the choice is given: either autonomy or determination; the protagonist must choose. In comedy, the subject can always rise above the contradiction. In comedy, it is us who decide the forms of behaviour; comedy needs no gods because comics are. We dispense justice and the penalty."[44] While in tragedy the protagonist's commitment to a set of values results in his or her death, in comedy the protagonist survives and freedom shines through.[45] Comedy thereby takes art to its limit: beyond comedy, there is no further *Aesthetic* manifestation of freedom, there is only religion and philosophy.

By way of an example, one might consider Roberto Benigni's tragicomedy *La Vita Bella* (1996) in which he plays Guido, a Jewish Italian bookseller who, upon being interned in a concentration camp with his son (Giosuè) and wife (Dora), constructs an imaginative and alternate worldview to shield his son from the true horror. Following a set of given tasks such as hide-n-seek, rewarded by points, the first child to reach a thousand points will win a tank. At the level of tragedy, Guido, whose virtue remains intact throughout the film, is eventually shot, overcome by the external circumstances. Yet at the level of comedy, he is able to rise above the contradiction between autonomy and determination to the extent he is also able to determine the external circumstances in the sense that in the end his fantasy

41. Ibid., 1199.
42. Ibid., 1205.
43. Ibid., 1201.
44. Law, "Hegel and the Spirit of Comedy," 117.
45. Huddleston, "Hegel on Comedy," 11.

construction is vindicated. When the US Army arrives to liberate the camp, at its helm is a Sherman tank in which the Giosuè is driven away to safety.

What then does Girard make of the distinction between comedy and tragedy? Comedy, Girard argues, lends itself to structural effects rather than what arises from an individual's character. In other words, comedy shifts the focus from the individual to the pattern of life itself. Comedy demands passions that are identical; whereas tragedy demands "unique sentiments."[46] And it is by virtue of its immediacy and "structural" component that Girard also considers comedy a radicalization of tragedy, only now for the opposite reasons: comedy is more crushing than tragedy: "[T]he vengeance of the gods, meaninglessness of destiny, and the malice of the 'human condition' may well crush the individual but not to the extent they do in the case of comic patterns which are truly 'structural' in the sense that they dominate individual reactions and fully account for them . . . whereas individual thinking is unable to take them into account. The structural patters of the comic therefore deny the sovereignty of the individual more radically than either god or destiny."[47]

Laughter, for Girard, is further along toward a negative reaction to a given threat. If, for Hegel, the tragic hero is crushed by external situation all the while maintain fidelity to a given set of values, for Girard, it is the *comic* who is more determinately crushed by a situation in which even the very values are destroyed. Whereas for Hegel, comedy is marked by a sovereignty of the subject to the extent they can change the determinate situation, for Girard, the comic's very being is eclipsed by the sacrificial mechanism and its arbitrary sway. For Hegel, comedy implies the radicalization of both the subjective and objective elements; Girard's view of comedy radicalizes only the objective and hence remains entirely on the side of the tragic.

Part III: Girard, Žižek, and the Broken Middle

Rose takes up her critique of Girard in *The Broken Middle* where she extends (considerably) her critique of dualisms in the light of Hegel. Only now, the speculative position is identified as the broken middle: "[A]ll dualistic relations to 'the other,' to 'the world' are attempts to quieten and deny the broken middle, the third term which arises out of misrecognition." This "third term" is law: "My relation to myself is mediated by what I recognize or refuse to recognize in your relation to yourself; while your self-relation depends on what you recognize of my relation to myself." The law, "in all its

---

46. Girard, "A Perilous Balance," 817.
47. Ibid., 816.

various historical adventures—[is] the comedy of misrecognition." And this makes the meaning of law inseparable from the meaning of *Bildung*, that is, education, formation, and cultivation, the work of which *is* the work of love.[48]

In *The Broken Middle*, Rose turns to Kierkegaard to develop a "phenomenology of law": How does Law appear to consciousness? The "middle" is a third space, not the agnostic and unitary space of secular liberalism, but a place of anxiety to the extent it is the sheer givenness of the political and ethical situation that resists any attempt to posit either a retreat into sanctified origins or utopian ends. The concern of politics is not to provide a solution that sutures the diremptions of modern life, such as morality and legality, religion and the state, because those fields, as Hegel appreciated, already arise out of the process of diremptions.[49] Her aim then is to recover anxiety within our political and ethical discourse, "re-assigning it to the middle."[50]

And it is precisely this type of anxious labor toward "Absolute knowing" that Girard resists. As Rose highlights, Girard is a gnostic, that is, a dualist, because the victim mechanism of scapegoating implies creation, in the first instance, is evil, the result of a "violent demiurge demanding violent sacrifice" in the face of a "chaos of undifferentiated mimesis" that can only momentarily be suspended.[51] All the while, the Godhead, the Christian exception to myth, the god of love, sees humanity not as sinful as such, merely unenlightened as to the truth of mimetic theory, although the sociological foundation in chaos remains. In other words, he overemphasized the distinction between the violence of the scapegoat mechanism (nature), and the love of God (grace) such that freedom is only ever freedom from the basic mechanism he posits of culture, that is, the negative rejection of the mechanism with only the Christian counter sacrifice as abstract principle. Theologically, as Milbank points out, this amounts to the adoption of an extrinsic God[52] and thus affirms the autonomy of the secular realm. As Andrew Shanks put it, Girard's is an attempt to think "from the outside about religion", rather than the type of thinking that "springs right from the very middle of a community's existential brokenness."[53]

---

48. Rose, *Mourning Becomes the Law*, 74–75.
49. Rose, *The Broken Middle*, 286.
50. Lloyd, "On the Uses of Gillian Rose," 699.
51. Rose, *The Broken Middle*, 147.
52. Milbank, *Theology and Social Theory*, 394.
53. Shanks, *Against Innocence*, 107.

The Severe Style

Little wonder Rose characterized Girard's writing in terms of the "severe style"—a cognate of what Kierkegaard called the ethical. How so? "The severe style" is taken from Hegel's aesthetic writings; it is her judgment upon his early Jena writings, serving as a propaedeutic to the political task. As Rose writes, "the political problem could not be solved in the severe style."[54] The

> severe style is that higher abstraction of beauty which clings to what is important and expresses and presents it in its chief outlines, but still despises charm and grace, grants domination to the topic alone, and above all does not devote much industry and elaboration to accessories. Thus the severe style still limits itself to reproducing what is present and available. In other words, while on the one hand, in *content* it rests, in respect of ideas and presentation, on the given, e.g. on the present sacrosanct religious tradition, on the other hand, for the external *form* it allows complete liberty to the topic and not to its own invention.[55]

To clarify the above, one could say that the severe style makes no concession to the role of subjectivity; to put the matter in Kierkegaard's terms, it is concerned with the *what*, not the *how* of subjectivity: the "severe style sharply repulses any subjective judgement."[56] So the point Rose is making is that Girard's work cannot answer the political question precisely because politics requires something of risk in negotiating the middle, that is, law; herein lies its "absence of irony—or its dramatic cognates, humor or facetiousness—in the presentation of a theory."[57]

The Standpoint of Faith

In *Hegel contra Sociology*, the severe style is contrasted with the speculative disposition towards the absolute ethical life; in *The Broken Middle* the severe style is contrasted with Kierkegaard's category of the "ethical," that is, the realm of universal law. Kierkegaard identified the religious stage with the exception to the rule; the religious stage invites the "suspension" of the ethical in a moment of faith, as exemplified for Kierkegaard by the Akedah.

---

54. Rose, *Hegel contra Sociology*, 51.
55. Hegel, *Aesthetics*, 616–17.
56. Ibid., 620.
57. Rose, *The Broken Middle*, 141.

For Girard, employing the *a priori* form of sacrificial reasoning, the story of Abraham and Isaac amounts to a condensed form of mimetic theory, charting both the call for infant sacrifice and its replacement by animal sacrifices, which itself stands not simply as a replacement for Isaac but a portent of the sacrifice to come in Christ: the end of animal sacrifice points to the end of the sacrificial mechanism *qua* sacrifice.

By contrast, Rose takes Kierkegaard's line: Abraham may well be accorded the title "father of faith," yet understood ethically, Abraham set out to "murder" Isaac.[58] What gives Abraham his greatness therefore cannot be his moral code, but rather must be the fidelity he maintains to God's word, that is, his ability to suspend the social in its ethical considerations, maintaining instead a passionate commitment to God: the teleological suspension of the ethical. As Rose says, expanding on Kierkegaard:

> [T]o adopt the standpoint of faith is to be willing to stake oneself in the middle, between the arbiter of law (the sovereign will) and the victim. Faith is this in-between: to occupy the middle is to take precisely a stance on love and violence. Faith: acknowledges violence in love and the love in violence because the law is in both: the violence in love—Abraham's exclusive, violent love of Isaac; the love in violence—his willingness to bind Isaac with faith not with resignation, not with the prospect of loss, but a free offering, freely given—oblation not sacrifice. It is this witness alone—this always already knowing yet being willing to stakes oneself again—that prevents one from becoming an arbitrary perpetrator or an arbitrary victim; that prevents one, actively or passively, from acting with arbitrary violence. Such witnessing is always ready—it is therefore the beginning in the middle: the middle in the beginning—holding itself alert in the anxiety and equivocation of each.[59]

Rose and Tragedy

Yet here the charge may be laid that Rose fails to appreciate fully the comic mode Hegel sets out in distinction to tragedy. As Milbank puts it, by situating herself within the broken middle, she both accepts Hegel's radicalization of Kantian dualisms while being resigned to them. For this reason her ethics come across as "chastend, tragic, and less jocular gloss, a form of postmodern impossibilism, the new opium of the intellectual . . . a Hegelian variant

---

58. Kierkegaard, *Fear and Trembling*, 30.
59. Rose, *The Broken Middle*, 148–49.

on hopelessness."[60] Indeed, if comedy amounts to the pathos of misrecognition, is not comedy turned into its very opposite? Take for example her conclusion to *The Broken Middle*: the more the middle is dirempted the more it becomes sacred in ways that figure its further diremptions. Said otherwise, we try to heal the splits by which we negotiate society with imagined "holy" middles (i.e., utopian goals) without appreciating the ways we further ratify the very splits. So, while comedy maintains a social-critical task to the extent it makes the failings of individuals and in particular the failings of contemporary society its prime focus, it also remains captive to them. Arguably, it is a reading further ratified by Rowan Williams evaluation of her comic sensibility when he situates her comedy under the "sadness of the King," that is, our brokenness.[61]

Or, by way of a further example, consider her critique of Holocaust piety in film. What she refuses in the representation of fascism is the standpoint of the voyeur, that is, one in which the viewer remains distant from the events, unimplemented, while allowing that subject nonetheless a cathartic revulsion or infinite pity to manifest—a case of what Girard would call, scapegoating. The point is not simply to defend our interests over and against the other, but to encounter violence legitimized by our own sense of the individual moral will. Hence her proclivity toward Kazuo Ishiguro's *The Remains of the Day* over Spielberg's *Schindler's List*. In the former, the attraction for German Nazism is drawn out through the organization of the English aristocratic household and the collusion of servants with masters; the viewer is not left intact. In the latter, the evil of the genocide is rendered into an unfathomable and unforgivable crime that precludes the inner tendency we can all bear toward fascism.[62]

A Kenotic Reading of Girard

There remains however another way to read Girard, which takes into account the kenotic trajectory of Hegel's thought. Recall Hegel's description of comedy *qua* representation: comedy marks the end of aesthetic representation (and thus art in general) in the sense that in comedy the actual self of the actor coincides with what he impersonates. There is a kenotic logic at play here that mirrors Hegel's kenotic Christology. According to Hegel, God initially divests himself of abstract substance by contracting into man (Jesus coincides with what he impersonates) to then be finally self-emptied on the

60. Milbank, "On the Paraethical," 78.
61. Williams, "The Sadness of the King," 1.
62. Rose, *Mourning Becomes the Law*, 54.

cross (the exemplary of love) such that "what dies on the cross is indeed God himself, not just his 'finite container' but the God of the beyond."⁶³ Following this double self-divestment, the single individual reestablishes the relation to the Absolute *qua* the community (Spirit) of believers (the synthesis of the individual and universal), and takes on the contingency of belief. As Žižek says, Spirit refers directly to the corporal body of faithful: "[the] Holy Spirit of their community."⁶⁴

For Žižek, ritual or ceremonial precepts often operate on the assumption of a metaphysical Other to which a given sacrifice is offered. Yet as Žižek remarks of the very title of Girard's work, *Things Hidden since the Foundation of the World*, while it implies in a gnostic vein some terrifying and mysterious power overseeing and sustaining the sacrificial process, it masks the realization that there is no big Other:⁶⁵ the law is grounded in its own tautology. And herein is the key to rereading Girard. Because the gospel story is told from the perspective of the innocent victim rather than the mob it renders the entire contingency of sacrificial violence transparent, it exposes the impotence of the ritual or a supposed Master to appease. In this way, it brings into question the entire efficiency of the scapegoat mechanism. In other words, there is a kenotic logic involved in Girard's hypothesis, such that once we discern the Christian revelation of truth in this regard, that is, the truth by which the sacred is deprived of its power; we step out from the mask of myth (sacrificial violence) and assume the subsequent responsibility. In this sense, to read Girard in kenotic terms is to say that we can no longer pretend that scapegoating is anything other than arbitrary violence to contain mimesis and our choice to participate in the mob is precisely that, a self-grounding choice. Or rather, read from the perspective of Žižek, Girard's work returns us to the primacy of the political, Rose's middle: "What the inexistence of the big Other signals is that every ethical and/ or moral edifice has to be grounded in an abyssal act which is, in the most radical sense imaginable, political. Politics is the very space in which, without any external guarantee, ethical decisions are made and negotiated [the broken middle]. The idea that one can ground politics in ethics, or that politics is ultimately a strategic effort to realize prior ethical positions, is a version of the illusion of the 'big Other.'"⁶⁶

In this way, Žižek makes good on Girard in a way that avoids the severity of Rose's critique. Seen from the perspective of Žižek, Girard's

---

63. Žižek, "Dialectical Clarity versus the Misty Conceit of Paradox," 257.
64. Ibid., 282–83.
65. Žižek, *Less Than Nothing*, 972.
66. Ibid., 963.

distinction between myth and gospel might be reworked in terms of Hegel's distinction between tragedy and comedy, where comedy functions precisely as a kenotic moment in which socio-symbolic is suspended, through the irruption of laughter. That is to say, one occupies the position of risk, from which the middle comes into view, this is the speculative moment, when the political coincides with the religious in a way which exposes their mutual relation in their lack of identity; there is no big Other.

Conclusion

By way of conclusion, one might pose the question: What might the foregiven argument mean for ecclesial self-understanding? Here, one need only recall Girard's account of laughter as the proto-kenotic gesture constitutive of society. That being the case, it might be argued that comedy, not tragedy, logically stands at the foundation of Creation and likewise, Christ was not born out of tragic necessity, rather, Christianity arose at the point at which God was tickled by Jesus, tickled by himself in the way that only the kenotic laughter of Trinitarian difference could account for, that the event of gospel truth has happened, and now it is up to us; laughter is not subsequent to our brokenness but the laughter of brokenness. This comedy of the absolute, I wager, stands as the propaedeutic to a given political task, restoring not just anxiety but *mirth* also to the speculative middle.

Bibliography

Abbinett, R. *Truth and Social Science: From Hegel to Deconstruction*. London: Sage, 1998.

Dudley, W. *Understanding German Idealism*. Stocksfield: Acumen, 2007.

Girard, René. "Perilous Balance: A Comic Hypothesis." *Comparative Literature* 87 (1972) 811–26.

———. *Violence and the Sacred*. New York: Continuum, 1975.

Greer, C. "The Problem of the Middle in Gillian Rose's Reading of Hegel: Political Consequences for the Theology of John Milbank." In *After the Postsecular and the Postmodern: New Essays in Continental Philosophy of Religion*, edited by A. P. Smith and D. Whistler, 189–208. Newcastle: Cambridge Scholars, 2010.

Hegel, G. *Aesthetics: Lectures on Fine Art*. 2 vols. Translated by T. M. Knox. Oxford: Clarendon, 1975.

———. *Elements of the Philosophy of Right*. Translated by H. B. Nesbit. Cambridge: Cambridge University Press, 1991.

———. *The Encyclopaedia Logic* (with the *Zusätze*). Translated by T. F. Geraets, W. A. Suchting, and H. S. Harris. Indianapolis, Cambridge: Hackett, 1991.

———. *Natural Law*. Translated by T. M. Knox. Philadelphia: University of Pennsylvania Press, 1975.

———. *Phenomenology of Spirit*. Translated by A. V. Miller. Oxford: Oxford University Press, 1977.

Huddleston, A. "Hegel on Comedy: Theodicy, Social Criticism, and the Supreme Task of Art." In *British Journal of Aesthetics* 54 (2014) 227–40.

Kant, Immanuel. *Critique of Pure Reason*. Translated and edited by P. Guyer and A. Wood. Cambridge: Cambridge University Press, 1998.

———. *Groundwork for the Metaphysics of Morals*. Translated and edited by M. Gregor and J. Timmermann. Cambridge: Cambridge University Press, 1998a.

Kierkegaard, Søren. *Fear and Trembling*. In *Fear and Trembling/Repetition*, translated and edited by Howard H. Hong and Edna V. Hong, 1–123. Kierkegaard's Writings 6. Princeton: Princeton University Press, 1983.

Law, S. "Hegel and the Spirit of Comedy: *Der Geist der stets verneint*." In *Hegel and Aesthetics*, edited by W. Maker, 113–30. New York: SUNY Press, 1983.

Lloyd, Vincent W. "On the Uses of Gillian Rose." *Heythrop Journal* 48 (2007) 697–706.

Mark, M. "Hegel's Theory of Comedy in the Context of Hegelian and Modern Reflections on Comedy." *Revue internationale de philosophie* 221 (2002/2003) 411–30.

Milbank, John. "On the Paraethical: Gillian Rose and Political Nihilism." *Telos* 173 (2015) 69–86.

———. *Theology and Social Theory: Beyond Secular Reason*. Oxford: Blackwell, 1990.

Rose, Gillian. *The Broken Middle: Out of our Ancient Society*. Oxford: Blackwell, 1992.

———. *Dialectic of Nihilism: Post-Structuralism and Law*. Oxford: Blackwell, 1984.

———. *Hegel contra Sociology*. London: Athlone, 1981.

———. *Mourning Becomes the Law: Philosophy and Representation*. Cambridge: CUP, 1996.

Schuster, A. "A Philosophy of Tickling." *Cabinet Magazine* 50 (2013). http://www.cabinetmagazine.org/issues/50/schuster.php.

Shanks, Andrew. *Against Innocence: Gillian Rose's Reception and Gift of Faith*. London: SCM, 2008.

———. "Gillian Rose and Theology: Salvaging Faith." *Telos* 173 (2015) 145–62.

Steinkoler, Manya. "Sarah's Laughter: Where Babies and Humour Come from." In *Lacan, Psychoanalysis, and Comedy*, edited by P. Gherovici and M. Steinkoler, 25–35. New York: Cambridge University Press, 2016.

Williams, Rowan. "The Sadness of the King: Gillian Rose, Hegel, and the Pathos of Reason." *Telos* 173 (2015) 21–36.

Žižek, Slavoj. "Dialectical Clarity versus the Misty Conceit of Paradox." In *The Monstrosity of Christ: Paradox or Dialectic?*, edited by Slavoj Žižek, John Milbank, and Creston Davis. Cambridge, MA: MIT Press, 2009.

———. *For They Know Not What They Do: Enjoyment as a Political Factor*. 2nd ed. London: Verso, 2002.

———. *Less than Nothing: Hegel and the Shadow of Dialectical Materialism*." London: Verso, 2012.

———. "The Truth Arises from Misrecognition Part I." In *Lacan and the Subject of Language*, edited by Ellie Ragland-Sullivan and Mark Bracher, 188–212. New York: Routledge, 1991.

Chapter 4

"The Tree Is Really Rooted in the Sky"
Beside Difficulty in Gillian Rose's Political Theory

KATE SCHICK[1]
Victoria University of Wellington

Gillian Rose's writings have the reputation of being difficult, a reputation that Rose relished.[2] Difficulty is layered upon difficulty with her insistence that a life well lived eschews *euporia*, the easy way, in favor of *aporia*, pathlessness. Rose calls us to embark on a journey of recognition that relinquishes our attachment to self-certainty and self-advantage and attends to the ways we are located, and complicit, in relations and structures of (mis)recognition.

It is easy for Rose's notion of recognition to seem demanding and austere or "joyless and difficult."[3] In this chapter, I argue that, while Rose's oeuvre is both difficult and demanding, it is neither joyless nor austere. The difficult *and* joyful aspects of Rose's thought are rooted in her radical Hegelianism

---

1. I am grateful to Amanda Russell Beattie, Greta Snyder, and Ben Thirkell-White for their helpful comments and advice.

2. Howard Caygill, "Preface," in Rose, *Paradiso*, 7–8.

3. I am grateful to my colleague, Brent J. Steele, for making this comment in response to a draft chapter and for pushing me to clarify and justify my contention that Rose's work is indeed difficult, but far from joyless.

and her insistence on a fundamentally different orientation to knowing and acting. Rose's speculative philosophy unsettles the confident epistemology of moral rationalism and advocates a slower, more difficult journey toward comprehension that starts with *what is*. She maintains that we must be willing both to *know again* and to *act again*, claiming that knowledge and action are "fallible and precarious, but risk-able."[4] Rose's deeply relational approach to knowing and acting is unsettling and countercultural; however, life lived relationally and vulnerably opens us not only to uncertainty and the pain of coming to know but also to love, beauty, and grace. The dance of recognition is "full of surprises":[5] it juxtaposes misrecognition and loss with joy and "overwhelming plenitude."[6] Seen and unseen bounties return Rose always to "the vocation of the everyday,"[7] which starts with *what is* and eschews messianic escapism; they accompany and sustain love's work on its imperfect journey towards a "good enough justice."[8]

This paper has two parts. In Part One, I outline the challenge of Rose's oeuvre, arguing that it layers *difficulty upon difficulty*: difficulty of theory and praxis. Rose refuses the seduction of rigid dualisms such as universal and particular, law and ethics, calling instead for a speculative negotiation of the "middle" between opposites that attends to the ways they inform and shape one another. This speculative negotiation works toward comprehension of *what is*; that is, it embarks on a journey of recognition that gradually comes to know, not through the positive accumulation of facts, but through an ongoing process that revisits and revises what is (inevitably only partially) known. Difficult praxis follows difficult theory. Instead of *euporia*, the easy way, Rose embraces *aporia*, or pathlessness—a willingness to sit with equivocation rather than follow prescribed or culturally sanctioned paths. Against the prevalent elevation of self-certainty and invulnerability as ideals to be achieved, Rose's work invites uncertainty and vulnerability. Her struggle-filled conception of recognition looks inwards as well as outwards to our complicity in perpetuating misrecognition; it works against the tidy, distant rationalism of Enlightenment thought. Rose's speculative philosophy also doggedly refuses postmodern despair or messianic utopianism, both of which neglect the politics of the everyday; instead, it calls us to risk political engagement in pursuit of (a good enough) justice.

---

4. Rose, *Mourning Becomes the Law*, 13.
5. Rose, *Judaism and Modernity*, 9.
6. Rose, *Paradiso*, 20.
7. Ibid., 21.
8. Rose, *Love's Work*, 116.

In Part Two, I outline the potential for joy that accompanies life thought and lived vulnerably. I argue that a countercultural understanding of reason as vulnerable opens us not only to pain but also to love, grace, and joy. Rose's embrace of pathlessness entails uncertainty, which can be uncomfortable; however, it can also be freeing, eschewing the counsel of perfection and inviting us instead to try, fail, and try again as we navigate our way toward a better justice. Although the aporetic way is "without a [predetermined] path,"[9] nonetheless the path can and should be ventured; indeed, the faith-filled life, the dogged and risk-filled engagement with ordinary politics, "lead[s] along the path of despair to the walkways of ripening olive trees."[10]

I take Rose's *Paradiso* as my primary text in this endeavor. Published posthumously, this unfinished work contains rich meditations on living otherwise under conditions of modernity. Rose describes her project as "a series of descants on friends and family who have somehow passed beyond purgatory, who have dwelt in the abyss, in hell, and have undergone purgation . . . I will write about goodness and its fruits."[11] Rose's philosophical memoir, *Love's Work*, invites us to keep our minds in hell and despair not;[12] *Paradiso* does likewise and gives us further companions for the journey.

Difficulty upon Difficulty: Theory and Praxis

Rose's speculative philosophy is demanding: she writes difficult theory and calls us to difficult praxis. In this section, I highlight two dimensions of the difficulty of Rose's thought. First, it is intellectually demanding: *difficult theory*. It advocates a "slow" philosophy that refuses easy paths in favor of an agonistic journey toward recognition of *what is*. This difficult path is "unsettled and unsettling": against the confident description and prescription of modern political thought, it advocates willingness to "[be] in uncertainties."[13] Second, it disturbs our sense of self: *difficult praxis*. The journey toward recognition asks us know differently: to "[hold] still"[14] for long enough that we come to know our selves and our complicity in shaping the social world. It also calls us to act differently: against prescription or paralysis, Rose calls us to take political risk in pursuit of a good enough justice.

9. Rose, *The Broken Middle*, 201.
10. Rose, *Paradiso*, 38.
11. Ibid., 22–23.
12. Attributed to Staretz Silouan, 1866–1938, epigraph to Rose, *Love's Work*.
13. Rose, *Paradiso*, 31.
14. Ibid., 37.

Difficult theory

Rose is emphatically against *euporia*, the easy path, and much of her oeuvre takes on the rigid dualisms adopted by modern philosophy. She is scathing both of Enlightenment thought and of postmodernism, arguing that both approaches impoverish reason: the former fashions it into a rationalist, instrumental caricature of itself, fostering its rejection by the latter. Against the instrumentalization or demonization of reason, Rose seeks to rehabilitate reason, calling us to a fuller understanding of reason as "relational, responsive and reconstructive."[15] Her radical Hegelian conception of recognition works towards comprehension of *what is*, rejecting grandiose theory in favor of agonistic engagement with the everyday.[16] Rose's refusal of the one-sidedness of much philosophical thought maintains that both rationalist prescription of universals and postmodern celebration of difference miss the "grey in grey"[17] of a subtler, more difficult, philosophy. Rose maintains that: "This subtle array, this grey in grey, would turn hubris not into humility but into motile configuration. Grey in grey warns against philosophy's pride of *Sollen*, against any proscription or prescription, any imposition of ideals, imaginary communities or 'progressive narrations.' Instead, the 'idealizations' of philosophy would acknowledge and recognize actuality and not force or fantasize it."[18]

Rose refuses both the confident prescription of universals and the despairing retreat from reason. Both paths, she maintains, are *easy paths*. They are simplistic and one-sided and too easily neglect the difficult work of negotiating actually existing social and political realities; they refuse the anxiety of the middle.

Rose's subtler and more difficult philosophy rejects the hubris of Enlightenment reason's claim to "absolute and universal authority" and its propensity to "[sweep] all particularity and peculiarity from its path."[19] Enlightenment approaches are determinedly rationalist: they elevate a specific way of knowing that occludes particularity and peculiarity, silences the historical, social, political, and economic conditions that create and

---

15. Rose, *Judaism and Modernity*, 4.

16. See also the discussion of the everyday in Solomon and Steele, which highlights the move away from "grand theory" toward "approaches that hold much potential for seeing abstracted global systems and structures through the lenses of lived, embodied and experiential everyday processes." Solomon and Steele, "Micro-Moves in International Relations Theory," 9.

17. Rose, *The Broken Middle*, xi.

18. Ibid.

19. Rose, *Love's Work*, 128.

sustain ethical problems, and obscures the self and its place in moral judgment. They doggedly pursue "useful knowledge"[20] that might be wielded to prescribe positive solutions to contemporary ethical and moral dilemmas. Useful knowledge, on this reading, is that which can be accessed, measured, and mobilized in the service of particular goals: the accumulation of "more facts"[21] that can be used to advance humanity toward more recognition,[22] more freedom, and more security.[23] Modern rationalism seeks certainty: it wants to know both *what has happened* and *what should be done*. Rose is profoundly critical of modern rationalism's relation to knowledge, arguing that it elevates useful knowledge as the "key to human salvation,"[24] and steadfastly pursues the accumulation of measurable facts in pursuit of this goal.[25]

Postmodern approaches also reject the hubris of Enlightenment reason, with its prescription of universals and evisceration of difference. In response, they pursue the laudable and "highly rational" goal of giving voice to the voiceless, of protesting on behalf of the powerless.[26] However, in challenging the narrow rationalism and overweening universalism of Enlightenment thought, postmodern approaches too often abandon reason itself, castigating it as exclusionary and oppressive. Rose argues that the "renunciation of reason, power, and truth"[27] strips postmodern thought of the ability to know and to judge, characterizing it as "despairing rationalism without reason"[28] and asserting that it risks becoming mired in "everlasting melancholia."[29] Although postmodernism is right to challenge the exclusionary universalism of moral rationalism, it goes too far: it "disqualifies any universal or shared notion of justice and the good."[30] Rose maintains that

20. Geuss, *Outside Ethics*, 3.
21. Morgenthau, *Scientific Man versus Power Politics*, 215.
22. Markell, *Bound by Recognition*, 180.
23. Drichel, "Introduction."
24. Rose, *Paradiso*, 25.
25. To illustrate, the rationalist tradition in International Relations engages with violence and losses as events that might be counted, analyzed, and theorized, reducing lived experience to data that might be mobilized to produce an account of *what has happened* and *what might be done*. In this endeavor, there is no place for a deeper and broader understanding of those factors that facilitated the violence and there is no place for recognition of those whose lives are quantified and theorized.
26. Rose, *Paradiso*, 43.
27. Rose, *Mourning Becomes the Law*, 11.
28. Rose, *Paradiso*, 42.
29. Rose, *Mourning Becomes the Law*, 11.
30. Rose, *Paradiso*, 43.

the outright rejection of reason and of the possibility of shared universals paradoxically works against postmodern goals, saying, "[H]ow can you launch a claim without a communality?"[31]

Rose's *difficult* philosophy—her "grey in grey"—has at its core a "radical"[32] reading of Hegel that takes his theory of recognition seriously and posits a fundamentally different relation to knowledge. On this reading, we are social beings who continually come up against and are shaped by our interactions with one another. Hegel's theory of recognition posits an ongoing, agonistic reaching toward comprehension that inevitably gets it wrong and requires knowing again. The need to *know again* is built into the very word recognition: Rose argues that Hegel's *Anerkennen* (re-cognition) "implies an initial experience which is misunderstood, and which has to be re-experienced."[33] Recognition works against ignorance, calling us to reexamine what we think we know (the "familiar or well-known"),[34] but inevitably misunderstand, and to know again as we work towards a fuller understanding of our social world. On this reading, recognition is marked by inevitable misrecognition, by the failure to fully know, and by an ongoing need to know again.

Difficult praxis

Rose's concept of recognition is "unsettled and unsettling":[35] it invites us on a vulnerable journey that works toward comprehension but is attuned to the inevitable need to re-cognize, to "know again."[36] Whereas modern rationalism seeks to know what has happened and what should be done, Rosean recognition claims that "wisdom works with equivocation."[37] Eschewing the rationalist desire for confident description and prescription—for the relentless pursuit and instrumentalization of useful knowledge—Rose advocates an aporetic or struggle-filled path that tarries with uncertainty. She characterizes this more difficult philosophy as requiring the "acceptance of pathlessness (*aporia*): that there may be no solutions to questions, only the clarification of their statement."[38]

31. Ibid.
32. Gillian Rose, *Hegel contra Sociology*, viii.
33. Ibid., 71.
34. Ibid.
35. Rose, *The Broken Middle*, 155.
36. Rose, *Hegel contra Sociology*, 71.
37. Rose, *Mourning Becomes the Law*, 2.
38. Rose, *Paradiso*, 42. See also the discussion in Rose, *The Broken Middle*, 199–215.

Being willing to be vulnerable—to "[be] in uncertainties"[39]—is an integral part of Hegelian recognition and works against the contemporary valorization of invulnerability and certainty. As Tarik Kochi puts it: "What is rational (or reasonable) is the realisation of the freedom of being which can only occur if the ego gives up its immediate solipsistic tendencies towards self-certainty and instead finds itself in, and gives itself to, the radical project of mutual recognition."[40]

Hegelian recognition requires that we embark on a journey where certainty is shaken and displaced. It works against hubris and against the elevation of security as an incontrovertible good; Rosean recognition offers no "new security, neither individual nor collective."[41] This is *difficult praxis*: it invites struggle-filled engagement with ordinary politics without the promise of problems solved or insecurities allayed. It relinquishes self-certainty in favor of uncertain pathlessness and equivocation.

The radical project of mutual recognition requires us to work toward comprehension of ourselves as well as the social world. Rose enjoins us not to remain "strangers to ourselves as moral agents and as social actors."[42] This too is *difficult praxis*; it asks us to look inwards as well as outwards and to consider our own complicity in oppressive social and political relations. Even with good intentions, Rose argues, we unwittingly participate in and validate norms that silence and structures that oppress. She insists that it is "possible to mean well, to be caring and kind, loving one's neighbour as oneself, yet to be complicit in the corruption and violence of social institutions."[43]

The painful difficulty of coming to know ourselves is illustrated powerfully in *Paradiso*, where Rose speaks of an unbearable travelling companion with whom she resolved never to travel again. Her companion's days and nights were marked by constant activity, by a "frantic insomnia"[44] that prevented her from stopping and "holding still."[45] Rose came to realize that her frenetic busyness masked a deeper laziness,[46] a refusal to do the difficult work of coming to know herself. As Rose puts it, her companion's activity

---

39. Rose, *Paradiso*, 31.
40. Kochi, "Being, Nothing, Becoming," 138.
41. Rose, *The Broken Middle*, 155.
42. Rose, *Judaism and Modernity*, 36.
43. Ibid., 35.
44. Rose, *Paradiso*, 37.
45. Ibid.
46. Rose maintains that she was, in truth, beset by "the most remorseless *acedia*—laziness, sloth, apathy" (ibid.).

was paradoxically rooted in "a deeper lack of will to action: that affirmation of the intensity of life which one finds—holding still—in whatever site surrounds one and whatever the soul sights in itself."[47] Allowing the soul space to hold still in "whatever the soul sights in itself" is difficult; in stillness, we come to know ourselves and the ways we engage with others and with our world. Allowing ourselves to hold still is risky; stillness requires vulnerability and risks coming face to face with pain we would rather not feel. Rose acknowledges this fear, but responds with the assertion that, "[i]f you don't feel pain, you won't feel anything else."[48] Being willing to sit with and acknowledge our pain, to own our distress, allows us to move beyond the fear that keeps us "mired in the swamp of *acedia*"[49] and instead to embrace the faith that would lead us through despair to joyous engagement.[50]

Rosean speculative philosophy is marked by faith: it doggedly commits to the difficult journey of coming to know. Her reflections on faith are framed by the concepts of negative and positive capability. Rose argues that faith is committed to pathlessness: "[F]aith is first and last negative capability, as Keats puts it, the capacity of being in uncertainties, mysteries, doubts, without any irritable reaching after fact and reasons."[51]

Negative capability is willing to tarry with uncertainty. By relinquishing the comfort of certain knowledge, this aspect of faith is profoundly countercultural. It is *difficult praxis*—"disturbing or even agonizing for the self"[52]—as we work toward recognition that challenges our perception not just of the world in which we live, but also of ourselves. Rose extends Keats's definition of faith by adding a second dimension, that of positive capability. She argues: "It is also positive capability, not developed by Keats, the enlarging of inhibited reason in the domain of praxis, of practical reason,

---

47. Rose, *Paradiso*, 37.
48. Ibid., 38.
49. Ibid., 41.
50. Ibid., 38.
51. Ibid., 31. Keats's exact definition of negative capability is being "capable of being in uncertainties, Mysteries, doubts, without any irritable reaching after fact & reason." Keats, *The Letters of John Keats*, 1:193–94.
52. Ou, *Keats and Negative Capability*, 2. Li Ou highlights the central core of negative capability as resisting the "instinctive clinging to certitude, resolution and closure." She continues: "To be negatively capable is to be open to the actual vastness and complexity of experience, and one cannot possess this openness unless one can abandon the comfortable enclosure of doctrinaire knowledge, safely guarding the self's identity, for a more truthful view of the world which is necessarily more disturbing or even agonizing for the self" (2).

Aristotle's *phronesis*, the educating of wisdom that knows when to pass unnoticed and when to act."[53]

Meeting negative capability with positive capability ensures that we do not become paralyzed by uncertainty. Positive capability knows *when to act*; however, it takes the *risk* of engaging politically without certain knowledge of what will eventuate: "Learning in this sense mediates the social and the political: it works precisely by making mistakes, by taking the risk of action, and then by reflecting on its unintended consequences, and then taking the risk, yet again, of further action, and so on."[54]

Political action, for Rose, cannot be prescribed; it too requires revisiting and revising: acting, evaluating, and acting again. She enjoins us not to seek perfection but rather to seek a good enough justice that allows space for imperfection, for failure, for trying again.

Full of surprises: Disturbing and joyful

Although Rose's work is challenging—layering difficulty upon difficulty—it is far from joyless. Rose provokes us to know and act differently—*vulnerably*—and argues that this will be both difficult *and* enriching. She maintains that we have domesticated reason, stripping it both of its difficulty and of its bounty. Against the instrumentalization and demonization of reason, Rose enjoins us to rehabilitate reason as relational: "Reason in modernity cannot be said to have broken the promise of universality—unless we have not kept it; for it is only we who can keep such a promise by working our abstract potentiality into the always difficult but enriched actuality of our relation to others and to ourselves. Whether disturbing or joyful, reason is full of surprises."[55]

For Rose, a deeply relational understanding of reason invites us on an unpredictable and uncertain journey that comes to know our relation to others and to ourselves. On this reading, reason is full of surprises—it can be both disturbing *and* joyful. This fuller conception of reason asks us to be willing to be vulnerable. We continue to risk knowing and acting—participating in structures of power—knowing that we will get it wrong and need to know, and act, again. Although embracing vulnerability entails the possibility of wounding, it also opens us to the prospect of love and joy. Simone Drichel argues that by failing to engage with our helplessness, our vulnerability, but instead rushing toward safety, we are "fleeing from and

53. Rose, *Paradiso*, 31–32.
54. Rose, *Mourning Becomes the Law*, 38.
55. Rose, *Judaism and Modernity*, 9.

defending against the very relationality that, to be sure, is always a potential source of pain and wounding, but that is also the condition of possibility for pleasure and satisfaction, and ultimately for ethical life."[56]

The epigraph to *Love's Work* is "Keep your mind in hell, and despair not."[57] Rose's speculative philosophy is against ignorance and against innocence. The injunction to keep your mind in hell asks us to start with *what is*: to unflinchingly face social and political realities and work toward a deeper understanding of the conditions that have created and sustain global challenges. The agonistic recognition to which Rose calls us is not moral rationalism's diligent but sanitized gathering of "more facts"[58] that can be mobilized to bestow "*more* recognition":[59] such endeavors silence that which falls outside useful knowledge and entail no risk to our sense of self.[60] Instead, she invites us to keep our minds in hell: to interrogate our complicity in practices and structures of misrecognition and to take the risk of acting politically in response.[61]

Alongside Rose's insistence that we face the unpalatable actualities of contemporary life and work toward recognition of *what is—difficulty upon difficulty*—is her contention that we must not take refuge in despair ("and despair not"). This is, in part, a refusal of what she perceives as postmodernism's "despairing rationalism without reason."[62] However, it is much more than a negative injunction: Rose's oeuvre is shot through with the recognition not only of "hell" but also of love, joy, and grace. Indeed, it is in part through difficulty—through "the always difficult but enriched actuality of our relation to others and to ourselves"[63]—that "goodness and its fruits"[64] are birthed. In *Paradiso*, Rose's meditations focus primarily on friends who have "passed beyond purgatory," who have "dwelt in the abyss, in hell, and have undergone purgation."[65] These friends have held still and allowed themselves to feel pain: they have begun to know themselves. They

---

56. Drichel, "Introduction," 13.

57. Attributed to Staretz Silouan, 1866–1938, epigraph to Rose, *Love's Work*. The last line of Rose's published final notebooks returns to this quote: "Keep your mind in hell and dN." Rose, "The Final Notebooks of Gillian Rose," 18.

58. Morgenthau, *Scientific Man versus Power Politics*, 215.

59. Markell, *Bound by Recognition*, 180.

60. Hutchings, "A Place of Greater Safety?"

61. See also the discussion in Schick, "Re-cognizing Recognition."

62. Rose, *Mourning Becomes the Law*, 7.

63. Rose, *Judaism and Modernity*, 9.

64. Rose, *Paradiso*, 23.

65. Ibid., 22–23.

have welcomed vulnerable reason, whose "ambivalent potentiality"[66] opens us not only to pain and wounding, but also to love, joy, and grace. Where distress retreats and joy and beauty advance, she does not allow her experience of these mysteries to take her away from ordinary political life.[67] She contends: "This does not make me ecstatic, unreal, unworldly: it returns me to the vocation of the everyday—to Miss Marple's sense of quotidian justice."[68] These fruits, in turn, return us to the fray, to engagement with the everyday.[69]

I argue that one of the keys to understanding the joyful aspects of Rosean recognition is to understand vulnerability's "ambivalent potentiality."[70] A fuller conception of vulnerability challenges the hegemonic perception of vulnerability as inextricably entwined with violence and therefore unwelcome. Being vulnerable entails a more difficult and courageous engagement with our selves and our social world; it shuts down "easy paths" that promise certainty and security. However, being vulnerable is inextricably entwined with relationality and thus opens us to the possibility of love and joy; vulnerable reason is "full of surprises"[71] and facilitates our "movement from loss to grace."[72] For Rose, vulnerable reason calls us to a different way of being and acting: it "reopens the way to conceive learning, growth and knowledge as fallible and precarious, but risk-able."[73] In what follows, I highlight the ways that "goodness and its fruits" are apparent in being and acting differently and argue that they nourish us on our imperfect journey toward a good enough justice.

---

66. Drichel, "Introduction," 23.
67. Rose, *Paradiso*, 20–21.
68. Ibid., 21. See also 102n99.
69. Ibid. Rose, *Love's Work*, 135.

70. Drichel, "Introduction," 23. See also Gilson, "Vulnerability, Ignorance, and Oppression." Note that Rose's work has clear links with recent feminist work on vulnerability, although Rose was intellectually and personally ambivalent towards feminism (as toward identity politics, more generally). See Rose, *Love's Work*, 131–33. Lloyd, ed., "Interview with Gillian Rose." See also Lloyd, "Gillian Rose, Race, and Identity," 119. However, I contend that Rose's work advocates vulnerable judgment and action and that this emphasis on vulnerability, contra certainty, stems in large part from her speculative reading of Hegel. Hegel's legacy for feminism is ambivalent: he was misogynist and excluded women from reason and history; however, despite this, (radical) readings of Hegel that take his theory of recognition seriously provide a rich resource for feminist thought. See Hutchings, *Hegel and Feminist Philosophy*.

71. Rose, *Judaism and Modernity*, 9.
72. Rose, *Paradiso*, 17–18.
73. Rose, *Mourning Becomes the Law*, 13.

To be human, for Rose, is to be relational. Rose argues that we cannot be thought in isolation from our relationship with others, from our embeddedness in communities and institutions. To think of ourselves as "isolated [selves] separate from community and corporation"[74] is to fall into Gnostic error[75] and to shy away from the work of coming to know ourselves and our location in social, historical, and political context. As human beings, we are always in the process of becoming and we become ourselves though interaction with others. As for Hegel, for Rose, "the moment of mutual recognition involves a 'speculative' realisation on the part of the ego that its identity already contains within it aspects of the other and that its being is really a relational, inter-dependent existence, a form of social being (*Gemeinwesen*)—the 'I that is We and We that is I.'"[76]

Being human, on this reading, entails taking part in a relational dance whereby our selves come up against other selves and whereby our understanding of self and other is gradually transformed. The dance of recognition renders self-certain identities less certain, as we become aware of our porosity, of the inescapable relationality and relativity of our beings.[77] Hegelian recognition, on this reading, is unsettling; our once-secure identities are shaken and increasingly open to contingency and difference as we navigate our world.

As relational subjects, we are vulnerable. We are open to the other and to all that this entails—to the possibility of wounding *as well as* the possibility of warmth and love. As discussed above, vulnerability's "ambivalent potentiality" is not well recognized in mainstream political theory and public discourse, where vulnerability is seen as a weakness to be shut down.[78] However, in working to shore up defenses and to become invulnerable, we also work against the possibility of warmth and love. Instead, we valorize "a certain kind of subjectivity privileged in capitalist socioeconomic systems, namely, that of the prototypical, arrogantly self-sufficient, independent, invulnerable master subject."[79] Understanding ourselves as vulnerable and

---

74. Rose, *Paradiso*, 25.

75. Rose characterizes Gnosticism as the default spiritual condition of pre-moderns, moderns, and post-moderns, saying that it is founded on rigid dualisms marked by its relation to (instrumental) knowledge, which it perceives as "the key to human salvation" (ibid.).

76. Kochi, "Being, Nothing, Becoming," 137. See also Hegel, *Phenomenology of Spirit*, 110.

77. Kochi, "Being, Nothing, Becoming," 136–37.

78. See, for example, the discussion of US defense policy in the wake of the 9/11 attacks in Butler, *Precarious Life*.

79. Gilson, "Vulnerability, Ignorance, and Oppression," 312.

relational subjects—as "shining-into-another"[80]—works against the destructive individualism of liberal capitalism.

Rose explores the dynamics of vulnerable relationality in the microcosm of the relationship between lovers. She speaks of the wonder and challenges of encountering the lover's "ever strange being, which comes up against you, and disappears, again and again, surprising you with difficulties and with bounty."[81] The dynamic of mutual recognition is played out in the context of the love relationship, as each partner comes up against the other and is transformed. As Lloyd puts it: "[I]n loving, when the relationship is between two individuals, there is dynamic feedback. Each presentation and representation is constantly forcing alterations in the two parties. The lover and the beloved, as they interact with each other, are constantly forced outside of themselves by the miracle of love, by the miracle enacted in the space between them. Neither party remains who she or he was before the interaction; each, through the interaction, is forced to become a new person."[82]

The relationship between lovers is intensely vulnerable—we are laid open to one another as we navigate life and love together. Rose remarks that "each party, woman, man, the child in each, and their child, is absolute power as well as absolute vulnerability."[83] Love's ambivalent potentiality is manifest in its joys and agonies, its difficulties and bounty, its limitations and failures.[84] In her reflections on the risks of loving, Rose remarks "If I am to stay alive, I am bound to continue to get love wrong, all the time, but not to cease wooing, for that is my life affair, *love's work*."[85]

Rosean recognition's invitation to a deeply vulnerable and relational way of being is both demanding and freeing: it does not expect or require perfection but, on the contrary, expects, and accepts, imperfection and failure. Rose enjoins us to work toward a good enough justice, aware of the unavoidable precarity and contingency of efforts to know and to act.

In Rose's meditations on friends and family in *Paradiso*, she reflects on their willingness or otherwise to *fail*. Let me return for a moment to the story of the unbearable travel companion, whose restless activity precluded rest for both travelers. Rose eventually confronted her with the disastrousness of the holiday; however, predictably, her companion was

---

80. Hegel, *Encyclopedia Logic*, 175, cited in Kochi, "Being, Nothing, Becoming," 137.

81. Rose, *Love's Work*, 54.

82. Lloyd, *The Problem with Grace*, 39.

83. Rose, *Love's Work*, 55.

84. Ibid., 54.

85. Ibid., 99.

unable to acknowledge any difficulties. Rose remarks: "How could she? For all emotional work—all the ironies and humour of failing each other—is inaccessible to her."[86] Her companion's inability to hold still, to turn her gaze inwards, goes hand-in-hand with "emotional dishonesty,"[87] with an inability to recognize or acknowledge the negative consequences of her frantic activity on her travel companion.

For Rose, being willing to fail is a cornerstone of a politically engaged life. After reflecting on the travel companion who was unwilling to hold still, acknowledge pain, or admit imperfection, she turns her attention to two Margarets, two "pearls of the soul"[88] who regularly do all three. Of these friends, Rose asserts: "Margarets refresh themselves frequently in the shifting pits of the underworld. When they become impatient and patient with the perennial penance aroused by zealous ministrations towards others, which are invariably generous and effective, but which swell the soul to God-like dimensions, then prayer is the practice that arrests the pride: its repose softens the stiffened soul."[89]

Her Margarets are willing to be still, to feel pain, and to fail. They regularly engage in prayer, counterbalancing their capable and "zealous ministrations towards others" with a practice that requires stillness and vulnerability. Their willingness to hold still goes hand in hand with a willingness to be discomforted, to feel pain ("these souls are perfected ... with regularity in the refining furnaces of pain")[90] and to fail ("Margarets know how to fail").[91] The quality of being willing to fail, of risk-filled engagement with the world, is a theme that recurs throughout Rose's work.[92] Her challenge to know and act differently—vulnerably and relationally—accepts that our knowing and acting is inevitably partial and gets things wrong. Just as we need to re-cognize, to know again, we also need to act again. Failure does not entail reproach or devastation; instead, it is a productive part of coming to know ourselves and our place in the world and of political engagement.

86. Rose, *Paradiso*, 38.
87. Ibid.
88. Ibid.
89. Ibid., 40–41.
90. Ibid., 41.

91. Ibid. See also Rose's reflection on Edna in ibid., 15–36 and her assertion that "Edna will not be able to sing the *Song of Songs* until she abandons this all too Greek *gnosis*, and allows herself to become less immaculate, to allow the imperfections throughout her physical and moral being to exist" (ibid., 31).

92. See, for example, Rose's autobiographical reflections in *Love's Work*. Love's work, for Rose, is "the work I have been charting, accomplishing, but, above all and necessarily, failing in, all along the way" (71).

Expecting, even welcoming, imperfection in this way *frees* us to take the "risk of recognition"[93]—of coming to know ourselves and our complicity in oppressive norms and structures—while continuing to be willing to "participate in power and its legitimate violence for the sake of the good."[94] Rose calls us to resist paralysis in the face of inevitable failure and loss, inviting mourning and political (re)engagement in its stead.

In *Paradiso*, Rose reflects on her deceptively accessible meditations on love, loss, and failure in *Love's Work*.[95] In this endeavor, she seeks to "pass unnoticed"[96] and to move "from loss to *grace*":[97] "[*Love's Work*] deploys sensual, intellectual and literary eros, companions of pain, passion and plain curiosity, in order to pass beyond the preoccupation with endless loss to the silence of grace. Miss Marple is the code-name for this movement from loss to grace ... [she] is what Kierkegaard calls a *knight of faith*, as distinct from what we mostly are most of the time—*knights of resignation*."[98]

In these reflections on loss—loves lost, the impending loss of her own life—Rose refuses to continually encircle these losses; instead, she passes beyond to the "silence of grace."[99] She rejects the temptation of endless mourning, or *melancholia*, which encircles trauma and refuses to pass beyond. Instead, she embraces *inaugurated mourning*, mourning that comes to know the contours of loss and suffering.[100] Inaugurated mourning works through endless loss and returns to "the city, renewed and reinvigorated for participation, ready to take on the difficulties and injustices of the existing city."[101] As a *knight of faith*, Miss Marple is not immobilized by failure or loss but reinvigorated for faithful engagement with the everyday: "As the sublime in the pedestrian, the knight of faith simply appears as whatever

---

93. Rose, *Mourning Becomes the Law*, 100.
94. Ibid.
95. Rose, *Love's Work*.
96. Rose, *Paradiso*, 17.
97. Ibid., 17–18; emphasis mine.
98. Ibid.; emphasis in original. Miss Jane Marple is a character in a number of Agatha Christie's crime novels. Rose describes her as "*exactly what she appears to be*: a proper, fussy, inquisitive, old lady ... [whose] success in establishing justice invariably depends on her being able to pass unnoticed while noticing everything herself." Rose, *Judaism and Modernity*, 222; emphasis in original.
99. Rose, *Paradiso*, 17.
100. Rose, *Mourning Becomes the Law*, 64, 69–76. Schick, *Gillian Rose*, 44–49, 57–80.
101. Rose, *Mourning Becomes the Law*, 36.

she is: she returns to her vocation beyond the endless anxiety of the test of salvation."[102]

The last pages of Rose's (unfinished) *Paradiso* return to the relation of law and grace, everyday and miracle, pedestrian and sublime. She meditates on a passage from Simone Weil's *Gravity and Grace*:[103] "It is the light falling continuously from heaven which alone gives a tree the energy to send powerful roots deep into the soil. . . . The tree is really rooted in the sky."[104]

In her reflections on Weil's image of the tree, Rose argues that it is "not a mystical appeal to the ineffability of the sky, but a relating of gravity and grace."[105] Weil's tree is "an analogy of the middle"[106] that refuses to divorce the ethical from the political, the supernatural from the everyday: "The pathos of gravity—of weight, ground, earth, city—channelled to grace—the response to ethical commandment—means that spiritual and religious life, supernatural, is not radically divorced from nature, being, logic and politics."[107]

The image of light falling speaks of grace, which Weil represents as "light or lightness, and as upwards motion."[108] This "light from heaven"—grace—does not call us to mystical contemplation, divorced from the everyday. Instead, it *nourishes* our negotiation of the everyday: "We know who we are only when we venture to live from that thirsty turning to the heavens where there is nothing to see yet everything to nourish us."[109] We turn to the heavens and, in turn, grace sends our roots downwards, drawing us toward *the city in which we reside*—to faithful engagement with ordinary life.

Despite key differences, both Rose and Weil capture grace's creative element of surprise and its call to know again. Weil's icon of the tree captures both the uncertainty of negative capability (suspended in the sky) and the courage of positive capability (putting down roots). One of the markers of grace, for Weil, is that it is not something one actively seeks, but rather that one opens oneself to through de-creation, "a kenosis of the self that makes room for the sudden access of God's grace."[110] There is a *passivity* to Weil's concept of opening oneself to the possibility of grace that sits ill with

102. Rose, *Paradiso*, 18.
103. Weil, *Gravity and Grace*.
104. Rose, *Paradiso*, 62–63.
105. Ibid., 62.
106. Rose, *Judaism and Modernity*, 218.
107. Rose, *Paradiso*, 63.
108. Macfarlane, "Gravity and Grace in Geoffrey Hill," 240.
109. Williams, "'The Sadness of the King,'" 35.
110. Macfarlane, "Gravity and Grace in Geoffrey Hill," 241.

Rosean political risk.[111] However, Geoffrey Hill's poetry and prose highlight a meeting point for Rose and Weil by signaling grace's invitation to re-know. First, the "work of grace,"[112] for Hill, induces a "shock of recognition" whereby we revisit what we thought we knew—re-know—in a form of knowledge that "escapes committal."[113] Rose and Hill's notions of grace meet here, in the notion of knowledge as "fallible and precarious."[114] Second, following Weil, Hill maintains that grace is not attained by "a willed questioning, but passively, by coming upon it abruptly, 'unlooked-for.'"[115] We don't *pursue* or *secure* grace; instead, we are surprised by grace. Although Rose resists passivity, Rose and Hill's notions of grace cohere in this element of surprise: both thinkers refuse rigid forms of knowing and being that can be pre-determined or predicted—they refuse the domestication of knowledge and remain open to "surprises."[116]

Conclusion

In this chapter, I have argued that Rose's speculative philosophy is both disturbing *and* joyful. Its radical relationality is "unsettled and unsettling,"[117] layering difficulty upon difficulty; however it is also joyful, opening us to one another and to the possibility of love, beauty, and grace as well as pain. Rose's vulnerable conception of reason alerts us to our fundamental fallibility: we expect to know *and* act again in response to (inevitable) misrecognition and failure.

Rose's subtle philosophy, her *grey in grey*, resists both the confident prescription of universals and the despairing retreat from reason—difficult theory. She invites us on an agonistic journey towards recognition that tarries with uncertainty and looks inwards as well as outwards at our complicity in violent structures and practices—difficult praxis. Against the instrumentalization or demonization of reason, she advocates its rehabilitation. For Rose, reason is not "dualistic, dominant and imperialistic" but "relational,

111. As we have seen, Rose's work castigates passivity and instead emphasizes "activity beyond activity," which "reopens the way to conceive learning, growth and knowledge as fallible and precarious, but risk-able." Rose, *Mourning Becomes the Law*, 13.

112. Macfarlane, "Gravity and Grace in Geoffrey Hill," 248.

113. Ibid., 249.

114. Rose, *Mourning Becomes the Law*, 13.

115. Macfarlane, "Gravity and Grace in Geoffrey Hill," 246. Hill, "Language, Suffering, and Silence," 253–54.

116. Rose, *Judaism and Modernity*, 9.

117. Rose, *The Broken Middle*, 155.

responsive and reconstructive."[118] It commits to the difficult journey toward comprehension and gradually "*comes to learn*."[119] However, although Rose's difficult theory and praxis is intellectually and personally demanding, it is also "full of surprises." It is disturbing *and* joyful—we navigate life together as vulnerable subjects, open to discomfort and failure *as well as* "goodness and its fruits."

To conclude, I return to Weil's icon of the tree, which captures the vulnerability inherent in Rose's difficult theory and praxis. I explore this image with reference to Rose's definition of faith as negative and positive capability—a willingness to accept our fallibility and imperfection yet to persist in engaging politically with the everyday. Weil's evocative image of the tree, rooted in the sky, powerfully communicates the uncertainty of Keats's negative capability. Rose emphasizes the courage that embracing uncertainty requires, saying: "What courage is summoned by this icon of the visible and the invisible. To be a tree. To be suspended in the empyrean, with no security, no identity, no community. Yet only this willingness to be suspended in the sky, to be without support, enables us to draw on the divine sources and sustenance which make it possible to put down roots."[120]

The tree is, first and foremost, "suspended in the sky . . . without support."[121] Indeed it is this *willingness* to be suspended in the sky that is one of the markers of a tree—its suspension "makes it possible to put down roots."[122] Being willing to be uncertain is difficult—"we feel lost, we are in the abyss"[123]—it requires courage to risk not knowing in the face of overwhelming pressure to know. Rose asserts: "We need to venture again the courage of suspense, not knowing who we are."[124] Being willing to accept uncertainty facilitates our ability to "put down roots," to embark on the courageous journey of re-cognition, of engaging with the here and now.

Rose twins the willingness to be uncertain—Keats's negative capability—with a willingness to risk acting politically despite this uncertainty—positive capability. Her reflections on Weil's suspended tree draw us resolutely to the risk-filled endeavor of political engagement in the here and now: "activity beyond activity" that resists passivity.[125] Rose asks us to

118. Rose, *Judaism and Modernity*, 4.
119. Ibid., 8; emphasis in original.
120. Rose, *Paradiso*, 63.
121. Ibid.
122. Ibid.
123. Ibid.
124. Ibid.
125. Rose, *Mourning Becomes the Law*, 13, 121–23.

"venture again the courage of suspense . . . *in order to* rediscover our infinite capacity for self-creation and response to our fellow self-creators."[126] The suspense of not knowing is a necessary part of the journey of recognition. Recall Kochi's characterization of Hegelian recognition as requiring that the ego "gives up its immediate solipsistic tendencies towards self-certainty and instead finds itself in, and gives itself to, the radical project of mutual recognition."[127] Vulnerable recognition holds in tension a courageous willingness to be uncertain—"the courage of suspense"—with a commitment to engagement and (re)discovery that takes the form of "self-creation and response to our fellow self-creators."[128] The ego comes up against other egos and, in the process of this struggle-filled, relational engagement, transforms our understanding of ourselves and of others. As part of that process, we do not shy from political engagement, despite not knowing what the outcome may be. As self-creators, we are in the process of *becoming*, an agonistic process that is both transformative and unsettling. This process requires *work*, "a working through, that combination of self-knowledge and action which will not blanch before its complicities in power—*activity beyond activity*, not passivity beyond passivity. For power is not necessarily tyranny, but that can only be discovered by taking the risk of coming to learn it—but acting, reflecting on the outcome, and then initiating further action."[129]

Bibliography

Butler, Judith. *Precarious Life: The Powers of Mourning and Violence*. London: Verso, 2004.

Drichel, Simone. "Introduction: Reframing Vulnerability: 'So Obviously the Problem . . .?,'" *SubStance* 42, no. 3 (2013) 5–7. doi:10.1353/sub.2013.0030.

Geuss, Raymond. *Outside Ethics*. Princeton: Princeton University Press, 2005.

Gilson, Erinn. "Vulnerability, Ignorance, and Oppression." *Hypatia* 26, no. 2 (2011) 308–32. doi:10.1111/j.1527-2001.2010.01158.x.

Hegel, Georg Wilhelm Friedrich. *Phenomenology of Spirit*. Oxford: Clarendon, 1977.

Hill, Geoffrey. "Language, Suffering, and Silence." *Literary Imagination* 1, no. 2 (1999) 240–55. doi:10.1093/litimag/1.2.240.

Hutchings, Kimberley. *Hegel and Feminist Philosophy*. Cambridge: Polity, 2003.

———. "A Place of Greater Safety? Securing Judgement in International Ethics." In *The Vulnerable Subject: Beyond Rationalism in International Relations*, edited by Amanda Russell Beattie and Kate Schick, 25–42. Basingstoke, UK: Palgrave Macmillan, 2013.

---

126. Rose, *Paradiso*, 63; emphasis mine.
127. Kochi, "Being, Nothing, Becoming," 138.
128. Rose, *Paradiso*, 63.
129. Rose, *Mourning Becomes the Law*, 121; emphasis in original.

Keats, John. *The Letters of John Keats, 1814–1821*. Vols. 1–2. Edited by Hyder Edward Rollins. Cambridge, MA: Harvard University Press, 1958.

Kochi, Tarik. "Being, Nothing, Becoming." In *New Critical Legal Thinking: Law and the Political*, edited by Matthew Stone, Illan rua Wall, and Costas Douzinas, 128–44. Abingdon, UK: Routledge, 2012.

Lloyd, Vincent. "Gillian Rose, Race, and Identity." *Telos* 173 (2015) 107–24. doi:10.3817/1215173107.

———. "Interview with Gillian Rose." *Theory, Culture and Society* 25, nos. 7–8 (2008) 201–18.

———. *The Problem with Grace: Reconfiguring Political Theology*. Stanford, CA: Stanford University Press, 2011.

Macfarlane, Robert. "Gravity and Grace in Geoffrey Hill." *Essays in Criticism* 58, no. 3 (2008) 237–56.

Markell, Patchen. *Bound by Recognition*. Princeton: Princeton University Press, 2003.

Morgenthau, Hans. *Scientific Man versus Power Politics*. Chicago: University of Chicago Press, 1946.

Ou, Li. *Keats and Negative Capability*. Continuum Literary Studies. London: Bloomsbury Academic, 2009.

Rose, Gillian. *The Broken Middle: Out of Our Ancient Society*. Oxford: Blackwell, 1992.

———. "The Final Notebooks of Gillian Rose." *Women: A Cultural Review* 9, no. 1 (1998) 6–18. doi:10.1080/09574049808578330.

———. *Hegel contra Sociology*. London: Athlone, 1981.

———. *Judaism and Modernity: Philosophical Essays*. Oxford: Blackwell, 1993.

———. *Love's Work: A Reckoning with Life*. 1st American ed. New York: Schocken, 1995.

———. *Mourning Becomes the Law: Philosophy and Representation*. Cambridge: Cambridge University Press, 1996.

———. *Paradiso*. London: Menard, 1999.

Schick, Kate. *Gillian Rose: A Good Enough Justice*. Edinburgh: Edinburgh University Press, 2012.

———. "Re-cognizing Recognition: Gillian Rose's 'Radical Hegel' and Vulnerable Recognition." *Telos* 173 (2015) 87–105. doi:10.3817/1215173087.

Solomon, Ty, and Brent J. Steele. "Micro-Moves in International Relations Theory." *European Journal of International Relations* 23, no. 2 (2017). doi:10.1177/1354066116634442.

Weil, Simone. *Gravity and Grace*. Translated by Emma Crawford and Mario von der Ruhr. 1st English ed. London: Routledge, 2002.

Williams, Rowan D. "'The Sadness of the King': Gillian Rose, Hegel, and the Pathos of Reason." *Telos* 173 (2015) 21–36. doi:10.3817/1215173021.

Part 2

Thinking the Absolute
Law, Education, Theology

Chapter 5

Mis(re)cognition of God and Man
The Educational Philosophy and Politics of Gillian Rose

Rebekah Howes

Rose cites Hegel's fundamental speculative proposition as being that "religion and the foundation of the state is [sic] one and the same thing."[1] What Rose is drawing attention to here in her book *Hegel contra Sociology* (first published in 1981) is the "logic" within which modern bourgeois freedom presupposes and also reproduces the separation between thought and the absolute. It is to say that "the *speculative experience of the lack of identity* between religion and the state is the basic object of Hegel's exposition."[2] This gives rise to the difficult suggestion that "the idea which a man has of God corresponds with that which he has of himself, of his freedom."[3] In contrast, Kantian and neo-Kantian logic, which is not speculative, appears to itself in and as the modern diremption of law and ethics whereby the thought of the absolute in politics and religion is the "re-presentation of the extreme subjectivity, the lack of freedom, in social and political relations."[4]

1. Hegel quoted in Rose, *Hegel contra Sociology*, 49.
2. Hegel quoted in ibid.
3. Hegel quoted in ibid., 92.
4. Hegel quoted in ibid.

Modern consciousness in Hegel and Rose, and in their speculative logic, is this contradictory self-relation of state and religion. We think and we live in the divorce between modernity's idea of God and its idea of freedom. Rose's retrieval of a thinking of the absolute in Hegel for modern social and political thought, which rests on the phenomenological experience of the relation between substance and subject, between objective ethical life (the state) and subjectivity (religious disposition) thus renews Marx's question, "How do we now stand in relation to the Hegelian *dialectic*?,"[5] to the historical and political contingencies which determine our thinking of, and our living with, the absolute.

That there are two logics here poses an immediate challenge for any attempt to conceive if and how Rose might be said to be something like a political theology. I am taking political theology here to mean, in its widest sense, the attempt to integrate discourse about God with an account of human interaction and meaning-making in the political sphere. But in the shadow of Rose's work it is the much more difficult task of a *speculative* theologizing about and within the "divorce in the idea of the absolute."[6] It involves, she says, the absolute "misconceived as the principle of political unity" and "misrepresented as a conception of God."[7]

In this way, Rose reads Hegel thinking as always already determined within the social, political, and historical conditions that represent this divorce. This is not simply a critique of determination but the contingency of our critique of determination *ad infinitum*. In the groundlessness that this imposes upon us, we are dependent on illusion and on our relation to illusion. This is one of the central insights in Rose regarding the identity of state and religion. Modern freedom, as the contradictory self-relation of state and religion, finds itself separated from its own formation and development in the broken middle of their relation. Rose's challenge to a political theology is, first of all, for it to find itself in the difficulties of thinking state and religion together and apart. Secondly, it is to know these difficulties as *philosophical*, as the "process or *Bildung*" of modernity "as it comes up against, again and again, its own positing of 'the world,' discovering outcomes the inverse of what it intended."[8]

In what follows, I will show that in working with these difficulties Rose finds a different logic of the thought of politics and God from within the illusions and misrecognitions of state and religion. With reference to the

---

5. Marx quoted in Rose, *The Melancholy Science*, 3.
6. Rose, *Hegel contra Sociology*, 92.
7. Ibid., 92–93.
8. Rose, *Mourning Becomes the Law*, 74.

work of Nigel Tubbs, a former student of Rose, I argue this to be the educational logic of *mis(re)cognition*. I will show that this logic comprehends not only the religious nature of modern bourgeois freedom to be correspondingly the political actuality of religion, but that therein the absolute has its political and spiritual truth in and as education. To this end, the examination seeks not to extract a political theology from Rose because, as we will see, her work undermines the thinking that would seek to posit the parameters of a political theology as "correction" to the various misrecognitions of secular liberalism and political theory. I argue instead that Rose holds to the educational difficulty of the relation between politics and religion and that it is education in Rose and in Hegel that works with difficulty as of absolute significance. Reading Rose in this way we are challenged to retrieve the speculative depth of her work in its fundamentally educative ambiguities, or in the consistencies of its inconsistencies, as a radical politics and faith.

Reading God and Politics in Rose

In "Gillian Rose and the Project of a Critical Marxism," Tony Gorman argues that Rose's early political engagement with Adorno and Lukács and the project of a Critical Marxism in *Hegel contra Sociology* (*HCS*), is, in her later words, ultimately abandoned.[9] This is due to the appearance of an "irresolvable aporia"[10] at the heart of Rose's attempt to retrieve a thinking of the absolute in Hegel for modern social and political thought. For Gorman, *HCS* "oscillates" between two modes of phenomenological reconstruction; one which advances a positive or speculative dialectic through the Hegelian notion of recollection and one which "withdraws" from it in an Adornoesque eschewal of all positive and thus abstract, utopian ideals or moments. This means that the radical critique of bourgeois property relations that emerges in the phenomenological reconstruction of the antinomies of modern social and political thought, leads to a "retrospective and resigned" politics that, fearing the reactive, becomes "decidedly irrational and voluntarist."[11] Where Rose sees a formative work in and within the aporias of these two modes, there is, in fact, for Gorman, only a "radical incompatibility" leading to political impasse.[12] Rose's project to link "a presentation of the contradictory relations between capital and culture" to "the analysis of the economy,"

---

9. These are *The Broken Middle*, *Judaism and Modernity*, *Mourning Becomes the Law*, *Love's Work*, and *Paradiso*.
10. Gorman, "Gillian Rose and the Project of a Critical Marxism," 32.
11. Ibid., 35.
12. Ibid., 32.

thereby to "comprehend the conditions for revolutionary practice,"[13] leads only to failure.

Gorman blames this on a "non-metaphysical interpretation" of the Hegelian Concept or Absolute, one that "fundamentally re-orders"[14] its constitutive terms—universal, particular, and singular—as they determine subjectivity's objective social transformation. The universal, in its speculative mediations of the individual in its particular sphere of needs, is displaced by the experience of the single individual who only "'witnesses' and 'negotiates' the 'breaks' between them."[15] This singularity of experience becomes the "anchoring" of speculative negotiation and so usurps the idea of absolute ethical life with merely a "form of perspectivism."[16] There is no longer an objective basis for reconstructing capitalist social relations.

This view is echoed in Peter Osborne's review of *HCS*. Rose's absolute is limited, he argues, because her phenomenological approach gets trapped within "the perspective it knows to be false."[17] Speculative exposition turns out to be the limit of "eternal repetition,"[18] which "remains impotent in the face of contemporary reality."[19] Rose maintains the subject-object relation, which allows her to "conceptualize the mediation of the objective within the subjective," but she "rules out the possibility of a theoretical mode in which the subjective is mediated within the objective . . . the only possible form of a materialist theory of subjectivity, culture and politics, which aims to go beyond the mere recognition of the 'deformations' of existing forms of phenomenal knowledge to theorize their real determinations and possible mode of transformation."[20]

In consequence, argues Gorman, Rose finds the absolute in the quotidian practices of a "form of virtue ethics."[21] She becomes the "knight of faith" who, in the name of love's work, "melds the love of eternity with the love of the world."[22]

Both of these critiques highlight some of the difficulties that continue to surround the reception of Rose's work regarding the nature and meaning

---

13. Rose, *Hegel contra Sociology*, 220.
14. Gorman, "Gillian Rose and the Project of a Critical Marxism," 28.
15. Ibid., 35.
16. Ibid.
17. Osborne, "Hegelian Phenomenology and the Critique of Reason and Society," 4.
18. Ibid., 14.
19. Ibid., 5.
20. Ibid., 14.
21. Gorman, "Gillian Rose and the Project of a Critical Marxism," 34
22. Ibid.

of the absolute in and for a radical politics. Her work continues to fuel the division between right-wing religious and left-wing political perspectives on Hegel (and Rose), including political theology. In particular, her exposition of the *lack of identity* between state and religion, which she was later to call "the broken middle," provides what Lloyd has called various "politics of the middle," which attempt to offer an "'alternative' political theory which does not privilege the sovereignty of individual or state, and which puts intermediary associations center stage."[23]

We see this in Andrew Shank's *Against Innocence, Gillian Rose's Reception and Gift of Faith*. Here the broken middle is a radical form of mediation in the difficulties of law and social engagement. We learn to live in the brokenness of conflicting ideas and experiences but also to find therein the possibilities for "true conversation, 'peace as justice,'" and the "holding acceptance of inner conflict."[24] The broken middle is a "peace negotiator"[25] and the absolute is to be found in the openness of each participant to the "perfect Honesty"[26] of the conversation. The broken middle is thus the "impulse" of a politics open to its own pure and "ideal solidarity"[27] and the openness of a religion for which solidarity "constitutes the proper absolute essence of the sacred."[28] Shanks is clear that this openness works against those readings of Hegel that see absolute knowing as the teleological tyranny of history. Similarly, in Katie Schick's *Gillian Rose: "A Good Enough Justice,"* the broken middle of our relations with others, the drama of recognition and misrecognition, offers us possibilities for "mutual transformation"[29] because we discover the intersubjective dimension of our difficult negotiations. But, I argue, these interpretations read aporia as a middle and not as a broken middle. When aporia is read as stasis, or as an alternative politics, or as conversation, or as the albeit difficult path of mutual recognition, the middle unwittingly betrays the difficulty of actuality which is being suppressed. This is to sidestep Rose's most significant intervention in Hegelian interpretation, which reveals a notion of the absolute in actuality. This suppression is where the question of a different kind of logic in her work is most acute.

---

23. Lloyd, "Complex Space or Broken Middle? Milbank, Rose, and the Sharia Controversy," 225.

24. Shanks, *Against Innocence, Gillians Rose's Reception and Gift of Faith*, 33.

25. Ibid., 32.

26. Ibid., 43.

27. Ibid., 44.

28. Ibid.

29. Schick, *Gillian Rose: "A Good Enough Justice,"* 101.

A Question of Logic

Hegel, writes Rose, "puts a trinity of ideas in place of Kant's transcendental method; the idea of phenomenology, the idea of absolute ethical life (absolute *Sittlicheit*), and the idea of a logic."[30] In chapter 1 of *HCS*, Rose demonstrates the Kantian and neo-Kantian transcendental reasoning that all social and political theorizing, including Marxism, falls into and how the sociological tradition therein reproduces dualistic ways of thinking. As such, the antinomies of sociological reason rest on the Kantian separation of validity and values.

A transcendental account is characterized by the logic of the in-itself. Philosophy has always, in various ways, defined truth according to this ancient logic. Truth is defined as unity and lack of relation, while that which is merely for-another is mediation and thus error. This idea of truth is carried in Aristotle's notion of the Prime Mover, which is its own condition of possibility. Necessity—that it must be itself—is the principle of non-contradiction and the all-too-easily taken-for-granted judgment of the absurdity of infinite regression. Metaphysics has traditionally rested on this logic of the in-itself, which is free from opposition, contradiction, and change. In the Kantian separation of the transcendental from the object, the same ancient and perennial separation of the in-itself from mediation is betrayed. This is because a transcendental account "necessarily presupposes the actuality or existence of its object and seeks to discover the conditions of its possibility."[31]

One might argue that Kant's critical philosophy holds within it the relativity of the in-itself in its observation of mutual negation wherein "concepts without intuitions are empty; intuitions without concepts, blind."[32] Nevertheless, against such a view, the contradictions experienced by reason when it tries to think itself are seen as error and ultimately overcome in a transcendental account of experience and the synthetic *a priori* judgment that holds to the pure in-itself free from mediation. Presupposing the distinction between finite, "knowable appearances"[33] and the infinite (the unconditioned, things-in-themselves), Kant ultimately serves to "justify infinite ignorance'[34] because in seeking to justify the true in-itself it is only available in the way that it appears to us. This leaves "the social, political and

---

30. Rose, *Hegel contra Sociology*, 45.
31. Ibid., 1.
32. Kant, *Critique of Pure Reason*, B74.
33. Rose, *Hegel contra Sociology*, 45.
34. Ibid., 44.

historical determinants of all knowledge and all action . . . unknown and unknowable."[35]

What Kant fails to do, unlike Hegel, is to make the experience of the logic of the in-itself the content of reason's self-examination, which would be rather the phenomenological "exposition of the course of [its] experience."[36] Phenomenological consciousness observes the contradictions between thought and truth in-itself and so truth and experience to be "the occasion for a change in that consciousness and in its definition of its object."[37] Consciousness in Hegel has two experiences of the in-itself. The first is of the object as "the moment of truth."[38] But the object turns out to be not merely in-itself but also *for* consciousness. The distinction from, and relation to, the object is the determining aspect of thought or is what knowing is, and this relation between the two is the "dialectical movement which consciousness exercises on itself and which affects both its knowledge and its object."[39] The second experience here is the one that we, the philosophical observer, have of this natural relation to the object. Our inquiry into the truth of knowledge concerns the object "knowledge" whose essence will also be being-in-itself and being-for-another. Both experiences are ones of loss because consciousness loses the object (in both cases) to the insight that what is known in-itself is mediation. Philosophical consciousness is the thinking that comes to know itself not only in the experience of negation but in and as the activity of negation itself, that is, what it observes it knows to be its own doing. Philosophical consciousness sees that natural consciousness is "always already" a shape of relation to and determination of substance and thereby the misapprehension of substance. But it sees that only in this way is the relation between substance and subject "the precondition of immanent change"[40] wherein a different understanding of, and relation to, truth in-itself arises.

The Adornian strain in Rose's reading of Hegel finds a different dynamic here. For Adorno, like Hegel, the relation between thought and the in-itself, what Adorno calls the "logic of the excluded middle," is the "hypostasized concept," the abstract in-itself of the object that the concept reduces to "a mere sample of its kind or species."[41] But "objects do not go

---

35. Ibid.
36. Hegel, *Phenomenology of Spirit*, 55.
37. Rose, *Hegel contra Sociology*, 46.
38. Hegel, *Phenomenology of Spirit*, 53.
39. Ibid., 55.
40. Rose, *Hegel contra Sociology*, 150.
41. Adorno, *Negative Dialectics*, 46.

into their concepts without leaving a remainder."[42] This remainder is the object's potential, or "what it would like to be."[43] Adorno called this potential between concept and object, rational identity thinking. Non-identity thinking is the awareness of the gap between concept and object, which collapses the logic of non-contradiction. Negative dialectics shows that it is the object itself and not the "organizing drive of thought'[44] that yields non-identity thinking and so how the object as a specific mode of cognition in capitalist social relations appears to itself as illusion. The immanent method is not a method in the ordinary sense of the term because "it does not begin by taking a standpoint'[45] over and against an object. But consciousness, in working on itself, sees the immanently dialectical experience of subject and object to be its own work and so to be already the medium for its thinking about the non-identity of concept and object. This is to see the social form that non-identity takes.

But, for Rose, Adorno's immanent method, "the consciousness of antinomies which makes the necessities of the antinomies it discovers transparent," is an "inherently paradoxical attempt to state a non-systematic objectivism objectivistically and without a system."[46] It can only "present the awareness of the limitations of the attempt—'the mind tearing at its bonds.'"[47] Negative dialectics conforms to the logic of the in-itself because negative dialectics itself is not allowed to be mediated. Adorno does not yield the dialectic to its own immanent movement to positivity whereby it would come to know itself differently and so he merely observes it. It is only in Hegel, if we do not protect the negative from itself, from its own contradictions, that we find "a different kind of identity."[48] It is in the relation between Adorno, Hegel, and Rose that a different resonance is found for the rhythms and negations of this logic of the in-itself.

Mis(re)cognition

Rose's interpretation of Hegel's early Jena texts shows why this is the case. It is here that she offers her idea of mis(re)cognition. Hegel needed a more adequate term for the motility of the relation between concept and intuition

42. Ibid., 5.
43. Gillian Rose, "How Is Critical Theory Possible?," 71.
44. Adorno, *Negative Dialectics*, 144.
45. Ibid., 5.
46. Rose, "How Is Critical Theory Possible?," 85.
47. Ibid.
48. Rose, *Hegel contra Sociology*, 63.

than the idea of "intellectual intuition" in Fichte and Schelling. For Kant, concepts referred to intuition, to objects as they appear in themselves. Concepts cannot be legitimated without intuition. This is why intuition is not justified from concepts alone. Fichte and Schelling recognized, however, that the primacy of practical reason in Kant did precisely this. It presupposed the act of an *a priori* intuition that makes possible the framework within which theoretical and practical reason operates. But Hegel shows that intellectual intuition also produces new dominations of the concept over intuition. The problem was that intellectual intuition could not express adequately enough the triune nature of the reflective consciousness, which rests on the dichotomy of concept and intuition.

Summarizing Rose's view here, she sees that if the object in-itself is the result of the movement of immediacy and mediation, then *we* can see that consciousness is the thinking that presupposes its object and posits itself in relation to it, making consciousness a reflection-into-self. In this way consciousness sees itself in the object but the seeing is a one-sided reflection because the object does not see itself in consciousness. This makes the object merely the "reflection of individual domination."[49] Intuition as a term is thus "too immediate, too pre-critical" whereas the prefix *re-* of recognition tells us there is an inescapable "miss-seeing" in the experience that implies that something has been re-experienced in order that it is "well-known."[50] Recognition presupposes the gaps represented by the relation between concept and object/intuition. Intellectual intuition or reflection cannot acknowledge that the concept is never united with intuition. The failure to do so is also the failure to see how difficulty actually arises in the experience of the concept and in what sense it constitutes the form and content of our knowing. Recognition, then, or the relation between immediacy and mediation, has a triune structure. It implies unity (immediacy), lack of unity (mediation, contingency), and also, crucially, the *third* partner of the relation, the *work* of the gap between them that consciousness performs on itself. Here is where the object is able "to look back, without, in its turn, subsuming or denying the difference of that at which it looks back."[51] Recognition, which refers to lack of identity, is therefore "mis(re)cognition,"[52] the movement of, and the relation to, immediacy and mediation within which consciousness is changed. In this *educational* culture of experience, "the relata are able to

---

49. Rose, *Hegel contra Sociology*, 71.
50. Ibid.
51. Ibid., 65.
52. Ibid., 71.

see each other without suppressing one another."[53] This triune structure is also the Hegelian "concept or absolute."[54] I will explain what this notion of education means in a moment.

On this reading, the pitfalls associated with the concept of recognition in Hegel can be seen. Recognition, and thereby mutual recognition, imply formal recognition. The independent self-consciousness in Hegel "who exists only in being acknowledged"[55] presupposes the reflection of individual domination. Recognition is already misrecognition, "the failure of mutual recognition on the part of two self-consciousnesses who encounter each other and refuse to recognize the other as itself a self-relation."[56] Consciousness appears to itself in and as the illusion of independence, which is the template in Hegel for the experience of positing in the master and slave dialectic. Recognition is thus a relation to actuality, which means it can only appear to us abstractly. But the relation to actuality is what "determines the relation to self and relation to other."[57] This is why "if actuality is not thought . . . thinking has no social import."[58] The experience of self and other is the illusion of independence, equality, or mutuality, which in fact masks the reality of loss or the other as present in the self. Awareness of this is awareness of the ways in which the self exports otherness and difficulty, the very conditions within which selfhood is configured. Mis(re)cognition, then, in acknowledging actuality, expresses the return of the self to the negative and educational beginning within which it is determined.

Mis(re)cognition as Education

To explain further the educational logic of mis(re)cognition, I want now to turn to the work of Nigel Tubbs whose reading of Rose takes up the challenge of interpreting her Hegelianism as a philosophy of education, and again, as the education of philosophy.[59] He writes that the ancient logic of

53. Ibid., 70.
54. Ibid., 63.
55. Hegel, *Phenomenology of Spirit*, 111.
56. Rose, *Mourning Becomes the Law*, 74.
57. Rose, *Hegel contra Sociology*, 204.
58. Ibid., 214.
59. Tubbs's theory of education in Hegel has its roots in Rose's retrieval of Hegelian speculative experience. It is developed and expanded in a series of books, most notably, Tubbs, *Philosophy's Higher Education*; Tubbs, *Education in Hegel*; Tubbs, *History of Western Philosophy*; Tubbs, *Philosophy and Modern Liberal Arts Education*. It is also to be found in a trajectory of Hegelian educational theory and practice in two undergraduate programs in Education Studies and Modern Liberal Arts at the University of

Mis(re)cognition of God and Man

truth in-itself bequeathed to the tradition a political logic of overcoming within the relation of master and slave. The master as the pure and independent mind is deemed to be "logically true"[60] when he "overcomes" that which threatens independence, that is, the dependence of the slave. Overcoming here is ownership of what is other, of that which would relativize the master's freedom "all the way down."[61] The logic of truth in-itself is thus a "propertied logic."[62] It "owns error by ensuring that the chaos of infinite regression is overcome in being owned."[63] The implications of this are far reaching. "Truth is property," he argues.[64] Posited in the form of a general logic truth in-itself eschews all that is not itself and thereby suppresses the education between and within the relation of master and slave that is self-relation. But mis(re)cognition expresses the truth that lives suppressed in and by propertied logic. It thus *commends* educational logic from within propertied logic. Rose's work, he writes, demonstrates the logic of overcoming as it constitutes the antinomies and contradictions of modern and post-modern thought. In it, she finds the educational logic within which the experience of the relation of the in-itself to mediation, "is its own truth, its own form and content."[65]

In addition, argues Tubbs, the logic of mis(re)cognition has its truth in the notion of the *Aufhebung* in Hegel. Despite the fact that there is little reference by Rose to its structure and meaning Tubbs sees its work at the heart of her rereading of Hegel's philosophy. *Aufhebung* tends to get translated as sublation. In the *Science of Logic*, Hegel writes that it has two meanings. The first is "to preserve, to maintain" but it is just as much "to cause, to cease, to put an end to."[66] In the recent book, *Hegel's Preface to the Phenomenology of Spirit*, Yirmiyahu Yovel describes the *Aufhebung* as the principle of the Hegelian system whereby every moment of the dialectic in "transcending its limits" reconstitutes or rebuilds itself.[67] "The new form negates its predecessor's inadequate form but incorporates its essence within itself" and so is a new shape of relation to self and object.[68] Most common readings of the

---

Winchester, UK.
  60. Tubbs, "Gillian Rose and Education," 128.
  61. Ibid., 131.
  62. Ibid., 128.
  63. Ibid., 129.
  64. Ibid., 128.
  65. Ibid., 130.
  66. Hegel, *Science of Logic*, 107.
  67. Yovel, *Hegel's Preface to the Phenomenology of Spirit*, 95.
  68. Ibid.

term tend to describe it as the higher element of the dialectical process. But it is also the term that expresses speculative experience and as such carries a much more difficult idea of where we actually end up in the process.

This is why Tubbs argues that the term sublation does not quite do justice to the educational nature of the *Aufhebung* in Hegel, making it a mostly misunderstood term. If it is read according to the thesis-antithesis-synthesis triad then we might well recognize the formative nature of the movement but not the most important feature of that education; the fact that the consciousness experiencing the movement of negation and the negation of negation is also changed. To remain a voyeur of the movement is to see or look for the result or synthesis as merely identity. It is easy, on this reading, to criticize the dialectic as overcoming and so as the domination of reason over difference, diversity, openness, and critique (and thereby to repeat the logic of identity in that critique). But, he argues, the *Aufhebung*, in accordance with the logic of mis(re)cognition, is the experience in and by which consciousness can "realize a determinate self-(re)formation."[69] This is what is most suppressed about philosophical experience in Hegel, that it is always this relation to the object (natural consciousness) and the relation to that relation (philosophical consciousness). Mis(re)cognition is the term that acknowledges actuality because it acknowledges the prevailing social and political relations that reproduce and reinforce the Kantian and neo-Kantian dichotomies and their corresponding property relations. The *Aufhebung* is the work of consciousness sustaining itself in the relation between natural and philosophical consciousness, the mind learning about itself in and as the truth of them both. This is why, asserts Tubbs, the "change of perspective" in Rose and Hegel is not "left as a tool of general logic. They pursue it as a different logic, an educational logic of form and content as learning."[70]

Thinking the Absolute

When Rose writes that "Absolute ethical life according to its Relation" means "relative ethical life,"[71] she is drawing attention to the ways in which the absolute is present but hidden in actuality. By "deriving the social relations and institutions which correspond to the domination of the concept over intuition and of intuition over concept, and of demonstrating the relativity of those institutions,"[72] Hegel shows that a different identity emerges for

69. Tubbs, *Education in Hegel*, 48.
70. Tubbs, "Gillian Rose and Education," 132.
71. Rose, *Hegel contra Sociology*, 62.
72. Ibid., 64.

the absolute from within the aporias and anxieties of those relations from which he begins. In this way, he establishes the logic of mis(re)cognition as the logic within which the absolute is comprehended in the totality of property forms and their social and political relations. This new educational logic has its truth in recollection or rather it is known to itself in and as the recollective activity of Spirit which does not deny the difference of what it looks back at but which achieves an absolute perspective on itself because it is learning. In recollection, thinking knows that the learning life is the substance and subject of what it is and does.

But to know how recollection is really educational we must be mindful that its activity as something positive is more than mere remembering. To do this, we must be asking a particular question, says Tubbs. How is it possible to "know the truth of something in what it is not"[73] without suppressing its negativity in its being known? Tubbs argues that remembering is the overcoming of forgetfulness by memory, that it is identity. But remembering cannot sustain the negativity of that which *is* what it *is not*. Read speculatively, remembering is recollection. It is the thinking that knows it gets caught in the contradictions of recollecting itself as something in-itself, because as an object to itself it falls within the logic of non-contradiction. That is, it loses itself in a way that merely remembering does not. But it makes that contradiction its content because it remembers what is lost but loses what it remembers to mediation. What is known in recollection is not a negativity overcome but preserved in and as "the groundlessness" of that which is retrieved. While this is a rather difficult formulation by Tubbs it does offer us a way of reading Rose that can see the aporetic movement of the absolute in negation and in and as the negation of negation as the "presence" of the absolute but not as something to be achieved.

If we return now to the speculative proposition of the identity of state and religion we can see the challenge that Rose's absolute poses to a political theology. Speculative propositions in Hegel demonstrate that "the identity which is affirmed between subject and predicate" in an ordinary proposition "is seen equally to affirm a lack of identity between subject and predicate."[74] At first, we experience the proposition as a contradiction. It is clearly not the case and nor could it be the case that subjective disposition is the objective and universal legal principle of freedom realized in the state. They are irreconcilable entities. Speculatively, however, we experience the historical and political contingencies that determine the separation. We see that the history of Christianity is the continued re-presentation of the relation between

73. Tubbs, *Education in Hegel*, 51.
74. Rose, *Hegel contra Sociology*, 48–49.

substance and subject. But, in addition, we also see that our own relation to the contradiction presupposes historical and political contingencies not immediately intelligible. The speculative proposition reveals the continued domination of the concept in Kantian and neo-Kantian logic, which makes the distinction between finite and infinite, "between knowable appearances and unknowable things-in-themselves."[75] This is the fate of substantial freedom and subjectivity, namely, that "our concept of the infinite is our concept of ourselves and our possibilities."[76] In modernity, the separation presupposes "the autonomous moral subject as free within the order of representations and unfree within its preconditions and outcomes."[77] But speculatively it is "the working out of that combination" for the contradiction that "any, natural consciousness falls into when it considers the object to be external, can itself provide the occasion for a change in that consciousness."[78] Thinking the absolute in Hegel acknowledges actuality as the foundation for "the critique of different kinds of property relations."[79]

Rose writes that Marx could not conceive of the social import of Hegel's absolute. By reading the identity of religion and the state nonspeculatively, he failed to see the lack of identity in Hegel's thought, which re-cognizes the social, political, and historical conditions between state and religion that the ordinary proposition suppresses. It means he is unable to develop a notion of actuality that would acknowledge the "culture" of a political vocation formed and deformed in and by prevailing bourgeois domination. This is to avoid actuality's "educative . . . political intent."[80] Marxism is fated to become methodological in its approach because it can only impose a *Sollen*, making it historically redundant. When actuality is masked by bourgeois freedom, the critical potential of actuality to reveal illusion is undermined. This is not to "point to a flaw"[81] in Marx's critique of capital, Rose writes, but to draw attention to the element of a *Sollen* in a theory that is unable to see how it is a re-presentation of substance and subject. Only the speculative exposition of state and religion acknowledges the ways in which substance and subject are lived as mis(re)cognition, for philosophy has to "continue to

---

75. Ibid., 45.
76. Ibid.
77. Rose, *Mourning Becomes the Law*, 57.
78. Rose, *Hegel contra Sociology*, 45–46.
79. Ibid., 204.
80. Ibid., 217.
81. Ibid., 219.

rediscover 'the passage of the concept [of the Absolute] into consciousness,' into misrepresentation."[82]

Perhaps we can see now that the logic of mis(re)cognition does not avoid the relativity of concept and object/intuition *ad infinitum*, that the absolute in Hegel is "also 'relative'"[83] because "it has a presupposition from which it begins.[84] But this means that now, in educational logic, the absolute in-itself as the form of non-contradiction is related to its negativity 'as content' or 'as realized."[85] This logic is avoided by a politics that seeks only answers or solutions to the world's problems, because it abstracts the questions from the law and culture of their determination. But does not education that deepens understanding appear weak in contrast to calls for radical social action? Maybe. But the limits of education in Rose are to be risked in order that they can be comprehended in and as the work of truth. Rose insists that we see the neo-Kantian logic that suppresses this difficult truth as spiritual and political education. "We live in the contradiction,"[86] between our idea of God and our idea of freedom and so our thinking and our failing to think the absolute lives in us as our own learning.

Conclusion

This essay has argued that the broadly Marxist critique of Rose as well as the more liberal and religious interpretations of her work, including political theology, suppress what is most at stake in comprehending the broken middle of state and religion, that is, the "culture" or the re-formation of the relation between subjective freedom (religion) and objective unfreedom (formal freedom) lived as the learning life.

In drawing attention to the two logics at work in Rose and Hegel, I have taken the idea of mis(re)cognition to be the educational "code-breaker" of any theorizing of a political theology in Rose. In other words, we have to work within educational logic if we are to reach an understanding of the modern relation between state and religion, or between God and man. This is to say that the absolute in Rose is both the comedy of recognition and misrecognition in its various "misadventures" and the comic and tragic life of reason making the experience of contradiction substantial.

82. Ibid., 181.
83. Ibid., 206.
84. Hegel, cited in ibid.
85. Ibid.
86. Ibid., 94.

"Comedy, as much as tragedy, is always divine comedy."[87] This is the "inner self-perficient"[88] logic of education lived, not in spectatorship, which is to reduce the work of self-relation to one side of its opposition—to theory or practice, openness or closure, resignation or faith, success or failure—but love's work. Neo-Kantian logic suppresses the way in which this logic opposes itself and therein fails to sustain its own learning. This is why philosophy in *HCS* demonstrates such "a ferociously sincere record of its own opposition with all that is stationary and which resolves life as knowledge."[89]

Despite the interest in Rose's contribution to social and political thought, including political theology, too many interpretations of Rose refuse to engage with this speculative work. If, as Tubbs argues, it is really the case that to understand Rose we have to read her backwards, like any good Hegelian would, then we are required to read the relation between the form and drama of her thinking as well as its results, as the work of the broken middle, the work that is "always already ancient" but "prepared and ready for comprehension."[90] Here the logic of negation and negation of negation is known to itself as learning, for it is the work and the life that is changed by that learning. In and as the "labour of the notion" in *HCS*, Rose is giving us this *experience* of learning, not just its results. This means that we begin with Rose always in the anxiety of beginning. But if "the only honest beginning is with difficulty,"[91] then we are, perhaps, compelled, like Rose, to be fiercely critical, and self-critical, of anything that fails to do justice to difficulty's educational work.

Bibliography

Adorno, Theodor. *Negative Dialectics*. Translated by E. B. Ashton. London: Continuum, 2007.

Gorman, Tony. "Gillian Rose and the Project of a Critical Marxism." *Radical Philosophy* 105 (2001) 25–36.

Hegel, G. W. F. *Phenomenology of Spirit*. Translated by Arthur V. Miller. Oxford: Oxford University Press, 1977.

———. *Science of Logic*. New York: Humanity, 1969.

Kant, Immanuel. *Critique of Pure Reason*. Translated by J. M. D. Meiklejohn. London: Everyman, 1993.

---

87. Rose, *Mourning Becomes the Law*, 64.
88. Rose, *Hegel contra Sociology*, 64.
89. Tubbs, "What Is Love's Work," 34–46.
90. Rose, *The Broken Middle*, xi.
91. Williams, *Wresting with Angels*, 62.

Lloyd, Vincent. "Complex Space or Broken Middle? Milbank, Rose, and the Sharia Controversy." In *Political Theology* 10, no. 2 (2009) 225–45.

Osborne, Peter. "Hegelian Phenomenology and the Critique of Reason and Society." *Radical Philosophy* 32 (1982) 8–15.

Rose, Gillian. *The Broken Middle*. Oxford: Blackwell, 1992.

———. *Hegel contra Sociology*. London: Athlone, 1981.

———. *The Melancholy Style, An Introduction to the Thought of Theodor W. Adorno*. London: Verso, 2014.

———. *Mourning Becomes the Law*. Cambridge: Cambridge University Press, 1996.

Schick, Katie. *Gillian Rose: "A Good Enough Justice."* Edinburgh: Edinburgh University Press, 2012.

Shanks, Andrew. *Against Innocence, Gillian Rose's Reception and Gift of Faith*. London: SCM, 2008.

Tubbs, Nigel. *Education in Hegel*. London: Continuum, 2008.

———. "Gillian Rose and Education." *Telos* 173 (2015) 125–43.

———. "What is Love's Work." In *Women: A Cultural Review* 9, no. 1 (1998) 34–46.

Williams, Rowan. *Wresting with Angels, Conversations in Modern Theology*. London: SCM, 2007.

Yovel, Yirmiyahu. *Hegel's Preface to the Phenomenology of Spirit*. Princeton: Princeton University Press, 2005.

Chapter 6

Between Hegel and Wittgenstein
Reflections in the Wake of Gillian Rose and Rowan Williams

Gavin Hyman

In 1981, Gillian Rose's book *Hegel contra Sociology* made a decisive intervention into debates on the political potency of Hegel's philosophy that had been swirling around philosophy and political thought for many years. Over this time, a division between Right and Left interpretations of Hegel had been taken for granted as the assumed backdrop against which debates on the political implications of Hegel's thought had proceeded: "Hegel's philosophy could be interpreted either as an endorsement of the status quo (what is *real* is rational) or as a charter for radical, even revolutionary, criticism (only what is *rational* is real)."[1] The significance of Rose's intervention was not that it endorsed one side of this divide over the other but, rather, that it called into question this very dichotomy itself. Both Left and Right readings were predicated on problematical interpretations of Hegel that paid insufficient attention to the role of the *speculative* in Hegel's thought.

This is not to suggest, however, that Rose sought to evade the question of the political potency of Hegel's thought. On the contrary, she wished to rescue Hegel from the slur that Marx had cast upon him. When Marx

1. Harvey, "Ludwig Feuerbach and Karl Marx," 293.

famously said that "philosophers have only interpreted the world, in various ways; the point is to change it," he may have been thinking primarily of Feuerbach, but the accusation clearly extended to Hegel. In one of her boldest and most counterintuitive moves, Rose argued that Marx had read Hegel through the very categories and frameworks that the latter had sought to repudiate. The result was not only to downplay the radicalism of Hegel's own thought, but also to produce a Marxist political philosophy that was actually *less* radical than Hegel's own. It was this Hegel—a Hegel who was even more radical than Marx himself—whom Rose sought to recover.

Rose insists that the recovery of this politically radical Hegel is inseparable from the thinking of the absolute. As she put it, "Hegel's philosophy has no social import if the absolute cannot be thought."[2] In other words, if the absolute cannot be thought, we are left only with our own representations, political and otherwise, and we have no standard or vantage point from which they might be judged.[3] We would be left with a politically paralyzing relativism, which would take us back to the old misreading of "what is real is rational," namely, that what is, is what ought to be. As Rose continues, "If the absolute is misrepresented, we are misrepresenting ourselves, and are correspondingly unfree. But the absolute has always been misrepresented by societies and peoples, for these societies have not been free, and they have re-presented their lack of freedom to themselves in the form of religion."[4]

The thinking of the absolute is inseparable from the *speculative*, and it is worth reminding ourselves of what Hegel, according to Rose, takes this to be: "To read a proposition 'speculatively' means that the identity which is affirmed between subject and predicate is seen equally to affirm a lack of identity between subject and predicate. This reading implies an identity different from the merely formal one of the ordinary proposition. This different kind of identity cannot be pre-judged, that is, it cannot be justified in a transcendental sense, and it cannot be stated in a proposition of the kind to be eschewed. This different kind of identity must be understood as a result to be achieved."[5] It is in the context of this understanding of the speculative that we should conceive of the attempt to realize absolute, as opposed to merely relative, ethical life. Relative ethical life is constituted by those forms of ethical life we take to be ultimate, but which are in fact misrepresentations that imprison us, and from which we need to be delivered.

---

2. Rose, *Hegel contra Sociology*, 98.

3. As Roth, *Knowing and History*, has pointed out, this was one of the major concerns of the French twentieth-century interpreters of Hegel.

4. Rose, *Hegel contra Sociology*, 98.

5. Ibid., 52.

For Rose, one of the most obvious and pressing forms of this distortion is that of bourgeois property relations. It is our thinking of the absolute, in this case absolute ethical life, which allows us to see particular forms of relative ethical life precisely *as* distortions, and which therefore opens up the possibility of our deliverance from them.

The difficulty is, of course, that the absolute cannot simply be *stated*, as though "shot from a pistol." The absolute is rather the achievement of a speculative identity, so it cannot be "pre-judged" but can only be worked toward as a "result to be achieved." Consequently, the political task cannot be that of directly confronting a relative form of ethical life with a statement or formulation of absolute ethical life. The political challenge with which we are presented here is precisely that of the ambiguous status of the absolute in relation to the language of ordinary propositions. On the one hand, the absolute cannot be "stated" or "formulated," but on the other hand, the absolute is by no means strictly unknowable. So the absolute cannot be "said," but neither can we remain silent. How is this ambiguous interstice to be negotiated? Rose identifies some of the difficulties facing Hegel here when she says that he

> could not "justify" in the Kantian sense the idea of absolute ethical life; he could not provide any abstract statement of it apart from the presentations of the contradictions which imply it. For an abstract statement would make manifest that this ethical life does not exist in the modern world. This would be to turn ethical life into an abstract ideal, an autonomous prescription, a *Sollen*, which would be completely "unjustified" because not implied by the contradictions between political consciousness and its social and historical bases. Hegel's solution to this dilemma was to emphasise the presence of ethical life, not the task of achieving it.[6]

So absolute ethical life cannot be formulated as an abstract ideal, as this would be to enact a false separation between theory and practice, instantiating an abstract theory detached from actual practice. Rather, absolute ethical life is *implied* by our *experience* of the contradictions to each instantiation of relative ethical life. It is "a unity which includes all the real property relations, all the lack of identities, in social life. It is only by acknowledging the lack of identity as the historical *fate* (*Bestimmung*) of a different property structure that absolute ethical life can be conceived."[7]

---

6. Ibid., 54.
7. Ibid., 62.

This understanding of absolute ethical life remains problematic, while at the same time embodying an advance: "Since relative ethical life and its corresponding media of misrepresentation do prevail, the initial question of how absolute ethical life can appear in a society based on specific property relations without itself appearing abstract and unreal *remains unanswered.*" But at the same time, "absolute ethical life has been *alluded to* as an unspecific unity of concept and intuition, intuition and concept, as a universal (*allgemeine*) in the community (*die Gemeine*) . . . . Real recognition requires different property relations. It is philosophy (science) which has been *intimating* this real unification."[8] So an absolute ethical life has been intimated and alluded to, and this intimation and allusion has exposed the need for different property relations, a different form of political representation, but how this absolute ethical life can appear "remains unanswered."

But how problematic is this in political terms? If absolute ethical life cannot (yet) be stated as such or cannot (yet) appear, what does this entail for political critique and action? If we cannot state the political form that provides the standard against which our current political configurations are found wanting, if we cannot specify the form of political life toward which we should be heading, is this not politically fatal? Hegel's thought may be politically invaluable insofar as it exposes the contradictions in our ethical, political, and legal frameworks, and may even provide the most radical critique of them, but if the absolute ethical life, towards which these failed relative ones point, cannot actually be stated, if as Rose recognises, "this alternative is never definitively explicated," does this not entail *passivity* in practical, conventional political terms? And would this not reinstate, albeit in a qualitatively different form, the political passivity of the Right Hegelians, from which Rose sought to deliver us? As Peter Osborne has expressed this, "[P]hilosophy cannot specify *concretely* what this new mode of transformation is. And so, I would argue, it cannot bring about such a transformation. A '*notion* of law' will not transform anything."[9] That is to say, political transformation is seen to be imperative, but the specific form of the mode of transformation is "unknowable in any ordinary sense of the word 'know.' It can only be known as the negation of all forms of determination which presuppose the independence of condition from conditioned. Hegel thus 'commends' an 'unstatable' alternative, and 'urges' us to seek it through the transformation of determinations which are 'unspecifiable'!"[10]

---

8. Ibid., 83–84 ; my emphases.
9. Osborne, "Hegelian Phenomenology," 14.
10. Ibid.

At this point, there would seem to be two possible ways forward. One would be to accept the diagnosis as a necessary outcome of the Hegelian phenomenological method, but to interpret this apparent passivity not as a renunciation of the political task, but as its radicalization. This would be to regard the desire for such practical political intervention and for some kind of narrative guide or template for such transformation as a disease of the non-speculative mind. It would be to remain caught up in the very modes of thinking that Hegel is seeking to overcome. As Rose says, "[F] or Hegel, actuality is posited or reflected in the ego . . . Hegel dissolves and maintains the ego in the world. Hegel cannot find another discourse because positing (*setzen*) is not the unconditioned act of the ego, but the law (*Gesetz*) of the formation of the ego and its cognition and miscognition."[11] Such non-speculative desires for active political interventions and "guides" for transformation must be given up because they are predicated on a non-speculative understanding of an active and detached ego attempting to impose itself violently on a passive world. To renounce such an ego is to renounce also a certain understanding of political action. Such a renunciation might appear to the non-speculative mind as a form of passivity, but to the speculative mind is a much more radical and thoroughgoing form of political transformation.[12]

For any serious reader of Hegel, such a response cannot wholly be ignored. Hegelian phenomenology does indeed entail a certain *surrendering* of the ego—a certain *dispossession*—that cannot but have consequences for how we conceive of political activity and transformation.[13] But dispossession does not entail dissolution; positing is the law of the *formation* of the ego, not its negation. And insofar as the ego has been formed or is being formed, some kind of agency still remains, people still have to make decisions, act, and interact, and through such activity bring themselves into being. If bourgeois property relations currently define our *Sittlichkeit*, we still have to make decisions and take actions—that can only be described as political—in this setting, and in ways that are not *fully* determined by this setting. If this is so, then the question raised by Osborne remains pertinent

---

11. Rose, *Hegel contra Sociology*, 212.

12. Such thought might more frequently be associated with Heidegger and his followers than with Hegel. It is the kind of political critique expressed, I think, by Hemming in his *Heidegger and Marx* and in his other numerous writings on Heidegger. But a more Hegelian version of it might also be seen in Žižek's espousal of a "Bartleby politics." See Žižek, *Parallax View*, especially the last chapter.

13. For further elucidation of this, see Butler, *Subjects of Desire*; and, especially, Malabou, *Future of Hegel*, chap. 11.

and requires some kind of answer, and this leads us to consider the second possible way forward.

What seems to be required, therefore, is some kind of substantive vision, a representation of absolute ethical life that, on Hegelian terms, is impossible, for reasons that Osborne has elucidated explicitly:

> The reason that it is unjustifiable even to conceive of an alternative form of ethical life is that to remain critical epistemologically, consciousness must posit no form of relation between itself and its objects which does not arise "naturally" out of its self-reflection upon the objects present to it in phenomenal knowledge.... (Despite her description of Hegelian philosophy as "the definitive political experience," in fact in contradiction to it, Rose acknowledges the political impotence of philosophy when she says that the "possibility of becoming ethical" depends on neither the recognition of determination, nor on any moral decision, but on a "transformation of intuition." The determination of which is, of course, by definition, beyond the individual consciousness.) So "absolute ethical life" (the social ideal) is an "unstatable" alternative.[14]

In his engagement with Rose's work, Rowan Williams seems to recognize the force of Osborne's criticism, even if he by no means wishes to concede to it completely. Williams thinks that Osborne has too easily assimilated Rose's position to Adorno's with its dialectic of perpetual negation, and that this has become a much less sustainable reading of Rose's work, especially in light of her later writings in which she has explicitly distanced herself from Adorno in this respect. But having acknowledged this, Williams remains uneasy, asking, "[I]s Osborne right in seeing in the phenomenological method itself an incapacity to think the concrete and so to think its transformation?"[15]

Williams's comments become a little gnomic at this point, and his criticisms of Rose are so gently expressed that they are difficult to discern. But if I am reading him correctly, what Williams seems to be saying is this: first, that Osborne's criticisms are not insurmountable ("much of what I have so far written might serve to answer this" [the question just quoted]); second, that Osborne "repeats the fundamental misunderstanding of Hegel by Marx"; and third, that speculative thinking does more than simply offer a critique through negation.[16] So Williams certainly does not wish to cede

14. Osborne, "Hegelian Phenomenology," 13.
15. Williams, *Wrestling with Angels*, 69.
16. Ibid.

the final word to Osborne. But at the same time, one can discern a note of unease, as though Osborne has identified a point of weakness that Williams believes still needs to be addressed. As his comments at this point segue from a discussion of Rose's work into an explicitly theological coda, the suggestion seems to be that an unequivocal invocation of theology may serve to address what might be regarded as Osborne's legitimate concerns. Furthermore, Williams seems to suggest, this theological coda may be invoked in a way that is consistent with, rather than in tension with, Rose's Hegelian methodology.

When Williams says, as we have just intimated, that speculative thinking does more than simply offer a critique through negation, he is suggesting that it simultaneously points in a more positive "substantive" direction, even if the absolute cannot be stated as such. In other words, we are not condemned, politically, merely to a process of infinite negation; this negation, in turn, points towards some kind of affirmation. Williams says that "[t]hinking is itself a learning of some sort of dispossession, the constant rediscovery and critique of the myth of the self as owner of its perceptions and positions.... Insofar as this is always critical thinking about particular historical varieties of unfreedom or inequality, it is in fact always suggesting specific kinds of historical liberation, directions in which we can look for change, even if the speculative alone doesn't and could never deliver a 'programme' for political action."[17] But if there is no such "programme," there is what Williams characterizes as a "constant," which he also says is perhaps a less alarming way of talking about the "absolute," that which is non-negotiable in our being thinking subjects. This "constant" is "that truth requires loss. Or to put it slightly differently, the constant is that existence as a subject is recognised or re-learned all the time as a process of self-displacement, a never-ending 'adjustment' in search of the situation where there is real mutual recognition and thus effective common action, because we have moved away from the illusions of rivalry."[18] He goes on to say that if this "absolute" (non-negotiable) understanding of what it is to be thinking subjects tells us something of how we are to construe the real, "if the phenomenology of consciousness in also an ontology," this specific ontology is well articulated by *theology*, a "narrative of the absolute's self-loss and self-recovery."[19]

Admittedly, this is a very compressed way of articulating some very complex moves, and Williams's account of it is only slightly less compressed than my summary of it. Clearly, each move is worthy of some considerable

17. Ibid., 70.
18. Ibid.
19. Ibid., 70, 71.

unpacking. But although Williams doesn't say so directly, what he seems to be suggesting is that this theology, in turn, can serve to provide the very thing which Osborne argued that Hegel's phenomenology lacked, namely, a substantive account of absolute ethical life that can serve to guide political discernment and action, and to which all such discernment and action is answerable. If Osborne is right to identify this lack in political terms in Hegel's phenomenological method, theology may serve to fill this lack, and do so in a way that remains broadly consistent with that Hegelian method.

But what does this provision of a theological coda mean in *philosophical* terms? Very broadly, I want to suggest that it is indicative of a need to supplement Hegel with Wittgenstein. What our previous discussion suggested was that Hegel (and Rose) stood in need, politically, of a substantive vision, a narrative, a language game, which Hegel (and Rose) can only indirectly and precariously affirm. This vision, narrative, or language game would certainly not be a posited and abstract political "programme," which Rose rightly warns against, but it would be authoritative (in some sense "absolute"?) that could serve to motivate political discernment and action, and to which such discernment and action would be answerable. If Hegel can only indirectly and precariously affirm such a thing, we find ourselves compelled to look in a different philosophical direction, specifically, I suggest, to Wittgenstein who bore witness to the indispensability of substantive narratives or language games, not least for ethics and politics. Such a narrative, Wittgenstein insists, would not be justified by anything beyond itself. It is justified solely by the fact that it functions as a form of life in which people participate, in which they believe, and for whom it is authoritative. Williams's provision of a theological coda, therefore, may not be strictly warranted in Hegelian (and Rosean) terms (Rose herself certainly desists from invoking such a supplement), but it may be seen to be warranted by the identification of a certain deficiency in the political potency of Hegel's (and Rose's) project. But can the invocation of such a theological supplement be made while at the same time remaining true to the fundamental insights of Hegelian phenomenology? To what extent would such an invocation stand in tension with Rose's Hegelianism?

The question of Hegel's understanding of theology is of course highly complex and much contested. But if we confine ourselves in this context to Rose's own distinctive reading of Hegel, there are at least two ways in which the invocation of a theological supplement of the kind sought by Williams might sit uneasily with it. First, it has to be said that the supplementation of Hegel by Wittgenstein, the supplementation of phenomenology with an authoritative narrative vision, does not in itself determine what the content of that narrative vision would be. Indeed, it is intrinsic to Wittgenstein's own methodology that philosophy would not be able to help in answering this question. Philosophy clarifies and elucidates the narratives and language games to which we are already committed, but it does not presage what those narratives and language games should be. What is it, then, that takes us to theology, as opposed to any other narrative or language game? Is there a certain arbitrariness about the narratives to which we are already committed, that we are committed to them simply because we always have been, or because of the arbitrary contingencies of taste, chance, psychology, and experience? Or is the commitment reminiscent of a Kierkegaardian leap of faith that is justified solely by the passionate intensity of the leap itself? Either of these possibilities would certainly sit uncomfortably with the methodology of Hegelian phenomenology, as Rose understands it. Would this not be yet another example of subjective positing?

To raise these questions is also to raise the question of "natural theology," which Williams has himself addressed in his recent book, *The Edge of Words: God and the Habits of Language*. The reason this is relevant is because intrinsic to the method of natural theology has been the conviction that theological commitment is not just arbitrary, not just a fideistic leap or a groundless faith in divine revelation. In its various forms, natural theology has sought to show how theological commitment is in some sense warranted, justified, or rational, in terms of our experience of the world. Williams is careful to distance himself from the Enlightenment rendering of natural theology, which seeks knowledge of God on the basis of reason alone, using arguments acknowledged by all, and eschewing the contested and partisan claims of revelation. He believes this to be philosophically unsustainable as well as an impoverished way of raising theological questions, but he also wants to ask whether there may not be an alternative way of understanding the tradition of natural theology. He says, "[T]here is indeed at the heart of all Christian theology, as Wittgenstein said about the Gospels, a story with an imperative attached. But the question is, what makes us able to learn to recognise such an imperative, let alone respond to it?"[20] What is it about our experience of the world (and Williams is particularly concerned with our use of language and representation) that leads us to recognize such a theological imperative, draws us to it, such that our drawing near becomes something other than an arbitrary leap?

Williams's study is constituted by an extended discussion of these questions, and he wants to claim that "to start from somewhere other than claims to revelation is not necessarily nonsensical or impious. It obliges us to pay attention to the ways in which language about God actually finds

---

20. Williams, *The Edge of Words: God and the Habits of Language*, 3.

its way into our speech, and so delivers us from discussing the language of belief in a vacuum."[21] His investigations are wide and far-ranging; as he explores the nature of our use of language, its freedoms and constraints, its relation to time and the material, the roles of "excessive" speech and the silences in its midst, he shows how language of God, far from being at odds with such practices, in fact seems to be presaged by them. He says, "Such an account does not deliver 'a proof of God's existence'; what it does is to map the territory of human speech in a way that enables us to see that what is affirmed in the language of specific religious ritual and reflection—in the language of 'revelation' if you will—*goes with the grain* of what matters most and is most distinctive in anything claiming to be an adequate picture of our human speaking."[22] Williams doesn't frequently discuss Hegel directly in this study, but the Hegelian resonances are evident throughout. Just as the narrative of theology "goes with the grain" of any adequate account of language, so too it "goes with the grain" of any adequate account of thought itself—such as that developed by Hegel.

We have already observed the ways in which, for Williams, the political turn to theology, far from being an act of subjective assertion or positing, is presaged by Hegelian phenomenology itself. Thinking about what it means to think leads us to construe ourselves and our reality in a certain way, which in turn will preclude certain accounts of ontology and commend others. This is the point we saw Williams to be making when he said that Hegel's phenomenology of consciousness leads us to discern that accounts of reality that posit humans as being self-sufficient, assertive, and competitive are mistaken and enslaving, while other accounts that construe reality as being constituted by "mutual recognition" and "self-loss and self-recovery" are true and liberating. If this is the case, we can say that this particular philosophical supplementation of Hegel by Wittgenstein, the supplementing of the phenomenological method with a substantive theological narrative, is neither arbitrary in relation to Hegel, nor is it in harsh juxtaposition with it. Rather, we may say that the theological supplement "goes *with* the grain" of Hegelian phenomenology, and may, in a certain sense, be seen as being consistent with it.

The second way in which this Wittgensteinian invoking of the ` of theology might sit uneasily with Rose's Hegelianism is perhaps less easily answered. To what extent would this be to invoke another *Sollen*, another "ought," which, in an abstract way, is "imposed" on lived and concrete actuality? There is, of course, for Hegel and Rose, a sense in which religion

21. Ibid., 17.
22. Ibid., 184.

does indeed "go with the grain" of the phenomenological and speculative experience, although there is, equally, a sense in which it is also "out of joint" with it. Central to this understanding is the distinction between "intuition" and "concept." Intuition involves a "seeing-into" nature, such that what is "seen-into" can look back *without* subsuming the difference of that to which it looks back. The concept, in contrast, is ideal, infinite, abstract.[23] Rose says that for Hegel, bourgeois property relations enact the concept subsuming intuition: it makes "particular" private property relations "universal," which it can never possibly be.[24] The "particular" is made universal, and the mismatch between this pseudo-universal and universality as such is hidden. Art and religion overcome this by reversing the operational structure: that is, by making intuition subsume the concept, such that unity or the universal predominates.[25] "Hence absolute ethical life is represented or intuited by art. But in a society based on private property relations, art, too, becomes a form of misrecognition. For if intuition predominates over the concept, art can only re-present a real social relation not a real unity. Art (and religion) is 'absolute' in the sense that it presents absolute ethical life, but it is also imagination (*Vorstellung*) or intuition, a form of misrecognition, because configuration (*Gestaltung*) or image (*Bild*) or intuition predominate."[26]

In bourgeois society, art is distorted, as it is unable to unify concept and intuition, meaning and form, emphasizes one or the other, and falls into contradiction. Religion *does* reconcile them *but* the identity is misrepresented as an ordinary identity in which intuition dominates, so that the reconciliation is exiled to another world "and thus makes our relation to both the world beyond and real existence one of impotent longing. Religion, unlike art, maintains the image or intuition, the promise of a real transformation, but at the same time preventing its actual development."[27] This brings out well the ambivalence intrinsic to Hegel's understanding of religion, at least as interpreted and presented by Rose. On the one hand, religion does its work in the medium of misrepresentation, intuition, and thus presents only relative ethical life. But on the other hand, to return to a passage quoted earlier, it also *alludes to* absolute ethical life "as an unspecific unity of concept and intuition, intuition and concept, as a universal (*allgemeine*) in the community (*die Gemaine*), and as a reform of religious

---

23. See Rose, *Hegel contra Sociology*, 69.
24. Ibid., 78.
25. Ibid., 79.
26. Ibid.
27. Ibid., 82.

thought. Real recognition requires different property relations. It is philosophy (science) that has been intimating this real unification."[28]

This suggests that Rose would not be entirely averse to the kind of theological supplement Williams has suggested would politically "complete" Rose's project. Insofar as it is able to allude to absolute ethical life, and the desired unity of concept and intuition, it may indeed be able to give some kind of intimation of the absolute ethical life that we have seen to be "unstatable" as such, but nonetheless politically necessary. At the same time, however, we can also see why Rose might be uneasy with an invocation of theology, insofar as it is ultimately a form of misrepresentation, in that it unifies in the abstract, with reconciliation "exiled to another world," leaving us with an "impotent longing." It seems that theology may well be invaluable insofar as it is "positioned" by phenomenology (in Hegelian fashion), but would become problematic if it became an outsideless and ultimate metanarrative (in Wittgensteinian fashion).

That the latter is indeed the case, for Rose, is well brought out in her sharp criticisms of John Milbank's approach to theology. Although the theological methodologies of Milbank and Williams are by no means synonymous, there is undoubtedly more that unites than divides them. Milbank has been clear that there is nothing more "ultimate" than theology itself, neither can theology cede or indeed share its status as the ultimate metanarrative. It is this that stands at the heart of Rose's reservations about Milbank's project and, in particular, the way in which it understands the question of violence. Rose's objection is not the standard postmodern criticism that the imposition of universal metanarratives is necessarily and inherently violent. Rather, her point is that violence is itself an inescapable feature of the human condition. Any attempt to identify, isolate, and "overcome" violence is a false idealization and is ultimately doomed to fail. As she says, "'[V]iolence' cannot be isolated without being posited as the lowest common denomination, whether good or bad; while if, on the contrary, it is presupposed, there is no need to theorize it as such. All isolating of 'violence' is therefore suspicious unless the ethical is suspended and its historical and legal precondition recognized."[29] For Rose, therefore, human decisions and actions cannot be undertaken with a view to "avoiding" or "overcoming" violence, for no such avoidance is or overcoming is possible. Rather, such decisions and actions have to be taken *in the midst of* violence, and a failure to recognize this will only give rise to inversions of intention, and will risk colluding with still greater violence in turn.

28. Ibid., 83–84.
29. Rose, *The Broken Middle*, 152.

Milbank, on the other hand, seeks to overcome an ontology of violence (nihilism) with an ontology of peace (theology). In effect, therefore, he installs a dualism in spite of his avowed aim to move beyond dualism. As Rose comments, he reinstates "the *age old* oppositions between law and grace, knowledge and faith, while intentionally but, it will turn out, only apparently working without the *modern* duality of nature and freedom."[30] The ultimate framing dualism of Milbank's project, as Rose sees it, is between the heavenly city (a city of peace, harmony, and reconciliation) and the earthly city (the nihilistic secular city founded on the murder of Abel).[31] Between these cities is instantiated the city of God (on pilgrimage *through* this world, but not *of* this world). Salvation and liberation is not something to be worked toward or worked through; rather, it has already been attained ("posited"), and the task is only to bring it into effect, bring it into being (through an "imposition" on fallen reality).

This "overcoming" of one world ("violence") by another world ("peace") is what Rose considers to be problematic. As Andrew Shanks has said, she is mistrustful of it "because she senses that this immediate reduction of everything to the elementary struggle between the two 'cities,' of God and man, merely serves, in the end, to mask and justify a basic reflex of recoil from the 'broken middle.'"[32] What we are being presented with, therefore, is a posited ideal, which stands in juxtaposition to a fallen reality. This posited ideal is imposed upon—in order to "redeem"—this fallen reality. What is missing is the "real" city, in which we dwell, struggle, and advance, and which is simultaneously both "ideal" and "fallen." As she says of Milbank's project: "[T]his explication of pilgrimage and inclusivity effectively destroys the idea of a city: its task of salvation deprives it of site; while its inclusive appeal deprives it of limit or boundary that would mark it off from any other city and their different laws: 'the city of God is in fact "a paradox, a nomad city" (one might say).'"[33] The real task of a city and its institutions—its "trade unions, local government, civil service, the learned professions: the arts, law, education, the universities, architecture and medicine"[34]—is *mediation*, and it is this mediation that seems to be missing in Milbank's theology: "Institutions seem to be absent from these 'cities' in the sense that [Milbank does not seem] to be much interested in the patient work of mediation—negotiat-

30. Ibid., 282. For more discussion of the dualism in Milbank's thought, see Hyman, *The Predicament of Postmodern Theology*, 70–73.

31. Rose, *Broken Middle*, 281.

32. Shanks, *Against Innocence*, 162.

33. Rose, *Broken Middle*, 281. Rose is here quoting Milbank, *Theology and Social Theory*, 392.

34. Rose, *Broken Middle*, 282.

ing between all manner of competing interests, *sittlich* and secular—that institutions, in general, are designed to accomplish."[35]

Rowan Williams, although generally appreciative and supportive of Milbank's work, can be seen to share at least some of these concerns. In a way that echoes some of Rose's concerns about Milbank's posited and rival "cities," Williams expresses his own reservations about "diagrammatic accounts of ideological options . . . we are not given any purchase on the specific points of strain or collision that gradually constituted the Church as historically and tangibly other than the orders it contests. It is as if this origination is the birth of a full-grown Minerva; and if narrative is *plotted*, a structured sequence of transformations, the metanarrative that is being sought is in danger of flattening out into a bald statement of timeless ideal differences."[36] These timeless ideal differences are between options or "cities" that are simply "posited" as being "there"; the way to our salvation is therefore to endorse and embrace one over and against the other. Williams says that Milbank presents us "with something 'achieved,' and left with little account of how it is learned, negotiated, betrayed, inched forward, discerned and risked."[37]

Speaking of a city of "total peace" that out-narrates the city of violence will not really help here, and Williams is particularly concerned about Milbank's contesting of the role of the tragic in ethics. He wonders whether the tragic is not in some sense unavoidable:

> If our salvation is cultural (historical, linguistic, etc.), it is not a return to primordial harmonics, purely innocent difference. We are always already, in history, shaped by privation, living at the expense of each other: important moral choices entail the loss of certain specific goods for certain specific persons, because moral determination, like any "cultural" determination, recognizes that not all goods for all persons are *contingently* compatible. The peace of the Church is going to be vacuous or fictive if it is not historically aware of how it is *constructed* in events of determination which involve conflict and exclusion of some kind.[38]

What Williams seems to be saying, therefore, is that this Wittgensteinian-style move to a theology that is an outsideless, complete, and ultimate metanarrative is in danger of both simplifying and distorting reality, and is

---

35. Shanks, *Against Innocence*, 164–65.
36. Williams, "Saving Time," 319–20.
37. Ibid., 321.
38. Ibid., 322.

in danger of forgetting so much of what Hegel's phenomenological method has elucidated.

So where does all this leave us? We saw in the first half of this chapter that Rose's Hegelian methodology stood in need of a substantive narrative vision if its political potency was not to be weakened. We suggested that Hegelian phenomenology stood in need of a Wittrgensteinian narrative supplement. We also saw that theology might be able to provide that supplement in a way that goes with, rather than against, the grain of Hegelian phenomenology. But in the second half of the chapter, we also saw the ways in which an appeal to theology might stand in tension with Rose's Hegelian insights, and might even serve to undercut and undermine them. Through Rose and Williams's criticisms of Milbank's invocation of a theological metanarrative, we saw that many Hegelian insights were in danger of being obscured. We seem, therefore, to be presented with something of an impasse. How might this be negotiated and how might a possible way through be found?

One possible answer, of course, would be to look to the theological methodology of Rowan Williams himself. Williams himself has said explicitly that his criticisms of Milbank's project "are designed not to challenge that project, but to ask how fully its own leading themes are enacted in its exposition; how much place is systematically given for the patience that contingency enjoins."[39] So Williams seeks to align himself with, rather than to distance himself from, Milbank's project. But he would seek to develop and extend that project in ways that would mitigate the excesses that threaten to undercut key Hegelian (and indeed certain theological) insights. So Williams's approach might indeed have the potential to steer us through some of the various hazards identified in this chapter, and to negotiate the impasse we have identified. But at the same time, to respond in this way— however much might be said for Williams's theological methodology in general—might also be at risk of glossing over what is perhaps the central question at stake in this discussion.

This question is one that has been identified by Vincent Lloyd, when he asks whether the method of the "broken middle" should be seen as "arising out of, and authorized by, tradition" or whether it should be seen as "playing out in several, equally important domains (e.g., secular and Christian theological)."[40] Rose, we might say, sees the broken middle as "playing out in several equally important domains" whereas Milbank (insofar as he is com-

---

39. Ibid., 325.

40. See Lloyd's "A Reply to Gavin Hyman," in the *Syndicate* discussion of my book *Traversing the Middle*. The final paragraph of this chapter is a reformulation of my own "A Reply to Vincent Lloyd" in the same place.

mitted to the broken middle) would see it as "arising out of, and authorized by, tradition." Williams would no doubt subscribe to the latter approach too, although, as we have seen, perhaps slightly more equivocally than Milbank. But what should we do when confronted with Lloyd's question, which is so pertinent to what we have been discussing in this chapter? If Rose's Hegelian phenomenology leads us, especially in political terms, to a theology that goes "with the grain" of Hegel's insights, while at the same time being somewhat in tension with them, what are we to say about the question of priority here? Does the middle emerge out of, as a consequence of, the (prior) theological or does the theological emerge out of, as a consequence of, the (prior) middle? There are things that we have said in this chapter that might be cited in support of both possibilities. On the one hand, it was the method of the middle—Rose's Hegelian phenomenology—that led us to theology as a way of addressing some of the potential political shortfalls that Osborne and Williams identified. The shape of the argument would seem to suggest that the middle is prior, is the given, and this is what leads to theology, which is seen as the best way of perpetuating and "perfecting" it. But on the other hand, does the very "fact" that theology is best able to do this (in the manner indicated by Williams's reconfiguration of "natural theology") indirectly suggest that it is actually theology that is prior, and that the middle, as a "given," is in fact a secondary manifestation of it? Our analysis in this chapter has done little to settle this question either way. But what if that turns out to be the very point? What if the question is ultimately unanswerable? What if the method of the middle itself demands that we refuse to give an unequivocal answer to this question? What if there is a necessary and unavoidable circularity here? What if our calling is to rest content with this circularity, this equivocation? If this is indeed the case, then the task of political theology, it seems, should be pursued not only *between* Hegel and Wittgenstein, *between* philosophy and theology, but also, perhaps, *between* Gillian Rose and Rowan Williams.

Bibliography

Butler, Judith. *Subjects of Desire: Hegelian Reflections in Twentieth-Century France.* New York: Columbia University Press, 1987.

Harvey, Van A. "Ludwig Feuerbach and Karl Marx." In *Nineteenth-Century Religious Thought in the West*, edited by Ninian Smart et al., 1:291–328. Cambridge: Cambridge University Press, 1985.

Hemming, Laurence. *Heidegger and Marx: A Productive Dialogue over the Language of Humanism.* Evanston, IL: Northwestern University Press, 2013.

Hyman, Gavin. *The Predicament of Postmodern Theology: Radical Orthodoxy or Nihilist Textualism*. Louisville: Westminster John Knox Press, 2001.

———. *Traversing the Middle: Ethics, Politics, Religion*. Eugene, OR: Cascade, 2013.

Lloyd, Vincent. "A Reply to Gavin Hyman." *Syndicate*. 25 December 2014. Accessed July 23, 2017. https://syndicate.network/symposia/theology/traversing-the-middle/.

Marabou, Catherine. *The Future of Hegel: Plasticity, Temporality and Dialectic*. Translated by Elisabeth During. London: Routledge, 2005.

Milbank, John. *Theology and Social Theory: Beyond Secular Reason*. Oxford: Blackwell, 1990.

Osborne, Peter. "Hegelian Phenomenology and the Critique of Reason and Society." *Radical Philosophy* 32 (1982) 8–15.

Rose, Gillian. *The Broken Middle: Out of Our Ancient Society*. Oxford: Blackwell, 1992.

———. *Hegel contra Sociology*. London: Verso, 2009.

Roth, Michael S. *Knowing and History: Appropriations of Hegel in Twentieth-Century France*. Ithaca: Cornell University Press, 1988.

Shanks, Andrew. *Against Innocence: Gillian Rose's Reception and Gift of Faith*. London: SCM, 2008.

Williams, Rowan. *The Edge of Words: God and the Habits of Language*. London: Bloomsbury, 2014.

———. "Saving Time: Thoughts on Practice, Patience and Vision." *New Blackfriars* 73 (1992) 319–26.

———. *Wrestling with Angels: Conversations in Modern Theology*. Edited by Mike Higton. London: SCM, 2007.

Žižek, Slavoj. *The Parallax View*. Cambridge, MA: MIT Press, 2006.

Chapter 7

One Absolute Substance

Joseph W. H. Lough

In his lectures on aesthetics[1] G. W. F. Hegel faults Immanuel Kant for reducing the sublime to an empty disembodied abstraction. Hegel by contrast felt that we needed "to grasp [the sublime] as grounded in the one absolute substance *qua* the content which is to be represented."[2] This grounding of the sublime in one absolute substance could be taken as a rejection of docetic tendencies immanent to uniquely Protestant inflections of divine presence. In such uniquely Protestant inflections, God may be present, but only *sub contrario absconditum*, hidden under the opposite. By taking the sublime as "the content which is to be represented" (*als dem darzustellenden Inhalt*), Hegel could be understood as inviting us to embrace a divine presence whose embodiment rather than hiding instead reveals what is to be represented, namely, the incarnate or embodied divine. Here I will explore an alternative interpretation. In this interpretation, what Hegel in his lectures called one absolute substance might better be understood as a misrecognized instance of the capitalist social formation; and what he there called the sublime might better be understood as a misrecognized

---

1. Hegel delivered his lectures on aesthetics in Heidelberg in 1818 and then in Berlin in 1820/21, 1823, 1826, and 1828/29.

2. Hegel, *Aesthetics*, 363; Hegel, *Vorlesungen über die Ästhetik*, 468. Wherever two references are offered for the same citation the first refers to the English edition, the second to the German. Wherever I offer my own translation, I will indicate so.

instance of the sublime value form of the commodity. In this respect, albeit in a misrecognized form, Hegel offers us valuable insights into the peculiar character of spirituality that prevails within societies governed by commodity production and exchange. In such societies, all bodies are necessarily grounded in one absolute substance. Could it possibly be otherwise? Should it be?

It is far from unusual that these two themes—totality and capitalism—should find expression in an essay that seeks to shed light on Gillian Rose. Over the years, many commentators have been drawn into the hermeneutical circle carved out by Rose's idiosyncratic treatments of Immanuel Kant, Johann Gottlieb Fichte, G. W. F. Hegel, and Karl Marx—even an archbishop.[3] Yet, to my knowledge, I may be the first economist to explore her mind. My interest therefore is likely to differ somewhat from others—chiefly Peter Osborne[4] and Tony Gorman[5]—who approach Rose from a more explicitly philosophical, post-Marxist vantage point. I share Osborne's and Gorman's interest in pursuing a critical Marxism and exploring Rose's contribution to this project. I also share their criticism of Rose's Fichtean inflection of Marx's mature social theory. This inflection has persisted for three reasons: first, in his pre-1848/49 theory, Marx displays a deep fondness for an emancipatory social subjectivity that, following Hegel, he believed immanent to the industrial proletariat. After the abysmal failures of 1848/49, Marx displayed significantly more caution over the emancipatory potential of working-class consciousness. The second reason the Fichtean inflection of Marx's mature social theory has persisted revolves around the specific historical trajectory of western Marxist social theory, which passed through Max Weber's Heidelberg on its way to Budapest. Weber's influence shines through on nearly every page of Georg von Lukács's *History and Working Class Consciousness* (1923), upon whose essay "Reification and the Proletariat" Tony Gorman argues that Rose erected her two studies, *Hegel contra Sociology* and *The Melancholy Science*. Third, and finally, inflected toward Hegel and not toward Fichte, Marx can appear to be defending a totalitarianism of spirit that he explicitly decried. When read through Weber-Lukács, by contrast, Marx can be read as defending a Kantian notion of freedom—freedom as the absence of constraint—thereby removing the suspicion that Marx shares Hegel's purported totalitarian tendencies.[6]

---

3. Williams, "Sermon."

4. Osborne, "Hegelian Phenomenology" (1982); Osborne, "Hegelian Phenomenology" (2015).

5. Gorman, "Gillian Rose."

6. See Lough, *Weber and the Persistence of Religion*, 57–72.

In my view, this line of reasoning is helpful up to a point since it casts light on the shifting theoretical frame not only for critical Marxism but also for Marx himself. Following Moishe Postone, I take this analysis in a slightly different direction. I suppose that Hegel is engaged in a project not altogether different from Adam Smith's, Jean-Baptiste Say's, David Ricardo's, and Thomas Malthus's. That is to say, I take Hegel to have been theorizing a world that was, in fact, becoming practically ever more integrated; a world that for this reason increasingly lent itself to rigorous mathematical modeling.[7] However, Hegel faulted French and British economists for failing to identify rationality as the driving force knitting this social totality together. In their view, the totality was generated by free exchange. In his pre-1848/49 writings, Marx was inclined to inflect Hegel in a Smithean manner; by focusing on the alienating dimension of bourgeois production and exchange, Marx could then present reappropriation (of alienated property and reified consciousness) as the overcoming of alienation as such.[8] After 1848/49, however, Marx increasingly came to see the value form of the commodity as the driving force behind comprehensive, rational, social integration. But he did not, on this account, regress to a Fichtean interpretation of agency. To the contrary, instead, as we will see, he reflected critically on the social and historical conditions under which human beings—shaped by and still shaping their world—can do so under constraints that do not give rise to self-domination. Insofar as Gillian Rose was seeking to redeem the distorted subject of Theodor Adorno's "Finale,"[9] Marx may himself have offered space to engage this fragment in chapter 48 of *Capital*, volume 3, when he speculates on the temporal conditions that make for freedom.[10]

Below in a concluding postscript I will explicitly engage the work of Gillian Rose. Before we reach this postscript, however, there is much ground to cover. In particular, we need to anchor Kant's and Hegel's interpretive categories more firmly to the social and historical landscapes in which they appeared, not in order thereby to more easily dismiss them, but in order to better appreciate their social and historical validity. I will then explore how the pre-1848/49 Marx of the *Vormärz* routinely adopted Kantian and Fichtean interpretive strategies in his interpretation and application of Hegel; strategies that led him to ontologize and transhistoricize proletarian social being. Following the failed revolutions of 1848/49, during his forced exile in London, Marx reevaluated his interpretation of Hegel and found it wanting.

7. Lough, "Subject of Rigorous Mathematical Economic Modeling."
8. Lough, "Marksistički Humanizam."
9. Adorno, *Minima Moralia*, 247.
10. Marx, *Capital*, 3:958–59.

In *Das Kapital* we find a much more faithful application of Hegel, but also an application that grounds Hegel's one absolute substance socially and historically. It is from this critical vantage point that I will then take up Rose's reflections on Hegel.

It might be thought that the one absolute substance to which Hegel called attention in his lectures antedated the capitalist social formation by centuries if not millennia and therefore that our ascription of it here to the capitalist epoch is, at best, heuristic and, at worst, simply wrong. Take popular stoicism, for instance, such as was nearly universally recognized throughout the late Roman Empire. Here God was felt to wield absolute power (ἐξουσία, *exousia*). All subordinate powers (ἐξουσίες, *exousiēs*) held what power they did hold—from the invisible powers of the heavens to the smallest particle—owing solely to their substantial participation in and subordination to God. Bringing one's thoughts, actions, and expectations—one's whole self—into conformity to "the powers that be" (ἐξουσίαις ὑπερεχούσαις, *exousiais hypereksousais*) was thus deemed both inevitable, but was also deemed every person's supreme political and moral duty. The further down this ontological ladder any being might fall, the less power it was by definition held to possess. Similarly, any being that might aspire to independence from or that might otherwise find itself separated from this ontological hierarchy not only bore evidence in its body of such perversion but also morally and legally would find itself at odds with what is.

Here ironically one of the best summaries of popular stoicism to have survived from the late Roman Empire is found in the Apostle Paul's Letter to the Romans:

> Let every person be subject to the governing authorities [ἐξουσίαις ὑπερεχούσαις]; for there is no authority [ἐξουσία] except from God, and those authorities that exist [αἱ δὲ οὖσαι] have been instituted by God. Therefore whoever resists authority [ἐξουσίᾳ] resists what God has appointed, and those who resist will incur judgment. For rulers are not a terror to good conduct, but to bad. Do you wish to have no fear of the authority? Then do what is good, and you will receive its approval; for it is God's servant for your good. But if you do what is wrong, you should be afraid, for the authority does not bear the sword in vain! It is the servant of God to execute wrath on the wrongdoer. Therefore one must be subject, not only because of wrath but also because of conscience. For the same reason you also pay taxes, for the authorities are God's servants, busy with this very thing. Pay to all what is due them—taxes to whom taxes are due,

revenue to whom revenue is due, respect to whom respect is due, honor to whom honor is due. (Rom 13:1–7)

There is to be sure an unmistakable verisimilitude between Hegel's one absolute substance and popular Roman stoicism's doctrine of absolute power. This is specially so if we take the Apostle's reference to "conscience" (συνείδησιν, *syneidēsin*) or "seeing together" in this passage as a concept parallel to the German *das Erhabene* or "the sublime." Upon this reading, conscience would reveal the content of absolute power in much the same way that the sublime, for Hegel, reveals the content of the one absolute substance. From here parallels could then be drawn to ancient Vedic literature, to the *Analects* of Kong Qui (aka Confucius), to the teachings of Lao Tzu, and so on with an aim to showing how and where Hegel's one absolute substance reappears universally next to the sublime in all world civilizations.

And, yet, as we shall see in a moment, not only does the Apostle's "conscience" differ in fundamental ways from Hegel's *das Erhabene* but so too does the popular Roman doctrine of absolute power differ substantially from Hegel's one absolute substance. Both to be sure describe inflections of power extending from the highest reaches of the heavens down to the smallest imperceptible particle. And yet where the Apostle's "conscience" holds no power save what brings the actions and thoughts of its bearers into conformity with "the powers that be," Hegel's sublime bears within itself the capacity of turning upon, annihilating, and reconstituting its own form of appearance, its own body. And it is this power over bodily destruction and reconstitution that invites us to explore its relationship to the sublime value form of the commodity in greater detail.

The Kantian Sublime

Here our point of departure must be the Kantian sublime, which Hegel in his lectures summarized as follows:

> Kant's view is that "the sublime, in the strict sense of the word, cannot be contained in any sensuous form but concerns only Ideas of Reason which, although no adequate representation of them is possible, may be aroused and called to our mind precisely by this inadequacy which does admit of sensuous representation" (*Critique of Judgment*, 1799, p. 77 [§ 23]). The sublime in general is the attempt to express the infinite, without finding in the sphere of phenomena an object which proves adequate for this representation. Precisely because the infinite is set apart from the entire complex of objectivity as explicitly an

> invisible meaning devoid of shape and is made inner, it remains, in accordance with its infinity, unutterable and sublime above any expression through the finite.[11]

The advantage that Kant found in this formulation was that it strongly suggested a vantage point from which the "absolutely large"[12] could be recognized by individuals embedded in and wholly subject to the laws that govern all things within the phenomenal world. *Sublime is what even to be able to think proves that the mind has a power surpassing any standard of sense.*"[13] Above we described this formulation as a uniquely Protestant inflection of divine presence. God cannot be present to our senses (*der Sinne*). And yet we can think the absolutely large. Thus God is present, though not to the senses.

However, it is not only the supra-sensual character of the sublime that catches our attention in the Kantian sublime. The "absolutely large" (*schlechthin groß*) could after all refer to nothing more sublime than the "infinite," which, although perhaps inspiring awe, need not annihilate or threaten to annihilate its own form of appearance. The absolutely large need not inspire fear. And yet fear is precisely what the sublime inspires. The sublime inspires fear—indeed *terror*—insofar as we recognize in the absolutely large its capacity to annihilate us. So, while we may wish to *contain* the absolutely large by reducing it to *infinity*, a merely endless succession, the sublime prohibits us from limiting its powers in this way.

> Hence, (since temporal succession is a condition of the inner sense and of an intuition) it is a subjective movement of the imagination by which it does violence to the inner sense, and this violence must be the more significant the larger the quantum is that the imagination comprehends in one intuition. Hence the effort to take up into a single intuition a measure for magnitude requiring a significant time for apprehension is a way of presenting which subjectively considered is contrapurposive, but which objectively is needed to estimate magnitude and hence is purposive. And yet this same violence that the imagination inflicts on the subject is still judged purposive *for the whole vocation* of the mind.[14]

---

11. Hegel, *Aesthetic*, 363; Hegel, *Vorlesungen über der Ästhetik*, 467.

12. Kant, *Critique of Judgment*, 103–6; Kant, *Kritik der Uteilskraft*, 169–72.

13. Kant, *Critique of Judgment*, 106 (emphasis in original); Kant, *Kritik der Uteilskraft*, 172.

14. Kant, *Critique of Judgment*, 116; Kant, *Kritik der Uteilskraft*, 182–83.

The violence (*die Gewalt*) that Kant contemplated in this encounter with the sublime is ontologically significant. Our encounter with the sublime contains us, but it also protects us, teaching us that what lies beyond our body and our senses, the sublime, holds the capacity to utterly destroy our bodies. And precisely for this reason Kant held it *purposive* (*zweckmäßig*) for the whole vocation of the mind.

For Kant, this *violence* is absolutely decisive. It is what distinguishes the sublime from the merely beautiful or attractive. "The beautiful," Kant noted, "prepares us for loving something, even nature, without interest; the sublime, for esteeming it even against our interest."[15] The sublime holds the power to destroy our bodies and for this reason we esteem the sublime, even against our interest (*was durch seinen Widerstand gegen das Interesse der Sinne*). Were we now to ask whether the incarnate body of the Lord reveals God, Kant would be compelled to respond in the negative. What it reveals is precisely the *incapacity* of bodies to reveal God. Solely by way of this *via negativa*, *sub contrario absconditum*, the body of the Lord reveals that *the mind has a power surpassing any standard of sense*.

We are now in a position to grasp the preface to Hegel's objection to the Kantian sublime. "This outward shaping which is itself annihilated in turn by what it reveals, so that the revelation of the content is at the same time a supersession of the revelation, is the sublime. This, therefore, differing from Kant, we need not place in the pure subjectivity of the mind and its Ideas of Reason; on the contrary, we must grasp it as grounded in the one absolute substance *qua* the content which is to be represented."[16]

In its embodiment, the sublime exhibits its own supersession, which is at the same time the content of its revelation. Bodily annihilation therefore is not only the consequence of divine presence—the recognition that God is not embodied—but is also, more comprehensively, the content that is to be revealed. If Martin Luther in the *Small Catechism* held that God's presence in body, in bread, in wine, in church only displayed God *sub contrario absconditum*, Hegel, the flamboyant romantic, will abjure. It is the annihilation and reconstitution of God's body in all of these instances that reveals God—that reveals *the sublime*—as the *self-moving substance that is subject*.

The One Absolute Substance

While poring over the documents compiled by Georges Espinas and Henri Pirenne, *Recueil de documents relatifs a l'histoire de l'industrie drapière en*

---

15. Kant, *Critique of Judgment*, 127; Kant, *Kritik der Uteilskraft*, 193.
16. Hegel, *Aesthetic*, 363; Hegel, *Vorlesungen über der Ästhetik*, 468.

Flandre (1886), French medievalist Jacques Le Goff believed that he had located the origins of this self-moving substance that is subject. "In Ghent, in 1324," reports Le Goff, "the abbot of Saint-Pierre authorized the fullers 'to install a bell in the workhouse newly founded by them near the Hoipoorte, in the parish of Saint John.'"[17] To the best of our knowledge this marked the first time anywhere that equal units of abstract time were used to measure the value of productive human activity. To economic historian David Landes, the installation of this single bell gave rise to a "revolution in time."[18] More importantly, at least for our purposes, the fullers' installation of this bell marks the point when substantive value began to pull free from the substances in which it had been imprisoned, to differentiate and isolate itself from these bodies. Where earlier social subjects everywhere had anticipated finding and had believed they did find value *in things*, 1324 shows how, at least in the parish of Saint John, social subjects were already beginning to isolate abstract time and, hence, abstract value from the bodies that composed their world. Evidently the revolution was already in full swing.

There can be little doubt why the abbot of St.-Pierre issued his request. When dispersed among the many homes where workers wove their cloth, the weavers themselves commanded the tools and the pace of their own weaving. The independence of their weaving made sense when the value of their work was measured in the substances out of which their products were composed, in cloth, and not in time. Under the new regime, the value of each unit of cloth, each yard, was measured instead by the abstract time consumed in its composition. Clearly such time was more easily accounted when workers wove under the watchful eye of the timekeeper,[19] a timekeeper who, in turn, was keeping track of time itself.

Regulation theorists are inclined to count the adoption of clock-time in the fourteenth century as evidence of the human preference for efficiency. Since work-discipline under regulated time achieves greater efficiency than the more diffused, worker-regulated outputting system that earlier prevailed, it made sense that owners of textile works would install clocks to regulate production.[20] And yet this raises the question why abstract time and abstract value, which had played no role anywhere in social mediation up to the fourteenth century, should suddenly find its legs when and where it did. The answer to this question is far from obvious. According to Landes, abstract time was the invention not of merchants, but of monastics;

---

17. Le Goff, *Time, Work, & Culture in the Middle Ages*, 45.
18. Landes, *Revolution in Time*, 73.
19. Postone, *Time, Labor, and Social Domination*, 209–10.
20. See, for example, Arrighi, *Long Twentieth Century*, 86–110.

monastics whose spiritual discipline required not an accurate accounting of time, but of the moments when specific practices, such as prayers, needed to be performed: "Monastic space was closed space—areas and corridors of collective occupancy and movement—so arranged that everyone could be seen at all times. So with time: there was 'only one time, that of the group, that of the community. Time of rest, of prayer, of work, of meditation, of reading: signaled by the bell, measured and kept by the sacristan, excluding individual and autonomous time.' Time, in other words, was of the essence because it belonged to the community and to God; and the bells saw to it that this precious, inextensible resource was not wasted."[21]

Yet, as Landes notes, keeping accurate time was a constant problem within cloistered communities. Water clocks froze, a problem that became even more pronounced during Europe's mini-Ice Age. Sundials were reliable only during daylight hours. And even the best candles burned at variable rates. It was therefore not until the serendipitous discovery of the Chinese escapement mechanism in the thirteenth century that cloistered monks finally found the perfect device for the required task. The escapement mechanism, driven by a spring or by weights, was eminently reliable, operating at all temperatures and at all hours of the day and night. Affixed to a wire or notched gear, the mechanism rang a small bell alerting Frère Jacques that it was time to awaken his brothers by ringing a larger bell.

David Landes has also mapped the spread of such timepieces in cloistered communities throughout Western Europe in the thirteenth and fourteenth centuries. The timepieces created a stir not least because they upset the temporal rhythms that governed the "hours" of non-cloistered workers, nearly all of whom were accustomed to rising at dawn and bedding at dusk. Owing to seasonal patterns, "dawn" and "dusk" were absolute points on a shifting horizon; "hours" were necessarily variable. Not so the "hours" for prayer. Townsfolk who otherwise had no special reason to rise before daybreak or bed down before dusk regularly found themselves awakened from their sleep either too early or too late.[22]

No one is suggesting here that the good brothers by adopting the escapement mechanism were seeking to foment a revolution in time. Quite to the contrary, they were seeking no more than to faithfully observe the "hours" cloistered monks everywhere had observed for centuries. And, yet, as Postone has noted, the fourteenth-century revolution in time had profound implications for how individuals outside these communities came to experience themselves, others, and their world. "The equality and

---

21. Landes, *Revolution in Time*, 69.
22. Ibid., 54–66.

divisibility of constant time units abstracted from the sensuous reality of light, darkness, and the seasons became a feature of everyday urban life (even if it did not affect all town dwellers equally), as did the related equality and indivisibility of value, expressed in the money form, which is abstracted from the sensuous reality of various products. These moments in the growing abstraction and quantification of everyday objects—indeed, of various aspects of everyday life itself—probably played an important role in changing social consciousness."[23]

We would even strengthen Postone's conclusion: without question, the revolution in time *did* play an important role in changing social consciousness.

From roughly 1320 to 1500, the daily rhythms of Europeans were diverted away from the annual circuit of heavenly lights, away from seasons, tides, animal migrations, and meteorological transitions, and bent instead toward the predictable chimes of the town bells. Life, all of life, was coming to be regulated by abstract time and abstract value. Town and country folk could not have known at the time, but capitalism was being born; a comprehensive regulatory and legal framework (the first ever born in Europe itself), but also a fully integrated, rational way of engaging with and experiencing the world of life and work was gradually emerging.

These changes displayed themselves in new ways of experiencing God, self, and others. Long before Martin Luther tacked his Ninety-Five Theses to the doors of All Saints, spiritual practitioners were growing accustomed to experiencing value less in the substances out of which things were composed than in the equal units of abstract time it took to compose them. They were growing accustomed, that is, to experiencing value as a *quantum* abstracted from bodies. Bodies, by contrast, were increasingly associated with mere matter, physics, biology. They were associated with the constraints and limitations that differentiated them, necessarily, from immaterial spiritual beings, which, although disembodied, were judged, precisely for this reason, to enjoy divine freedom. Bodies, in other words, were coming to be associated not with conduits of grace, but as constraints upon freedom, and barriers to divine knowing and being.

Everywhere one looks, and not simply in the rapid spread of international laws and regulations governing capital circulation, there is evidence of this profound shift in spiritual experience. It is apparent in the disappearing wounds of the risen Lord in both sacred iconography and in sacred speech.[24] It is apparent in the simultaneous eroticization and elision of the

---

23. Postone, *Time, Labor, and Social Domination*, 213.
24. Widdicombe, "Wounds of the Ascended Body."

breasts of the Mother of God.[25] It is apparent in the gradual translation of Mary from a sacred body into an angelic soul.[26] And it is apparent in the growing discomfort spiritual practitioners were experiencing over the presence of God in the bread and wine of the Holy Sacrament. When at the end of the fifteenth century an ever-growing number of communicants announced their desire to reexamine and rearticulate the relationship between divine grace and material bodies, these communicants were merely giving voice to the profound shifts in social subjectivity—including spiritual subjectivity—to which their changed and changing practical circumstances were giving rise. Still, the appearance of these novel forms of spiritual subjectivity raises an important question: How should we describe a unique spiritual form that retreats from and turns upon its own material form of appearance?

By the time critical philosophy took up this question in the eighteenth century, the world where divine beings occupied earthly bodies already lay in *their* distant past, which is to say that, for them, divine embodiment had come to be completely subject to abstract time and value. Europeans were of course well aware of the myriad peoples around the globe that, stuck in the past, still anticipated and still believed they found divine grace and guidance in bodies. Yet, when viewed from the vantage point of abstract time it was clear that these communities were trapped at a stage of human development that fell far short of the universal. Eighteenth-century critical thinkers were also acutely aware of their own bodies, their own particularity, their own history, not as conduits of divine grace and guidance, but as sources of corruption, limitation, and superstition. By its very nature the universal could not express itself adequately even in their own enlightened bodies. And, yet, these same thinkers were also acutely aware that it was only along a specific historical trajectory—their own—that this problem was even raised to consciousness. Two centuries later, it still haunted Europe's best thinkers.[27]

25. Miles, *Complex Delight*.

26. Ellington, *From Sacred Body to Angelic Soul*.

27. We naturally think here of the opening sentence to the Introduction of Max Weber's sociology of religion: "Universalgeschichtliche Probleme wird der Sohn der modernen europäischen Kulturwelt unvermeidlicher- und berechtigterweise unter der Fragestellung behandeln: welche Verkettung von Umständen hat dazu geführt, daß gerade auf dem Boden des Okzidents, und nur hier, Kulturerscheinungen auftraten, welche doch—wie wenigstens wir uns gern vorstellen—in einer Entwicklungsrichtung von *universeller* Bedeutung und Gültigkeit lagen?" (Everyone born into the modern European cultural sphere inescapably and legitimately is faced with the question: what set of circumstances account for the fact that precisely in the West, and only there, cultural manifestations have arisen that fall—or so we tell ourselves—in a developmental line that enjoys *universal* significance and value?) Weber, "Vorbemerkung," 1; trans.

Nevertheless, it is important that we appreciate how the directional dynamic in which Europeans placed their own specific historical trajectory should itself be understood as a product of Landes's revolution in time. When they stripped bodies of substantive value and instead credited abstract time as the source of value; or, even better, when they harnessed their own productive activity to the equal units of abstract time hammered out on mechanical clocks, Europeans lent social validity to a form of value constituted only through the methodical, iterative destruction of bodies. When viewed from the vantage point of eighteenth-century critical thinkers, communities that failed to advance in this way—communities whose members were anchored to substantive notions of value—could not help but appear arrested in their historical development. Only those communities accustomed to *utilizing* bodies to create abstract value—abstract value, which then in turn needed to be reinvested in the constitution of new bodies, bodies which were themselves destined for destruction—only communities that displayed this virtuous directional dynamic could lay legitimate claim to the universal, a universal that lay not in isolated, particular bodies but in the abstract value that knit all bodies together into a comprehensive, integrated whole.

Here we might pause to consider St. Thomas's *Summa Theologica*, part three, where Thomas devotes page after page, chapter after chapter, explaining not how God could be present in things, but rather to explaining why only some things—seven—are sacraments.[28] Or consider the brilliant iconography of the Mother of God from the Middle Ages, breasts exposed, nourishing and caring for Her Church.[29] These socially and historically specific examples find parallels all across the globe and across time. They illustrate how communities everywhere experienced value prior to the fourteenth century: embodied, substantive, limited, and particular. This is not to say that the universal was not a problem for communities prior to the emergence of capitalism, namely, popular stoicism in first-century Rome. Nor is it to suggest that bodily mortification or attempts to transcend the limits of the body were unknown prior to the fourteenth-century revolution in time. Protestantism did not invent religious asceticism. What was new—*is* new—is the social reproduction and regulatory elaboration of a form of practice, commodity production and exchange, whose overall effect was to transfer value from the bodies in and through which communities once experienced value to the equal abstract units of time logged produc-

---

author.

28. Aquinas, *Summa Theologica*.
29. Miles, *Complex Delight*.

ing these bodies. Beginning in Ghent in 1324 and from there spreading to other regions of northern Europe, leaping the Channel to England, and from there spreading throughout the rest of the world, social actors learned through practice that the sublime had no body.

When in 1790 Kant observed how "sublimity is contained not in any thing of nature, but only in our mind, insofar as we can become conscious of our superiority to nature within us, and thereby also to nature outside us,"[30] he was simply repeating what everyone knew to be true from practice: the sublime cannot occupy bodies. And, yet, it was precisely this isolation of the sublime from its material form of appearance that Hegel found so troubling, for it left that which we have reason to want to know better than anything else—ourselves—completely lacking for explanation. Where a mere four centuries earlier communities knew by way of the substances out of which things—including divine things—were composed exactly what they were and were meant to be, now these substances told them absolutely nothing. To which Hegel boldly objected: "This, therefore, differing from Kant, we need not place in the pure subjectivity of the mind and its Ideas of Reason; on the contrary, we must grasp it as grounded in the one absolute substance *qua* the content which is to be represented."[31]

But this raises the question: How precisely is it that the sublime content of the one absolute substance can be grasped? How does it lend itself to being known? Here is Hegel's account from the "Preface" to his *Phenomenology of Spirit*:

> Further, the living Substance is being which is in truth *Subject*, or, what is the same, is in truth actual only in so far as it is the movement of positing itself, or is the mediation of its self-othering with itself. This Substance is, as Subject, pure, *simple negativity*, and is for this very reason the bifurcation of the simple; it is the doubling which sets up opposition, and then again the negation of this indifferent diversity and of its antithesis [the immediate simplicity]. Only this self-*restoring* sameness, or this reflection in otherness within itself—not an *original* or *immediate* unity as such—is the True. It is the process of its own becoming, the circle that presupposes its end as its goal, having its end also as its beginning; and only by being worked out to its end, is it actual.[32]

---

30. Kant, *Critique of Judgment*, 123; Kant, *Kritik der Uteilskraft*, 188.
31. Hegel, *Aesthetic*, 363; Hegel, *Vorlesungen über der Ästhetik*, 468.
32. Hegel, *Phenomenology of the Spirit*, 10; Hegel, *Phänomenologie des Geistes*, 13.

Not only can what is *original* or *immediate* (*ursprüngliche oder unmittelbare*) not be known; it cannot even know itself. And, therefore, if for no other reason, speaking of "the True" in this context is simply incoherent. Deprived of its body—of the sublime content revealed in the one absolute substance—mind is empty. And, yet, Hegel did not yet grasp how this—his own description of the living Substance—might itself be evidence of its own historical and social specificity. As he surveyed the vast history of the sublime spirit—in art, in philosophy, in science, in religion, in politics—wherever he looked, no matter what his object, Hegel believed he could discern the same movement, the same logic, externalizing, differentiating, "this self-*restoring* sameness, or this reflection of otherness within itself . . . being worked out to its end"—the True. He did not see, in other words, that this logic was itself socially and historically specific, peculiar to the capitalist social formation.

The Sublime Value Form of the Commodity

Initially, at least, in the years leading up to the revolutions of 1848/49 and for some time thereafter, Karl Marx adhered fairly closely to Hegel's line of analysis, even—perhaps especially—where he fashioned himself Hegel's fiercest critic. So, for example, although he treated Hegel's *Philosophy of Right* as little more than an idealization of the existing Prussian state, it was Hegel's logic, both in general and in detail, that Marx featured in his own critique of bourgeois private property. Consider, for example, Hegel's critique of civil society (*bürgerliche Gesellschaft*) §§182–256. Hegel grounded his criticism in the particularity of private aims. "The concrete person, who is himself the object of his particular aims, is, as a totality of wants and a mixture of caprice and physical necessity, one principle of civil society."[33]

> Particularity by itself, given free rein in every direction to satisfy its needs, accidental caprices, and subjective desires, destroys itself and its substantive concept in this process of gratification. At the same time, the satisfaction of need, necessary and accidental alike, is accidental because it breeds new desires without end, is in thoroughgoing dependence on caprice and external accident, and is held in check by the power of universality. In these contrasts and their complexity, civil society affords a

---

33. Hegel, *Philosophy of Right*, 122; Hegel, *Grundlinien der Philosophie des Rechts*, 339.

spectacle of extravagance and want as well as of the physical and ethical degeneration common to them both.[34]

Clearly Hegel took this "spectacle" (*das Schauspiel*) as a general criticism of civil—which is to say "bourgeois"—society. For herein bourgeois society "destroys itself and its substantive content" (*zerstört in ihren Genüssen sich selbst und ihren substantiellen Begriff*). Bourgeois society, in other words, contains within itself the seeds for its own destruction.

Likewise for Hegel, as for the pre-1848/49 Marx, the supersession of this particularity arises from within the sphere of labor. As mere private persons (*als Bürger*), individuals find a world structured to serve their own private interests. These others—persons, laws, and institutions—mediate their private ends; and in this sense, these others count for them as a "universal" adequate to these purely private ends. "This end is *mediated* through the universal which thus *appears* as a *means* to its realization. Consequently, individuals can attain their ends only in so far as they themselves determine their knowing, willing, and acting in a universal way and make themselves links in this chain of social connections."[35]

And, yet, because they only "know" this "universal" to the extent that it serves their private ends, they know it only in its particularity. They do not yet know it as the universal in which they and others compose a whole. Their interaction with and dependence upon others is implicit. "In these circumstances, the interest of the Idea—an interest of which these members of civil society are as such unconscious—lies in the process whereby their singularity and their natural condition are raised, as a result of the necessities imposed by nature as well as of arbitrary needs, to formal freedom and formal universality of knowing and willing—the process whereby their particularity is educated up to subjectivity [*die Subjektivität in ihrer Besonderheit zu* bilden]."[36]

Bourgeois individuals thus become aware that they are particulars within a whole, "a universality of knowing and willing" (*Allgemeinheit des Wissens und Wollens*). Through this engagement with others and this recognition of mutual dependence within a universal to which all particularities contribute, private individuals are lifted up out of their particularity and come to recognize the universal. "This form of universality—the

---

34. Hegel, *Philosophy of Right*, 123; Hegel, *Grundlinien der Philosophie des Rechts*, 341.

35. Hegel, *Philosophy of Right*, 124; Hegel, *Grundlinien der Philosophie des Rechts*, 343.

36. Hegel, *Philosophy of Right*, 124–25; Hegel, *Grundlinien der Philosophie des Rechts*, 343.

Understanding, to which particularity has worked its way and developed itself, brings it about at the same time that particularity becomes individuality genuinely existent in its own eyes. And since it is from this particularity that the universal derives the content which fills it as well as its character as infinite self-determination, particularity itself is present in ethical life as infinitely independent free subjectivity. This is the position which reveals education [*die Bildung*] as a moment immanent in the Absolute and which makes plain its infinite value."[37]

Since many English readers will likely take this term narrowly to refer only to formal, institutional instruction, "education" might, in this context, be an unfortunate choice for translating the German *die Bildung*. Here, Hegel clearly means *formation* more generally, as when, for example, a savvy investor must take cognizance of all of the individual factors required to produce any good and, therefore, must also take cognizance of a universe of independent producers who produce those factors along with the conditions under which these factors are produced. When we take cognizance of these seemingly isolated and independent conditions—when we recognize how our own decisions are dependent upon and wedded to the decisions of these others—we are compelled to recognize that our freedom is dependent upon theirs. And this recognition "reveals education [or formation, *die Bildung*] as a moment immanent to the Absolute and which makes plain its infinite value."

And, yet, as Hegel himself recognized, the relationship between formation or education (*die Bildung*) and freedom (*die Freihiet*) that he wished to draw here still remained obscure. If freedom is more than simply the necessity or inevitability of shaping and being shaped by the universal; if it consists of something more than merely the implicit recognition of this mutual constitution or universal dependence and inter-dependence; if it refers also to freedom from such inter-dependencies, then how might our universal interdependence give rise to such freedom? Hegel's provisional answer appears in §§197–98 where he connects the iterative process of mastering a practice—work—both with an awareness of mutual interdependence upon other practitioners, but also with a growing interest in and capacity for transferring these increasingly rationalized and rational practices to machines. The universal engagement entailed in labor, when coupled with the recognition of how each practice is rationally related to every other—that is to say, recognition of the interconnected universe of production shared by all producers—gives rise to actual freedom *from* (and not merely *through*)

---

37. Hegel, *Philosophy of Right*, 126; Hegel, *Grundlinien der Philosophie des Rechts*, 345.

One Absolute Substance

necessity. "Practical education [*praktische Bildung*], acquired through working [*Arbeit*], consists first in the automatically recurrent need for something to do and the habit of simply being busy; next, in the strict adaptation of one's activity according not only to the nature of the material worked on, but also, and especially, to the pleasure of other workers; and finally, in a habit, produced by this discipline, of objective activity and universally recognized aptitudes."[38]

When all labor is integrated in this way, once all laborers are aware of their interdependence upon one another, they are now in a position to seize their freedom.

> The universal and objective element in work, on the other hand, lies in the abstracting process which effects the subdivision of needs and means and thereby *eo ipso* subdivides production and brings about the division of labour. By this division, the work of the individual becomes less complex, and consequently his skill at his section of the job increases, like his output. At the same time, this abstraction of one man's skill and means of production from another's completes and makes necessary everywhere the dependence of men on one another and their reciprocal relation in the satisfaction of their other needs. Further, the abstraction of one man's production from another's makes work more and more mechanical, until finally man is able to step aside and install machines in his place.[39]

From here it is then a relatively easy step to Marx's 1844 *Philosophical Manuscripts* and, ironically, to his *Critique of Hegel's Philosophy of Right*, which owes so much in nearly all respects to Hegel's own critique of the Kantian sublime.

In 1844, Marx was happy to more or less lift the Kantian sublime from its natural home and transfer it wholesale to the working class. Since in his view alienation lay at the root of class conflict, this alienation could only be resolved by the Subject of History returning to and therein realizing its Self in the completion of the industrial working class—its return to its Self.

> Whenever real, corporeal *man*, man with his feet finally on the solid ground, man exhaling and inhaling all the forces of nature, *establishes* his real, objective *essential powers* as alien objects by his externalization, it is not the *act of positing* which is the

---

38. Hegel, *Philosophy of Right*, 129; Hegel, *Grundlinien der Philosophie des Rechts*, 352.

39. Hegel, *Philosophy of Right*, 129; Hegel, *Grundlinien der Philosophie des Rechts*, 352–53.

subject in this process: it is the subjectivity of *objective* essential powers, whose action, therefore, must also be something *objective*. A being who is objective acts objectively, and he would not act objectively if the objective did not reside in the very nature of his being. He creates or establishes only *objects*, *because* he is established by *objects* —because at bottom he is *nature*. In the act of establishing, therefore, this objective being does not fall from his state of "pure activity" into a *creating of the object*; on the contrary, his objective product only confirms his *objective* activity, establishing his activity as the activity of an objective, natural being.[40]

Marx's pre-1848/49 interpretation therefore entailed little more than shifting Hegel's center of gravity ever so slightly from the One Absolute Substance to the working class so that, in effect, the content that Hegel ascribed to the sublime—the content whose substance Kant had denied, but whose social and historical validity Hegel demonstrated—Marx simply transferred to the universal Subject-Object of history, the industrial working class: *objective, natural being*.

The revolutions of 1848/49 completely disabused Marx of this conceit. During his forced exile in London, he carefully worked over texts that in the *Vormärz* had seemed clear, but now in retrospect appeared murky. Why hadn't the industrial working class seized upon their historical destiny? Why hadn't increased efficiencies yielded the freedoms promised in Hegel's *Philosophy of Right*? Why did each increase in efficiency give rise instead to a shift in marginal benefits upward and to the right, giving rise in the end to no more than a new plateau? In London, Marx became a historian—which is to say, he became a Hegelian—and this, in the end, proved his downfall.

An Alternative Emancipatory Vision

Marx's migration back to Hegel over the course of the 1850s is everywhere apparent. The revolutions of 1848/49 were a watershed after which the governments of Western Europe with near universal acclaim dropped their anachronistic restrictions against non-noble participation in the civil service and liberalized their trade and industrial policies. Seemingly overnight, the economic lethargy that had in large measure given rise to the events of 1848/49 gave way instead to a prolonged and impressive period of general economic growth. When, therefore, Marx sat down to write his magnum

---

40. Marx and Engels, *Economic and Philosophical Manuscripts*, 336; Marx and Engels, *Ökonomisch-Philosophische Manuskripte*, 577.

opus, *Das Kapital*, the story he told was worlds removed from the stories he and Engels had penned in the 1840s. The story told in *Das Kapital* was not about how capitalism had failed, but why it had proven so spectacularly successful and why it was likely to prove successful into the indefinite future. Obviously this was not a story likely to inspire hope and courage among Communists in Europe, England, or the Americas. And, so, not surprisingly, both critics and partisans alike have found it more convenient to draw upon or take pot shots at Marx's *Vormärz* writings, where, either seriously or comically, the Subject-Object of history, the industrial working class, marches victoriously into an emancipated future.

Nowhere, however, is this tragicomic image shred more completely than in Marx's own retranslation of Hegel's description of the Subject of history. Recall how in Hegel this Subject doubles itself, constituting its own object, which it then can legitimately recognize and by which it can, in turn, be recognized. Recall how the fault Hegel found in Kant's delineation of the sublime falls to Kant's failure to identify and preserve a body whose content could reveal One Absolute Substance. And recall Hegel's own discovery of how the freedom immanent to the sublime arises within an iterative, historical process in which workers become aware through practice of a technical elaboration of labor that might free them from necessity. These efficient workers might then have become the agents and subjects of freedom. They might have constructed the mechanisms—the machines—that would then have taken their place. But this would assume that value was something specific and substantive, so that, once enough value had been accumulated, workers would slowly but inevitably become obsolete. Value, however, was not substantive. When, therefore, Marx came to translate Hegel's universal Subject into a language that made social and historical sense, he would ascribe this universal subjectivity not to the industrial working class (which fit his *Vormärz* interpretation), but rather to the actual Subject of History, the sublime value form of the commodity:

> [Value] is constantly changing from one form into the other, without becoming lost in this movement; it thus becomes transformed into an automatic subject. If we pin down the specific forms of appearance assumed in turn by self-valorizing value in the course of its life, we reach the following elucidation: capital is money, capital is commodities. In truth, however, value is here the subject of a process in which, while constantly assuming the form in turn of money and commodities, it changes its

own magnitude, throws off surplus-value from itself considered as original value, and thus valorizes itself independently.[41]

Labor for Marx was no longer the Self-moving Substance that is Subject. That ship had sailed. It sailed in 1848/49. In *Kapital*, by contrast, this role is now assumed by the sublime value form of the commodity that "suddenly presents itself as a self-moving substance which passes through a process of its own, and for which commodities and money are both mere forms."[42]

Bourgeois Private Property and the Condition for Freedom

Two profound consequences followed from this shift in perspective. In the *Vormärz* Marx had been content to transfer Hegel's alienation-and-return dynamic without amendment to the industrial working class and to its "coming into its own," its "completion"—its *Aufhebung*. This *Vormärz* preoccupation with alienation-and-return was the driving force behind Marx's equally prominent preoccupation with bourgeois private property—*alienated* property—which, with the return of the industrial working class to itself, would likewise be restored to its non-alienated condition. In his new interpretation, capital takes the place of the one absolute substance whose content now is no longer the industrial working class, but is instead the sublime value form of the commodity. As the passage above indicates, it is not the working class then that returns to itself; rather is its value that returns to and completes itself. The Self-Moving Substance in that case is not the industrial working class, but capital; and the comprehensive, integrated, rational social totality is not the collective workers integrated into a comprehensive whole, but is instead fully integrated capitalist society. The comprehensive collectivization and socialization of all relations is not therefore an outstanding task for a future non-alienated working class; rather now is it a task always and already immanent to the capitalist social formation itself. But this also explains why alienated bourgeois property relations retreat almost completely from the foreground in Marx's mature, post-revolutionary social theory.

The second and in many ways even more profound consequence following from Marx's shift away from Hegel's alienation-and-return narrative is that he no longer conceptualizes the violent defeat of the bourgeoisie as a

---

41. Marx, *Capital*, 1:255; Marx, *Kapital*, 1:168–69.
42. Marx, *Capital*, 1:256; Marx, *Kapital*, 1:169.

precondition for social emancipation. Here, once again, Marx returned to Hegel and, more specifically, to Hegel's *Philosophy of Right*, §198, no longer as critic, but as disciple. If labor is the form that domination takes within societies regulated by commodity production and exchange, then a society composed entirely of laborers producing abstract value for themselves and one another—the complete socialization of the forces and relations of production—is entirely compatible with this peculiar form of *self-domination*. When in §198 Hegel identified freedom with the conditions under which laborers step aside and install machines in their place, he pointed to a form of freedom grounded not in the return of labor to itself—not in the dialectic of alienation-and-return—but rather to a form of freedom grounded in freedom from necessity.[43] Now Marx was inclined to agree with Hegel. Here is Marx in volume 3 of *Capital*:

> The realm of freedom really begins only where labour determined by necessity and external expediency ends; it lies by its very nature beyond the sphere of material production proper. This realm of natural necessity expands with his development, because his needs do too; but the productive forces to satisfy these expand at the same time.... Freedom, in this sphere, can consist only in this, that socialized man, the associated producers, govern the human metabolism with nature in a rational way, bringing it under their collective control instead of being dominated by it as a blind power; accomplishing it with the least expenditure of energy and in conditions most worthy and appropriate for their human nature. But this always remains a realm of necessity. The true realm of freedom, the development of human powers as an end in itself, begins beyond it, though it can only flourish with this realm of necessity as its basis.[44]

Where Marx differed from Hegel—and this was decisive—was that Hegel still grounded the gradual unfolding of freedom in the efficiencies he believed were immanent to the one absolute substance. For Hegel, as we have seen, gradual, iterative integration of all factors, where these factors become practically aware of their dependence upon and interdependence with one another, necessarily gives rise to efficiencies through technical innovation. These efficiencies in turn inevitably make it possible for workers

---

43. Hegel's freedom-necessity dyad owes itself in part to the Aristotle revival then sweeping Europe, as evidenced in and facilitated by publication of Aristotle's works in a definitive German edition by the Prussian Royal Academy, commenced in 1831 and completed in 1870. It was to this edition of Aristotle that Marx also returned while in London, informing his own reevaluation of freedom (see Ferrarin, *Hegel and Aristotle*).

44. Marx, *Capital*, 3:959; Marx, *Kapital*, 3:828.

to step aside and install machines in their place. For Marx, by contrast, since he counted abstract value a social substance transcendentally related to but separated from its material forms of appearance, he also recognized that efficiency would always be relative to the social relations that prevailed in any specific community. Abstract value would therefore always lend itself to recalibration to fit ever new efficiency horizons. Since abstract value—and not substantive value—was the aim of commodity production and exchange, Marx therefore came to doubt that workers would ever in fact be able to step aside, innovation notwithstanding.

It was therefore not private property that workers needed to seize, but time; and not even time in any absolute sense. Like Hegel, Marx also no longer contemplated a fundamental breach within temporality. For Marx therefore the precondition of freedom no longer lay in the violent overthrow of the bourgeoisie, but rather in legislating a shorter work day. "The true realm of freedom, the development of human powers as an end in itself, begins beyond [labor], though it can only flourish with this realm of necessity as its basis. The reduction of the working day is the basic prerequisite."[45] Not violent revolution and seizure of private property, but legislation and seizure of time.

Not surprisingly, given Marx's return to Hegel, *Kapital* is virtually devoid of the strident *Vormärz* anti-Hegelian vitriol that characterized so much of Marx's writing in the 1840s and early 1850s. He is chastened, almost humbled, by the spectacular success of capitalism in the late 1850s and 1860s. And, yet, his recuperation of Hegel is not without consequence. It marks more than a simple return. Hegel had mistaken the One Absolute Substance for a transhistorical universal. He had therefore supposed that the embodiment of the sublime would be a critical stage in the reintegration of particularity into the universal, a critical passage into the *realization* of an embodied universal *in time*. Marx's contribution, however small, to this Hegelian formulation is to identify the social and historical limits to the sublime itself—to point out that the subject or agent of universal history is composed by a socially and historically delimited set of circumstances: the reduction of value to abstract time and abstract labor socially generalized in the production and exchange of commodities. The fate bodies must endure in such a social formation was already prefigured by Hegel in his critique of the Kantian sublime.

45. Marx, *Capital*, 3:959; Marx, *Kapital*, 3:828.

A Postscript for Gillian Rose

While composing this reflection on Hegel's One Absolute Substance I have attempted to keep a sympathetic eye on Gillian Rose's considerable contribution to our science, broadly conceived. I am not, nor do I claim to be, a philosopher in any sense; but claim merely to be an economic historian of a fairly average sort. When it was first suggested that I might contribute to this volume I was therefore both flattered and terrified. What, after all, might a common economic historian have to say about one of history's leading philosophers, not to mention one of his leading contemporary interpreters?

And, yet, reading Hegel next to Gillian Rose has helped me to see, again, where my own science, economics, and my own faith, Christianity, have brought me to walk a path at odds with other scholars with whom on other points—perhaps most points—I might otherwise agree. For example, I find myself for the most part in agreement with Rose's critique of Kant and Fichte, whose disembodied sublime I count as evidence of their blindness to the sublime value form of the commodity. I am also sympathetic with Rose's historically grounded reading of Hegel, whose critique of the bourgeois state and bourgeois rationality have been so misunderstood over the years, not least by the pre-1848/49 Marx and his twentieth-century epigones.[46] Perhaps most surprising of all, however, is how closely Rose's readings of Georg von Lukács, Theodor Adorno, and Jürgen Habermas parallel my own readings of now more than a decade ago.[47] Here I am in near full agreement with Rose: Kant fixed a tightly bound noose about the neck of critical sociology, a noose that only Hegel and (I would argue) the mature Marx appear capable of loosening.[48] This noose, I have suggested, was composed of the empty, abstract, yet sublime value generated when productive human activity came to be measured in equal units of abstract time. From that point forward human action could be measured—and measured quite accurately—but its value appeared either banal (measured in inches, pounds, and seconds) or opaque: "The rigid dichotomy between the sensuous world (the finite, nature) and the supersensuous world (the infinite, freedom) prevents the comprehension of either. By degrading empirical existence in order to emphasize that the infinite is utterly different, the infinite is itself debased. For it is deprived of all characterization, and hence turned into an empty abstraction, an idol, made of mere timber."[49]

---

46. Lough, "Marksistički Humanizam."
47. Lough, *Weber and the Persistence of Religion*, xi–xii, 48–49, 57–66.
48. Rose, *Hegel contra Sociology*, 26–41.
49. Ibid., 104.

And, yet, because she is inclined to attribute this dichotomy to critical reflection itself; or, rather, because she is inclined to trace the social validity of this critical reflection to the contradictions implicit in bourgeois private property relations, Rose no less than Hegel is inclined to conceptualize the resolution (*die Aufhebung*) of this contradiction in terms of "a higher third" that preserves the particular in the absolute and the absolute in the particular. To be sure, such a resolution is preferable to the transcendental alternative, which contemplates resolution through mutual annihilation or, as in Fichte, a transcendental resolution that leaves the material form of appearances virtually unchanged: "This leaves the ordinary world just as it is, 'but with a negative sign,' in all its relations of domination. Thus to be 'free' from the empirical world is to be 'imprisoned' in the dualism between inconsequential 'freedom' and the sensuous world."[50]

And yet Rose's analysis begs the question of the practices out of which this dichotomy had arisen in the first place, not only in practice, but therefore also in critical reflection. If we are correct to see in the isolation of sublime value from its material form of appearance evidence of a practical taxonomy unique to the capitalist social formation, then there may be some value in wondering how differently shaped practical taxonomies might give rise to questions quite different than the ones that struck eighteenth-century thinkers as "natural" and "straightforward." Perhaps a substance conceptualized along absolute lines makes sense only within the narrow confines of a social totality bent by commodity production and exchange.

Rose's deference toward Hegel in this regard touches two areas in particular: the path to emancipation from the bifurcation in Kant and Fichte to which she rightly calls attention; and the forms of religious subjectivity and practice that might survive this emancipation. Both areas it so happens are intimately related and both come to light in an especially clear way once we take more careful note of the fourteenth-century revolution in time we have examined above.

Consider for a moment Hegel's—and therefore Rose's—preoccupation with bourgeois private property. As we have already seen, in the *Vormärz* Marx too shared this preoccupation.[51] While we might appreciate Rose's review of the close relationships between "personality," legal "persons," and "private property," in our view it is a mistake to draw too close a parallel of bourgeois property relations and personhood to Roman property relations and personhood. By focusing on the relationship between "personality"— that is, the legal characteristic of being a "person"—and private property—

---

50. Ibid., 107.
51. Ibid., 84–97.

which only legal persons can own and alienate—Hegel (and Rose) loses sight of the radically different social forms shaping Roman "persons" on the one hand and eighteenth-century European "persons" on the other. Against the backdrop of the capitalist social formation's One Absolute Substance, personality takes on an entirely different meaning than it enjoyed even under Roman hegemony. In a non-capitalist social formation, particularity is inflected differently, not in contrast to the universal, but, rather, as constitutive of an expanding, yet limited, social, political, and cultural horizon that is explicitly composed of private households bearing relationships to one another, but especially to the household of Caesar. Here, recalling the Apostle's defense of popular Roman stoicism, we can see how popular Roman stoicism displayed a very different experience not only of private property and personhood, but also how it suggests how different Rome's social landscape was from the social world in which Kant, Hegel, or Marx were embedded.

In Imperial Rome, each household along with all of its members individually were felt to bear a relationship, however near or distant, to the household and person of the Emperor. By equating this popular stoic cosmology and the experience of personhood it entails with eighteenth-century personhood, Rose loses sight of the very categories she was eager to decipher; the abstract individual whose substantial existence—whose particular body—had become a complete enigma.

In Imperial Rome, however, precisely the body was not an enigma. In late Empire, particularity held no mystery. This mystery emerged a full millennium later, after sublime value had successfully migrated from specific bodies and had become the content of the One Absolute Substance; only then will such purely private bodies and their private effects come under criticism precisely from the vantage point of the One Absolute Substance, capital. Hegel's criticism of bourgeois private property arose within and therefore was adequate to social relations composed precisely within societies characterized by commodity production and exchange—the isolation of abstract value from its material form of appearance. Personality in these societies is peculiar because, on the one hand, it is completely devoid of content—the abstract legal person; but, for this very reason, on the other hand, personality is completely enigmatic in those substantial particularities that do in fact differentiate persons from one another. Not only in Imperial Rome, but everywhere prior to the fourteenth century, the *differentia* distinguishing individuals from one another are simply not problematic. Rather, they are expected.

We find veiled reference to this transformation of social subjectivity and personhood in the first volume of Marx's *Kapital*, where Marx counts spiritual subjectivity a reliable instrument for measuring social subjectivity more generally. Here, in 1867, Marx no longer cast so broad a net as to lump all Christians together in one bundle. To the contrary, already in the 1850s Marx had come to question his earlier reliance upon Feuerbach and Feuerbach's merely reflective understanding of social subjectivity, including religious subjectivity. Now Marx was eager to more carefully specify and differentiate among forms of social subjectivity. "For a society of commodity producers, whose general social relation of production consists in the fact that they treat their products as commodities, hence as values, and in this material [*sachlich*] form bring their individual, private labours into relation with each other as homogeneous human labour, Christianity with its religious cult of man in the abstract, more particularly in its bourgeois development, i.e. in Protestantism, Deism, etc., is the most fitting form of religion."[52]

As though eager to have his readers catch him in the act of gross historical error, Marx here calls attention to his anachronistic reading of Christianity, thereby ensuring that we will notice that it is not Christianity as such that is guilty of eliminating human particularity, but Christianity in its specifically "bourgeois development" (*bürgerlichen Entwicklung*), Protestantism and Deism to be exact. Were he following Hegel's formal/legal analysis of personality, we would anticipate Marx here to fault Christianity, especially in its "bourgeois development," not for its "cult of man in the abstract" (*Kultus des abstrakten Menschen*), but for its differentiation among private agents by the private property they own. Instead Marx was eager for us to recognize how very differently personhood and personality are inflected under conditions of commodity production and exchange. For Marx it mattered little whether, as in Kant and Fichte, we are talking about the transcendental subject, or, as in Schlegel or Schleiermacher, we are talking more specifically about the spiritual personality. In both instances, the body drops from consideration, leaving only the vacant divine or human spirit dangling in the thin air.

Presumably Rose could have benefited from Marx's more socially and historically rigorous reading of Hegel since it would appear to reinforce her own criticisms of Kant and Fichte. But we can also understand why she might have preferred her own reading, which preserves the contradiction in a perpetual state of *Aufhebung*. Our reading re-embeds the dualisms with which both she and Hegel were preoccupied in socially and historically specific ways that might not have been to either of their likings. So, for example, Rose was inclined to take the oppositions—particular/universal,

---

52. Marx, *Capital*, 1:172; Marx, *Kapital*, 1:93.

finite/infinite, faith/knowledge, immanent/transcendent—and treat them as evidence not of a specific and relatively recent historical and social constellation (our reading), but as couplets enjoying something close to transhistorical validity.

Take, for example, her charge (Hegel's?) that "Kant and Fichte have destroyed the meaning of both religion and freedom."[53] Clearly such a charge differs from the more global charge that Christians everywhere at all times are inclined to deny embodied divinity. Yet, this is precisely the direction Rose took her argument, as in, for example, the following: "The abstract, pure concept of infinity in Kant and Fichte is 'the abyss of nothingness in which all being is engulfed.' The infinite is opposed to being, that is, to the finite, to all determination, and hence is nothing itself ('nothingness'). This nothingness is imposed on all being ('the abyss . . . in which all being is engulfed'). This 'signifies' the 'infinite grief' of the finite: the individual feels abandoned by a characterless, omnipotent and hence impotent God. This experience of 'infinite grief' is re-cognized as the historical meaning of Christianity *in the present*."[54]

So far, so good; for at this point, we might still be contemplating a historically and socially specific inflection of Christianity in the eighteenth and nineteenth centuries. But Rose then goes further: "The feeling that God is dead or absent has always been central to Christian religious experience, because in the Christian religion the absolute is misrepresented as beyond human life, not present in it."[55] Here "the absolute" leaps out of its historical clothes and spreads itself over the full sweep of Christian experience, as though "the absolute" were something other than a historically and socially specific category and as though "Christian religious experience" encountered this transhistorical category in its natural, disembodied home, rather than, as seems more likely, under Christians' own historically and socially specific circumstances. In our view, neither "the absolute" nor "Christian religious experience" enjoys any meaning apart from the meanings spiritual practitioners at various times find in them.

More than this, however, Rose's leap from Kant and Fichte to all Christian experience everywhere displays a profound misunderstanding of the force of Christian religious experience prior to the fourteenth century where religious practitioners routinely sought and found God present in the bodies that filled their world. For such practitioners, divine presence in human life was simply not problematic, not in the least. But it also suggests

53. Rose, *Hegel contra Sociology*, 110.
54. Ibid., 110–11.
55. Ibid., 111.

a transhistoricization of the dichotomies that we have instead credited to a highly specific social and historical landscape. If we are correct, then we should find evidence in the firsthand reports of spiritual practitioners prior to the fourteenth century of a different inflection of embodied value. And this, I would argue, is precisely what we find. Let us return briefly therefore to the beginning.

I began these reflections, somewhat ironically, by calling attention to the popular stoic thought embedded in, of all places, the Apostle Paul's Letter to the Romans. Here the Apostle invited us to entertain a notion of substantive being that connected all individual beings together in a strict hierarchy, where the place occupied by each being was carefully calibrated to the power each possessed. Hegel's "one absolute substance" differs from that suggested in popular stoic ontology, I argued, insofar as there is no corollary in popular stoicism to the sublime value that, in Hegel's account, displays the content of this substance. Presumably this is because in popular stoicism content and value are deemed inseparable.

I want to conclude by calling attention, again somewhat ironically, to a different Pauline text, this one found in the Apostle's First Letter to the Corinthians. The text commands our attention because in it the Apostle appears to directly contradict his advice to the Romans respecting the obedience they owed to the powers that be. Here, to the contrary, Paul specifically calls attention to the offense Romans must necessarily take in the Christian community's "foolish" foregrounding of "Christ crucified" (1 Cor 1:21–22); offensive both on account that gods are not overcome by powers weaker than themselves and on account of the Apostle's claim that "God's foolishness is wiser than human wisdom, and God's weakness is stronger than human strength" (v. 25). Such could be taken as no more than an *apophatic* reflection that aimed to elevate spiritual practitioners out of their particularity and unite them with a God who transcends death. Except that the Apostle then invites his readers to take note of their own deficiencies: they are, he says, "foolish" (μωρὰ), "weak" (ἀσθενῆ), "low-born and despised" (ἀγενῆ καὶ ἐξουθενημένα); indeed, according to the Apostle, the Corinthians "are not" (μὴ ὄντα), all of which would bring anyone the least familiar with popular stoicism to conclude that these "members of Christ's body" are forsaken by the gods. More troubling still is why the Apostle says God chose these foolish, ill-born, and despised ciphers. God chose these ones "to shame the strong" and "reduce to nothing things that are" (ἵνα τὰ ὄντα καταργήσῃ). That is to say, the same Apostle who in his Letter to the Romans counsels obedience to the Roman pantheon of powers here identifies the foolish, low-born, and despised as the instruments through which these very same powers will be brought down, not in spite of their relative lack of being, but because of this lack.

Paul will then go on to point out that this ontological reversal was not only not known, but could not be known to "the rulers of this age" (τῶν ἀρχόντων τοῦ αἰῶνος; 1 Cor 2:8). Again, this divine unknowing has also been interpreted *apophatically*. "Among the mature we do speak wisdom, though it is not a wisdom of this age or of the rulers of this age, who are doomed to perish. But we speak God's wisdom, secret and hidden, which God decreed before the ages for our glory" (1 Cor 2:6–7). How else can "secret and hidden" (ἐν μυστηρίῳ) wisdom otherwise be interpreted? And yet, this too misses the point, since it ignores Paul's claim that this wisdom has been revealed on the cross—not in a Kantian sublime, which, by its nature has no substance, but rather in the substance that is the cross; which explains why rulers trained in popular stoicism to despise weakness cannot see it. "These things God has revealed to us through the Spirit" (1 Cor 2:10) needs to be interpreted therefore as a rejection of popular stoicism and, by inference, a rejection of any social form that credits blind power with divine status.

When the cross is interpreted transcendentally, the embarrassment is removed, but so also is its content. This I take to be Rose's point. Dead gods exercise power in this case through a perpetual *via negativa*, a path of negation, which cannot help but misrepresent the absolute "as beyond human life, not present in it." She was mistaken, however, to feel that this "has always been central to Christian religious experience." It has not. Indeed, had this absent presence been central to Christian religious experience, the foolishness of the cross would have been eliminated from the outset and Christianity could have assumed its place—perhaps even a prominent place—alongside the long list of *apophatic* Roman mystery cults. Which is not to deny that the church, today as ever, is brimming with Christians whose embarrassment over divine embodiment runs so deep that, like Rome's rulers, they too seem to prefer divine unknowing to knowledge of the cross. But this is to ascribe heterodoxy and heresy to an institution, the church, that at nearly every turn, until very recently, has officially announced a preference for divine embodiment over disembodied divine unknowing of the sort made transcendentally necessary in the thought of Kant or (even more) Fichte.

Whether such an embodied Christianity is even possible under conditions of capitalist modernity is far from certain. Since the fourteenth century, it has become increasingly difficult for social actors—especially social actors whose social subjectivity has become so tightly bound to and inseparable from the sublime value form of the commodity—to imagine, much less experience, divine embodiment. Gods have no bodies; bodies are not divine. But let us suppose, for the sake of argument, that social actors proved successful practically decoupling abstract value from productive human action; say, by shortening the work day. And let us suppose that breaking the stranglehold of abstract value on social life also released a flood of alternative valuations—aesthetic, environmental, familial, gastronomical, astronomical, and so on—so that in the place of Hegel's One Absolute Substance there appeared instead a wide range of substances, bodies, differently inflected, whose relationships to one another, while not incoherent, were also not rigidly specified or assigned. In this case, we might well imagine spiritual practitioners seeking and finding *not* One Absolute Substance—for under these circumstances such a substance would prove genuinely incoherent—but substances they had reason to believe conveyed grace to their communities: embodied grace, divine *things*.

Hegel leads us up to this threshold. Gillian Rose brilliantly illuminates it. But she pulls to a halt at the sight of one absolute substance, unable to move any further. Only a practical transformation in social life of the sort Marx imagined at the end of *Capital*, where individuals necessarily bound to abstract labor, time, and value gradually eliminate these constraints; only then might embodied grace appear as more than a clever philosophical or spiritual paradox. Until that point, however, there may be some value in knowing that other communities, elsewhere, at other times, experienced the divine in dramatically different ways, not because they were stuck at an earlier stage of human development, but because they had not yet learned that value—and specially divine value—cannot occupy bodies.

Bibliography

Adorno, Theodor. *Minima Moralia*. New York: Verso, 2005.

Aquinas, Thomas. *Summa Theologica*. Translated by Fathers of the English Dominican Province. Benzinger Bros. ed. Christian Classics Ethereal Library. http://www.ccel.org/ccel/aquinas/summa.html. Notre Dame, IN: Christian Classics, 1981.

Arrighi, Giovanni. *The Long Twentieth Century: Money, Power, and the Origins of Our Times*. New York: Verso, 2010.

Ellington, Donna Spivey. *From Sacred Body to Angelic Soul: Understanding Mary in Late Medieval and Early Modern Europe*. Washington, DC: Catholic University of America Press, 2001.

Espinas, Georges, and Henri Pirenne. *Recueil de documents relatifs a l'histoire de l'industrie drapière en Flandre II*. Brussels: Kiesling et Cie, Imbrechts, 1886.

Ferrarin, Alfredo. *Hegel and Aristotle*. Cambridge: Cambridge University Press, 2001.

Gorman, Tony. "Gillian Rose and the project of a Critical Marxism." *Radical Philosophy* 105 (2001) 25–36.

Hegel, G. W. F. *Phänomenologie des Geistes.* Philosophische Bibliothek 114. Leipzig: Dürrischen Buchhandlung, 1907.
———. *Phenomenology of the Spirit.* Translated by A. V. Miller. Oxford: Oxford University Press, 1977.
———. *Philosophy of Right.* Translated by T. M. Knox. Oxford: Oxford University Press, 1978.
———. *Grundlinien der Philosophie des Rechts oder Naturrecht und Staatswissenschaft im Grundrisse.* Frankfurt: Suhrkamp, 1986a.
———. *Vorlesungen über die Ästhetik.* Vol. 1. Frankfurt: Suhrkamp, 1986b.
———. *Aesthetics: Lectures on Fine Art.* Volume 1. Translated by T. M. Knox. Oxford: Oxford University Press, 1988.
Kant, Immanuel. *Kritik der Urteilskraft.* Vol. 10 of *Werkausgabe.* Frankfurt: Suhrkamp, 1974.
———. *Critique of Judgment.* Translated by Werner S. Pluhar. Indianapolis: Hackett, 1987.
Landes, David. *Revolution in Time: Clocks and the Making of the Modern World.* Cambridge, MA: Harvard University Press, 1983.
Le Goff, Jacques. *Time, Work, & Culture in the Middle Ages.* Translated by Arthur Goldhammer. Chicago: University of Chicago Press, 1980.
Lough, Joseph. *Weber and the Persistence of Religion: Capitalism, Social Theory, and the Sublime.* London: Routledge, 2006.
———. "Marksistički Humanizam: Kritička Procjena." *Tranzicija: Časopis za ekonomiju I politiku tranzicije* 17, no. 36 (2015) 7–23.
———. "The Subject of Rigorous Mathematical Economic Modeling: Critical reflections on GWF Hegel and Robert Lucas, Jr." *Tranzicija: Časopis za ekonomiju I politiku tranzicije* 16, no. 33 (2014) 1–16.
Marx, Karl. *Das Kapital: Kritik der politischen Ökonomie.* Vol. 1. Berlin: Dietz, 1962.
———. *Das Kapital: Kritik der politischen Ökonomie.* Vol. 3. Berlin: Dietz, 1964.
———. *Capital: A Critique of Political Economy.* Volume 1. Translated by Ben Fowkes. New York: Penguin, 1976.
———. *Capital: A Critique of Political Economy.* Volume 3. Translated by David Fernbach. New York: Penguin, 1981.
Marx, Karl, and Frederick Engels. *Economic and Philosophical Manuscripts of 1844.* In *Works*, 3:229–346. London: Lawrence & Wishart, 2010.
———. Ökonomisch-philosophische Manuskripte aus dem Jahre 1844. In *Werke*, 40:465–588. Berlin: Dietz, 1968.
Miles, Margaret. "An Image of Salvation: God's Love, Mother's Milk." *Christian Century* (2008) 22–25.
———. *A Complex Delight: The Secularization of the Breast, 1350–1750.* Berkeley: University of California Press, 2008.
Osborne, Peter. "Hegelian Phenomenology and the Critique of Reason and Society." *Radical Philosophy* 32, no. 8 (1982) 8–15.
———. "Hegelian Phenomenology and the Critique of Reason and Society." *Telos* 173 (2015) 55–67.
Postone, Moishe. *Time, Labor, and Social Domination: A Reinterpretation of Marx's Critical Theory.* New York: Cambridge University Press, 1993.
Rose, Gillian. *Hegel contra Sociology.* New York: Verso, 2007.

———. *Mourning Becomes the Law: Philosophy and Representation*. New York: Cambridge University Press, 1996.

Weber. Max. "Vorbemerkung." In *Gesammelte Aufsätze zur Religionssoziologie*. Vol. 1. 2nd rev. ed. Tübingen: Mohr/Siebeck, 1922. ET: "Author's Introduction." *Protestant Ethic and the Spirit of Capitalism*. Translated by Talcott Parsons. London: Routledge, 2005.

Widdicombe, Peter. "The Wounds of the Ascended Body: The Marks of Crucifixion in the Glorified Christ from Justin Martyr to John Calvin." *Laval théologique et philsophique* 59, no. 1 (2003) 137–54.

Williams, Rowan. "Sermon by the Archbishop of Canterbury Christmas Day 1996." December 25, 1996. Accessed July 2, 2017. http://www.anglicannews.org/news/1996/12/sermon-by-the-archbishop-of-canterbury-christmas-day-1996.aspx.

CHAPTER 8

"A Frenzy of Self-Deceit"[1]

Commodity Fetishism, Labor, and Rose's Critical Marxism

Joshua B. Davis

The theory of commodity fetishism is the most speculative moment in Marx's exposition of capital. It comes nearest to demonstrating in the historically specific case of commodity producing society how substance is ((mis)-represented as) subject, how necessary illusion arises out of productive activity.[2]

—Gillian Rose

Revolution involves controlling the motion of capital.[3]

—Moishe Postone

---

1. This is Hegel's phrase, "The law of the heart and the frenzy of self-conceit," from *Phenomenology of Spirit*, 221ff. Rose translates this as "self-deceit"; see *Hegel contra Sociology*, 178, 191, and 233. Solomon translates it as *self-denial*; see *In the Spirit of Hegel*, 507 and 620.

2. Rose, *Hegel contra Sociology*, 232.

3. Postone, "Labor and the Logic of Abstraction," 329.

The God that does exist is the god of the workers.

—ERNESTO CARDENAL, 1983[4]

Gillian Rose is much closer to Marx than is often recognized, closer even than she seems to have realized herself. Her summary dismissal of Marx as "Fichtean" in *Hegel contra Sociology* and her relentless and discerning attack on *Marxism* as a culture, plays so well against the bowdlerized Marx of the doctrinaire Left that one can almost forgive readers for believing Rose had succeeded in routing Marx himself. But we should not forget that Rose identified Miss Marple as her exemplar of Kierkegaard's knight of faith, her "singular one." So her attentive readers ought to be attuned to that facetiousness that otherwise allows her true intentions to pass unnoticed. Rose's critique of Marx may not be what, on its face, it appears to be.

Peter Osborne noticed it. In his most recent reflections on Rose, written almost forty years after registering his initial disapproval, Osborne points to the palpable ire Rose showed toward Derrida's *Specters of Marx* in her essay "The Comedy of Hegel and the *Trauerspiel* of Modern Philosophy." Osborne remarks that, in a surprising gesture, after she had in his estimation "shelved" the project of critical Marxism, Rose unleashes a flurry of Marxist orthodoxy against Derrida. She links her reading of the speculative proposition, Hegel's *Geist*, and the triune formation (*Bildung*) of reason to Marx's treatments of commodity fetishism, labor, and class antagonism.[5] Though this treatment of Marx is enough to lead Osborne to reconsider how far he believed Rose had departed from Marx, he nevertheless concludes that she ended up in a place that was incompatible with the Marxist project. But it is interesting to bear this question of Rose's ongoing relation to Marx in mind, in light of her lectures on critical theory and the Frankfurt School, the recordings for which are in Rose's archives at the Sussex library.[6] In her

---

4. In *The Verso Book of Dissent*, 288.

5. See Osborne, "Gillian Rose and Marxism," 58–62.

6. I am grateful to Andrew Brower Latz for sharing with me his transcriptions of the lectures. They have been an invaluable reference for this essay. Any errors in my reading and interpretation of Rose are, of course, my own. The University of Sussex Library houses eleven tape recordings of Rose's lectures in two groups. Six lectures from a 1979 series titled The Frankfurt School:

1. Marxist Modernism. 4159, class R8056.
2. The Politics of Realism: Georg Lukács. 4160, class R8057.
3. The Greatness and Decline of Expressionism: Ernst Bloch. 4161, class R8058.
4. The Battle over Walter Benjamin. 4162, class R8059.

lecture, "Does Marx Have a Method?," for example, Rose states that after writing *Hegel contra Sociology*, she was prompted to reread Marx's whole oeuvre after encountering Braudel's declaration that Marx never used the word *capitalism*.[7] This rereading led her to recognize that her initial critique of Marx needed to be more nuanced, even going so far as to affirm the possibility of reading Marx as exactly the kind of speculative, Socratic thinker she argued in *Hegel contra Sociology* that we need.[8] What, then, given the Rose of *The Broken Middle*, are we to make of Rose's relationship to Marx?

At a most basic, methodological level, Rose shares with Marx an adamant commitment that a critical theory capable of understanding the imbroglio of modern social relations must disclaim any critique mounted from a position outside those relations. Both Marx and Rose understand modern bourgeois social life to be, in fact, created and reproduced through the very positing of such an "outside," and therefore any attempt to move beyond bourgeois social life by leveraging some "pure" position outside those relations is doomed from the start. Instead, the critique of bourgeois society must emerge from within them, through relentless analysis, and as a process of disclosure.

That method, as Rose realized, is perilous because it is equivocal. It is a method that risks misrecognition—by both readers and practitioners. The risk is not just that one's meaning will be misinterpreted. It is that one's standpoint of critique will be mistaken for a timeless and necessary aspect of human life, that the standpoint of critique will not itself be recognized as the primary object of the critique. In Marx's case, labor is the standpoint of critique, which traditional Marxism has mistaken (as I will argue below) for an essential, transcendental dimension of human social life from which to overthrow capital.[9] In Rose's case, the "broken middle," what she calls

---

5. The Dialectic of Enlightenment. 4163, R8060.
6. The Search For Style: Adorno, Kafka or Mann? 4164, R8061.

Five lectures from a multi-lecturer series titled Sociological Theory and Methodology:
1. Introduction to Critical Theory (1986) 7658.
2. The Dispute Over Marx and Weber (1987) 7702.
3. Does Marx Have a Method? (1987) 7703.
4. The Unity of Sociological Thinking (1986) 7812.
5. Simmel, Lukács and German Critical Theory (1982) unnumbered.

7. Rose, "Does Marx Have a Method?"
8. Ibid.
9. The principal statement of this reading was set out in Postone, *Time, Labor, and Social Domination*. But I have also learned from the variations of this reading in Elson, *Value*; and Larsen et al., *Marxism and the Critique of Value*. The latter develops Postone's articulation of the point, while Elson's is distinct from Postone's and has some significant differences from him in detail, though the overall point is consistent.

the "ancient" diremption of law and ethics, is that standpoint of critique, which I want to argue is mistaken by even Rose's most attentive readers as a basic, transhistorical condition of human consciousness and social life from which to mount the continued struggle for the just and rational city.[10]

I call attention to this commonality in Rose and Marx for two reasons. First, on the whole, I intend to take issue in this essay with the view that Rose settled her account with Marx (and the Frankfurt School) with the completion of *Hegel contra Sociology*. Osborne has argued that the distinctively Marxist element of her project—that is, an objective, material critique of social relations—drops out of her work around the time of the publication of *The Broken Middle*, when her work takes a different direction.[11] I am not convinced this is the best way to read Rose's development, but it is a consistent theme, or at least implicit assumption, among both readers sympathetic to Osborne's critique and those, like Rowan Williams, who are not. This interpretation of Rose's development seems to have been adopted by her readers in theology and religious studies,[12] who rarely discuss her critical Marxism and seem to assume it was abandoned.[13] The turn to theology and religion that those among this latter group find amenable, is for her Marxist admirer-critics a clear indication that any sustained focus on commodity fetishism, bourgeois social relations, and talk of the non-reformable revolution has been supplanted. And this seems to be the conclusion of her

10. Vincent Lloyd's essay in this collection makes a similar claim, and can be read as agreeing with John Milbank on this point. See Milbank, "On the Paraethical."

11. Three texts are central to this reading. Osborne, "Hegelian Phenomenology." Osborne revisited his argument thirty-five years later in "Gillian Rose and Marxism." Osborne's latter piece takes into account the detailed and excellent analysis set out in Gorman, "Gillian Rose and the Project of a Critical Marxism."

12. One of the more striking aspects of the reception of Rose's work in religious studies and academic theology is its almost total focus on this later period of her writing. It is true that the early period is not neglected, but it tends to be reduced to a set of general directives against the desire for purity, which is construed as a latent totalitarianism, and commending the virtues of antifoundational reason. See in particular Shanks, *Against Innocence*.

13. Perhaps the best example of this is found in Williams's two essays on Rose. Williams has a profound appreciation for Rose's work, and he is always a close and meticulous reader, but he mentions Marx in these essays only to agree with her dubious criticisms of him in *Hegel contra Sociology* and in doing so to defend her against the Marxist critique levied by Osborne. One does not get the sense from Williams, which Osborne does have, that she identifies her project as a critical form of Marxism. See Williams's engagement with Osborne's critique in Williams, "Between Politics and Philosophy." The summary of Rose's work that appears in Williams's most recent essay on Rose gives a most modest (one might even say evasive) mention of Rose's position on bourgeois property right, and every mention of Marx is negative or dismissive. See Williams, "The Sadness of the King."

religious admirer-critics, too. In good traditional Marxist fashion, these writers no doubt see these theological elements as ideology, while her admirer-critics in religion will tend to see this as a step beyond vulgar Marxist reductionism. I will register my objection to both of these assessments, calling attention to the formative, educative nature of speculative reason and immanent critique in both Marx and Rose.[14] On this basis, I do not think that we read Rose well unless we read her project, from beginning to end, as a critical development and elaboration of Marx. This leads to my second point.

While I believe that we must read Rose from beginning to end as a critical Marxist, I do not believe her later work, her embrace of the *broken middle* and recognition theory, is a successful or even a salutary development of those commitments. That is, I do not think that Rose departed in later work from the core of her critical Marxism, but rather adopted a style and voice that was justly "enraged and invested."[15] Liberalism as the objective ethical reality of bourgeois law and fascist totalitarianism as the political drive to resolve its contradictions[16]—these are Rose's preoccupations. The fact that the existential and ethical dimensions of this reality take center stage in the later work only underscores the fact that these issues had a decisive claim on her life and that she believed they constituted the crucial moral questions of modern politics and social life. It is the ethical questions of how we are to understand ourselves as moral agents and of what we are to do within the "iron cage" of bourgeois law and the liberal state that take center stage.[17]

This is how I believe we should read Rose's later work. Nevertheless, I do not think her answers—the anxiety of beginning, the equivocation of the ethical, and the agon of authorship—are adequate, not simply for moving beyond those conditions (as Osborne and Gorman convincingly argue), but as a critical analysis of that condition. In this respect, I think her Marxist critics are right, though not quite for the reasons they give for their conclusions. I will argue, instead, that analysis of the broken middle and the ethics of mutual recognition are inadequate because of, ironically, an equivocation that Rose makes between the standpoint and object of critique when, in her later work, she applies commodity fetishism to ethical reasoning. It is not that Rose is guilty of the charge she levies at Adorno, that he is guilty of

14. This is a reading made by Nigel Tubbs and developed in this collection by Rebekah Howes. See Tubbs, "Gillian Rose and Education."

15. Rose, *Mourning Becomes the Law*, 75.

16. Rose identifies these elements in *The Broken Middle*, xi. The connection between liberalism and fascism is developed by Landa, *The Apprentice's Sorcerer*.

17. See Max Weber, *The Protestant Ethic and the Spirit of Capitalism*.

standing outside the dialectic and not submitting himself to it. But it is to say that at the crux of her appeals to the ethical significance of the broken middle is an assumption that concrete human labor is "outside" the contradiction of law and ethics, and thus the resolute occupation of the brokenness of the middle is the only plausible way to act to disrupt the compulsion to an abstract and mystifying form of social mediation. I will argue that it is this misunderstanding of concrete labor that breeds the plausible misrecognition of Rose's project as cosmopolitan or end-of-history liberalism, rather than a unique critical Marxism that aspires to performatively enact a non-reformable revolution within critical social theory.

What I hope to show is that in order to understand Rose's project as a whole we must recognize that she maintains a positive relationship, if not to *Marxism*, then to Marx himself. But I will also argue, at the close of the essay, that the necessary corollary to this conclusion is that we must do the same for Rose's turn to theology. By correcting her reading of the role of concrete labor in the commodity fetish we can also clarify the status and value of theology in her later work, such that theology and Marx, together, can be recognized as integral to her project as a whole.

Rose and Critical Theory

Most scholarship on Rose acknowledges an important shift in her thinking during the decade between *Dialectic of Nihilism* (1983) and *The Broken Middle* (1992). *The Melancholy Science* (1979) and *Hegel contra Social Theory* (1981) set out a project of critical Marxism built on Hegel's speculative reason rather than Neo-Kantian dualism, and *Dialectic of Nihilism* advanced that claim by arguing for the unrecognized jurisprudential determination and essence of all critical philosophy. But although Rose makes it explicit that she understands *The Broken Middle* as a development of the arguments of *Hegel contra Sociology* and *Dialectic of Nihilism*,[18] she also makes a clear turn toward what Tony Gorman describes as a subjective "inwardness and an ethic of singularity"[19] that is a strong contrast to the phenomenology of social relations set out in the first three books. That same focus on inwardness and ethics continues in the essays collected in *Judaism and Modernity* (1993) and the posthumous publications *Mourning Becomes the Law* (1996), *Love's Work* (1997), and *Paradiso* (1999).

Her early project is so rich that it is worth rehearsing its major elements. Osborne recognized the extraordinary ambition of the project quite

---

18. See in the introduction to *The Broken Middle*, xiv–xv
19. Gorman, "Gillian Rose and the Project of a Critical Marxism," 25.

early, in his review essay of *Hegel contra Sociology*, noting that Rose was calling for a wholesale reformulation, root and branch, of the entire philosophical foundations of critical theory. She wanted to identify the impasse that modern social theory had encountered and locate its cause with its unchallenged neo-Kantian premises. By contrast, Hegelian speculative reason supplied a different critical frame, one that did not exploit but disrupted the various binaries of ideal/real, validity/value, necessity/freedom, theory/practical upon which social theory was erected, and did so by comprehending them as inflections of bourgeois law. Rose argued that these binaries were mistaken for transcendental conditions of consciousness and social life, but they were, in fact, effects produced by the social internalization of the distinction in Roman private law between persons (*persona*), who were owners of property, and things (*res*) that are owned.[20] The neo-Kantian foundations of social theory did not just presume this distinction, but its various theories served to conceal recognition of that fact. As a result, social theory became an instrument for the reproduction of bourgeois law. In this respect, as Osborne put it, Rose was developing "an Hegelian or 'philosophical' equivalent to Marxian critique."[21] And Rose was peculiar among critical theorists in that she focused on—perhaps indebted to her Jewish heritage—the unrecognized role that law and jurisprudence played in modern philosophy, politics, and social theory. She put that theme to work with great explanatory power in *Dialectic of Nihilism*, where she argues that the "Nietzscheanism" of poststructuralist arguments is in truth an unrecognized expression of the bourgeois legal form. That argument became the basis for the role that law played throughout the work that followed.

Osborne argues that her initial project of a critical Marxism was from the outset riven by a tension. On the one hand, there was the role that Rose saw for Hegelian speculative thought as a critique of society, which was phenomenological in form, and therefore focused on consciousness. In that work, she was able to break open the closed binary form of neo-Kantian reason, and expose it to its social determination. The trouble, Osborne argued, was that Rose made the same mistake for which she chastises Lukács, that of believing a change in consciousness is a sufficient condition for social transformation, for revolution.[22]

Rose wanted to deploy the immanent phenomenological critique to hamstring our capacity for producing abstract illusions that conceal the real

---

20. For Rose's presentation of this process of internalizing oppositions as the status of legal persons, see *Mourning Becomes the Law*, 73.
21. Osborne, "Gillian Rose and the Project of a Critical Marxism," 12.
22. See ibid., 59–60; and Rose, *Hegel contra Sociology*, 229–35.

contradictions of social life. Of particular importance about these illusions was not just that they are deceptive, but that they serve as an engine for reproducing our social contradictions, even when we think we are acting in opposition to them. Rose's prime example here is Lukács, who does not realize that his revolutionary proletariat functions as a regulative ideal (*Sollen*). On the one hand, he locates the proletariat's revolutionary potential in a change in their consciousness and not in the social relations that determine that consciousness. On the other hand, inasmuch as he imagines the proletariat mending the broken mediation of labor and culture, his very ideal of proletariat as the universal subject of history is a product of bourgeois social life, which it actually works to reproduce through its opposition to it. Rose wants to deploy Hegel's speculative reason in a way that disrupts this tendency to reproduce illusion, a way that compels social theory to remain integral to the concrete life that bourgeois social life mystifies. Yet, Osborne argues, no matter how successful that phenomenological analysis is, it too does its work within abstract consciousness and so cannot provide a political basis for moving beyond bourgeois social relations, even though it can reveal the truth about those relations.

While this is an understandable, and on the whole obligatory, objection for an orthodox Marxist to make, it is too prejudicial. Rose is working in the tradition of the Frankfurt School, and this means that her most fundamental concern is salvaging Marx by rethinking him within historical conditions that seem to have disproven traditional Marxism. Those conditions were, for the Frankfurt School, the dissolution of the Second International and the transformation of industrial capitalism into a bureaucratic structure sustained by the State.[23] Weber's "iron cage" of legal-rational authority was axiomatic for the Frankfurt School's assessment of the reality of these conditions, and they sought to expand Marx's analysis beyond the conditions of industrial capitalism within which he wrote, and into the realm of culture itself.[24] They developed a renewed critique of capital's bureaucratic, state organization, and conceived of commodity fetishism as a cultural force, showing how capital's contradictions and crises formed human subjectivity, art, and ethical action.[25]

---

23. See Postone's discussions in "The Subject and Social Theory."
24. Ibid., 66.
25. Ibid., 64–67. Postone has also noted that one of the primary motivations for developing this focus on the cultural and subjective dimensions of the commodity form was to shore up Marxist analysis and combat the turn toward existentialism and phenomenology many intellectuals made during the middle of the twentieth century, showing that these trajectories were not only unnecessary to a substantive account of individuality and culture but also that they were illusory.

With this cultural interpretation of capital as a social form, and not just as an objective condition of class antagonism, property relations, and market distribution, then we can recognize that the contradictions endemic to labor and production permeate the whole of social life. From this standpoint, traditional Marxist analysis, which is limited to industrial production and market distribution, can be recognized as playing a key role in obscuring the engine of capitalism and its social mediation, rather than illuminating them.[26] Adorno, Benjamin, Bloch, and Brecht, for example, all explored the nuances of this phenomenon in aesthetic theory, where forms of art, like Expressionism, which were developed to oppose bourgeois life, could be analyzed to show that they are complicit effects of bourgeois life.[27] Rose rehearses this history in *The Melancholy Science* and her lectures on critical theory show that she gave it special importance, spending a good deal of time outlining where they identified the ethical and theoretical deadlock.[28] In doing so, Rose was linking their work with her reading of Hegel, namely, that all modern, bourgeois law is reducible to subjective positing, a *Sollen*,[29] As such, every attempt to transform our social relations will, without recognizing, addressing, and undermining this fact, simply reproduce the abstract form of bourgeois social mediation.[30]

Rose's project set out to theorize, confront, and overcome this problem.[31] And this problem is made up of a far more snarled set of issues than Osborne's and Tony Gorman's objections allow. Gorman summaries the complaint, and Osborne concurs, that Rose's own strategy for subverting these conditions does not have sufficient grasp of the "difference between the comprehension of the social in phenomenological reflection and its theorization by the critique of political economy."[32] But that objection does not address the fundamental problem that Rose is concerned with: the ethical imperative of how to act, given the impasse between thought and action

26. See Postone, "Rethinking Marx's Critical Theory."

27. Rose, "The Politics of Realism: Georg Lukács"; Rose, "The Greatness and Decline of Expressionism: Ernst Bloch."

28. Ibid.

29. See *Broken Middle*, xi.

30. *Hegel contra Sociology*, 229–35.

31. The tendency to overlook this is evident in Milbank's curious assessment that Rose subscribed to the "end of history thesis," which may in a different light suggest something about the influence that Frankfurt School pessimism had on her. Nevertheless, Milbank does not take seriously enough the extent to which Rose's entire project, from beginning to end, can be read as at root a rejoinder to that pessimism, a continuation of the Frankfurt School's project as a direct repudiation of its failures.

32. Gorman, "Gillian Rose and the Project of a Critical Marxism," 36n40, quoted in Osborne, "Gillian Rose and Marxism," 60.

that is created by bourgeois social relations.[33] If, in other words, traditional Marxist analysis of capital's contradictions is not adequate to account for the sociocultural formations that continue to occlude comprehension of those contradictions, then Rose is neither simply stuck within phenomenology nor failing to attain a critique of political economy, but establishing the sine qua non for any transformative ethical act within these particular social determinations. Rose is analyzing the ethical question of how to act, of what to do, under these conditions, which neither phenomenology nor the critique of political economy alone can supply.

I am arguing that we cannot grasp the full ethical force of Rose's concept of the *broken middle*, much less the role she gives to recognition theory, unless we see both as elaborations of her original project of critical Marxism. These concepts develop out of her use of Marxist categories and analyses, and are consistent with her attempt to find a more adequate response to the predicament the Frankfurt School had identified. In the next section, I will carry this argument for continuity forward by looking in some detail at Rose's treatment of the commodity fetish. I will suggest that her later work on the broken middle and recognition theory is a repetition of the critique of commodity fetishism in another form and serves as an ethical response to the cultural deadlock, the diremption of law and ethics, that she understands to be the cornerstone of the commodity form. On the basis of how she interprets the commodity fetish we will be in a better position to identify why Rose's ethical proposals remain inadequate, as Osborne and Gorman are right to claim, but why her turn to political theology is exactly the right and indispensable supplement to the entire critical Marxist project.

The Commodity Fetish

Rose agrees with the strategy Lukács set out in "Reification and the Consciousness of the Proletariat," which treated the commodity fetish as the heart of fragmented social mediation and subjective domination.[34] Com-

---

33. That said, Osborne's and Gorman's critique of Williams's defense of Rose against this charge of failing to register the difference between phenomenology and the critique of political economy certainly applies to Williams's own reading of Rose and recognition theory in general.

34. Rose is very clear to call attention in *Hegel contra Sociology* to the fact that Lukács made this connection between Marx and sociology from Georg Simmel's *The Philosophy of Money*, which treats money in the context of a sociology of culture. It was through Simmel that Lukács discovered Marx, who became a source of the Frankfurt School's whole project, in some sense, and especially the critiques of Lukács that developed in Adorno.

modity fetishism recurs throughout Rose's body of work.[35] In *Hegel Contra Sociology*, for example, Rose states how central she takes the idea of commodity fetishism to be: "This is why the theory of commodity fetishism, the presentation of a contradiction between substance and subject, remains more impressive than any abstract statements about the relation between theory and practice or between capitalist crisis and the formation of revolutionary consciousness. It acknowledges actuality and its misrepresentation as consciousness."[36] In her lecture "Does Marx Have a Method?," she links the critique of the commodity fetish to her own treatment of speculative reason.[37] Marx can be read, she says, not just as a dogmatic or instrumental dialectician, but as a speculative, Socratic thinker, who leads abstract consciousness from its immediate experience to awareness of how it has been formed by social realities it was previously unaware of, and finally to a comprehension of those social conditions. We can see this, she says, in the fact that Marx begins with the reality of commodities and then "traces the path of their formation back to their origin in specific social relations between people."[38] Once this is done, he then retraces "the paths from the origin of our immediate experience by showing that people treat themselves and others as commodities."[39] The result is that he makes our "familiar immediate experience unfamiliar and makes us aware how deeply we have accepted this strange familiarity."[40]

Rose draws a deep, structural connection between commodity fetishism, bourgeois law, and Roman private law. The distinction between person (*persona*) and thing (*res*) operative within the commodity form is itself jurisprudential, originating in Roman private law. In Roman private law, *persons* are defined as agents with the right to own property, even if what is owned happens to be a human being.[41] In this regard, the commodity form

35. The later lectures (given in 1979 and 1986–1987) give a good portrait of any development in her readings of figures between *Dialectic of Nihilism* and *The Broken Middle*.
36. Rose, *Hegel contra Sociology*, 233.
37. Rose, "Does Marx Have a Method?"
38. Ibid.
39. Ibid.
40. Ibid.
41. In a lecture dated 1982 and collected with the series entitled Sociological Theory and Methodology, she makes sure to note that Marx and Weber would have studied Roman law in detail as undergraduates and "were very well aware that the distinction between persons and things is a distinction from Roman law" (ibid.). She then emphasizes the point about naturalization of immediate experience by calling attention to the fact that almost everyone attending the lecture would have been a person according to Roman law, none of the women and none of the men with living fathers.

is first of all a matter of law, an effect of a certain kind of jurisprudence. Rose argues that this legal distinction is the condition of possibility for the commodity, wage, or money forms to arise in the modern ways they do because bourgeois law is the universalization of this otherwise contingent legal category of Roman personhood.[42] Bourgeois law universalizes the Roman notion of legal personhood. When it does, it sets a contradiction as the cornerstone of modern society: every member of society has the inherent right to except his [sic] person and property from the universal society, but it is only his participation in universal society that secures the right to that exception.[43] This is the modern expression of the diremption of law (substance) and ethics (subject), which produces the "necessary illusions" (Adorno) of commodity fetishism.

Rose understands the commodity fetish to arise out of a specific legal form, then, but how does she understand it to work? In "Does Marx Have a Method?," she follows Lukács in thinking it in terms of Marx's distinction between concrete and abstract labor, or the objectification (reification) or concrete labor. Exchange, she says, takes place "because the concrete labor that went into the commodity (e.g., taking the apple from the tree) is transformed into labour in the abstract, the socially necessary labour time for its production, or value as such. This value, which appears in exchange, seems to be a natural property of the commodity, like its taste, but is the expression of the social relations between people."[44] It is important for my purposes here to note that Rose understands Marx to analyze the commodity as arising out of "the social relations between people, concrete labour," while "social or universal relations between things are lived as the material or concrete relations between people."[45] It is our "concrete labor," she says, that is reified (*thing-ified*, objectified), making it buyable and sellable as an abstract quantity (value). When concrete labor is objectified in this way, we are all diremped, living lives in which we are at one and the same time both persons and things—personal owners of property and things to be bought and sold—in the objective substance of social life.[46]

According to Rose, the heart of commodity fetishism is that "[p]eople treat concrete human labour as if it were a thing.... [T]his way of treating real, social concrete relations as if they were things would prevent people

42. Ibid.
43. See Williams, "The Sadness of the King," 24. *Dialectic of Nihilism*, 11–24.
44. Rose, "Does Marx Have a Method?"
45. Ibid.
46. Ibid.

from really understanding the structure of capitalism."[47] On Rose's reading of Marx, the most important dimension of the commodity is the transformation of qualitative social activity of labor into an abstract, formal, and quantitative equality between goods—formal in the same way that persons are in bourgeois law—that hides the real inequality between labor and capital.[48] Rose emphasizes that this objectification of concrete labor happens not just in production and distribution of goods but in circulation and consumption as well, which means that it is just as much a process of cultural formation.[49]

Tony Gorman's analysis of Rose's reading of Lukács and Adorno on the commodity fetish is invaluable. He sheds a great deal of light on why Rose concludes *Hegel contra Sociology* as she does, based on how she positions herself in relation to the differences between these two thinkers. Gorman points out that Rose agrees with Adorno that Lukács's view of labor is nostalgic for an illusory "harmony" of precapitalist forms of production[50] and that Lukács retains a residual idealism in the link he draws between social transformation and the development of proletarian consciousness.[51] Nevertheless, Gorman notes, Rose agrees with Lukács, as I noted above, that the commodity fetish arises in the abstract objectification of concrete labor, and is not primarily, as Adorno argued, a matter of use-versus exchange value.[52] On this basis alone, Gorman calls Rose's position "neo-Lukácsian."[53]

It is this focus on concrete labor, and the direct connection Rose understands it to have to law and sociality, that, I argue, she is leveraging in the later work. For example, by invoking the "single one" who suspends the law (Kierkegaard) and thereby effects a transvaluation of value (Nietzsche), Rose is not turning in a facile way from objective materiality into subjective

---

47. Rose, "The Dispute over Marx and Weber."

48. Postone characterizes the difference between the abstract and concrete dimensions of labor in these quantitative and qualitative terms. See Postone, "Labor and the Logic of Abstraction," 327.

49. Rose, "Simmel, Lukacs, and German Critical Theory." Rose shows in this lecture that she recognizes a clear distinction between works like *The German Ideology* and *The Communist Manifesto*, which rely upon a base/superstructure analysis of the labor-capital relation, and the position that Marx took from the time of the *Grundrisse*. Rose further recognizes that Marx's position develops from the *Grundrisse*, which begins with the money form, to *Capital*, which unfolds the critique of capital from the commodity form.

50. This is also true of Milbank and Williams

51. Gorman, "Gillian Rose and the Project of a Critical Marxism," 26.

52. Ibid.

53. Ibid.

interiority.[54] The situation is much more complex, because, under the conditions of the commodity, on Rose's read, it is only the single one who can disclose the qualitative actuality of concrete labor—the work of love—beyond abstract value. The single one suspends the law of abstract equality, and thus his/her labor can appear as a noncommodity, and s/he lives as a nonreified person, in excess of the contradictions of bourgeois social life.

Where is it that this reading runs aground?

Lukács and Postone: Rethinking the Link between Labor and Value

I want to suggest that the problem with Rose's neo-Lukácian interpretation of the commodity fetish is that it requires her to treat labor as a natural, transhistorical reality of human life and experience. It is true that it is a common reading of Marx to take labor as an essential aspect of human life, but it is peculiar for Rose not to submit that notion to critical analysis. Rose never once considers that the way she deploys concrete labor is itself an illusion of bourgeois sociality. This is how Moishe Postone, the political economist and philosopher, has argued we are to interpret Marx's writings from the *Grundrisse*, forward. Postone argues that Marx never considers the commodity in its abstract dimension alone, but always "analyzes [it] as both abstract and concrete."[55] Contrary to Rose's Lukacsian reading, concrete labor and abstract labor are the two inseparable aspects of the commodity form.[56] Though the distinction may appear subtle, it has quite important consequences given the prevalence of classical Marxist and Lukácian readings of *Capital*. Where Rose, with classical Marxism and Lukács, locates the fragmentation of social mediation in the objective, social, and cultural misrepresentation (substance) of concrete human labor (subject), Marx identifies abstract and concrete labor (subject) as the constitutive aspect of the proletariat, which produces and reproduces capital as a totality (substance), thus creating the distinctively modern form of domination and unfreedom.[57] The commodity, then, is not, on this interpretation, a distorted objectification of concrete labor, but the material embodiment of the contradiction of the universal (value) and particular (labor), or law/substance

54. Ibid., 25.

55. Postone, "The Subject and Social Theory," 78. See Joseph Lough's essay in this collection for a more detailed recounting of this reading of Marx's body of work and development.

56. Postone, "The Subject and Social Theory," 78.

57. Ibid. See Rose's discussion of Simmel and Lukács in *Hegel contra Sociology*.

and ethics/subject, in our social relations. A commodity does not just come into existence as an objectification of labor but is constituted as the expression of the contradiction between abstract and concrete labor. This means that the commodity is an inherently unstable, yet profoundly dynamic expression of bourgeois life and law. Capital, in turn, is the commodity in its dynamic circulation through those social relations.[58] And labor is the means by which the commodity is produced and reproduced (concrete labor), as well as the human activity that mediates the commodity's movement through society (abstract labor).[59]

Postone's argument is that this distinction between concrete and abstract labor is not a description of a timeless human metabolic activity of transforming nature, but is a contingent reality that only exists in capitalism, where this contradiction between abstract and concrete labor replaces all other forms of mediation, like kinship or feudalism, which have existed in the past.[60] In this account, it is not that objectification deforms labor and its products, but that both abstract and concrete labor together constitute the reality of the commodity as an object and form of dynamic social mediation. In its dynamic movement, the commodity perpetually transforms social life, but in a way that "reconstitute[s]... its own fundamental condition as an unchanging feature of social life .... The historical dynamic of capitalism ceaselessly generates what is 'new,' while regenerating what is the 'same.' This dynamic both generates the possibility of another organization of social life and yet hinders that possibility from being realized."[61] It is within this closed circuit—which Rose was right to recognize with Hegel, as the problem of reflection—that the value labor produces becomes self-valorizing, taking on a life of its own as it moves through society. Labor is compelled, dominated even, by the very value that it produces. Labor must reproduce that value at increasingly accelerated rates of efficiency and growth, which become not only impossible for labor alone to sustain, but which have the effect of rendering labor itself obsolete in the reproduction of value. Lukács got the matter backwards. Lukács looks forward to a day where subjective labor and objective culture will be reconciled in a universal proletarian culture. But, according to Postone, Marx looks forward to a day when proletarian labor is abolished altogether as the medium of capital's self-reproduction.

58. Postone, "The Subject and Social Theory," 76.
59. Ibid. See Postone, "Anti-Semitism."
60. Postone, "Rethinking Marx (in a Post-Marxist World)." http://www.obeco-online.org/mpt.htm.
61. Postone, "The Subject and Social Theory," 79.

Capital's self-valorization also has important implications for thinking the connection between the commodity fetish and Hegelian speculative reason and the Absolute. The most important point is that capital is, in its movement and self-identity, identical to Hegel's *Geist*.[62] The Absolute here is not Lukács's proletariat, but capital itself. I have pointed to the fact that Rose's essay "The Comedy of Hegel and the *Trauerspiel* of Modern Philosophy" gives a more nuanced and attentive reading of Marx than *Hegel contra Sociology*, and is also the text in which she link commodity fetishism and Hegel's *Geist*. The objection she levies against Derrida is that he has "forgotten Marx's materialism and Hegel's *Logic*, on which Marx's account of commodity fetishism depends."[63] She summarizes:

> Without positing a suprasystemic origin, Marx expounds the inequality between those who sell their labour-power as a thing, as a commodity, and those who own the means of production. It is this discrepancy between the formal equality of the wage-contract (and equally of the form of money) and the substantial inequality of the parties to the contract that initiates the exposition of the capital/wage-labour relationship. The theory of commodity fetishism serves to explain the way this dynamic inequality generates further social and political forms which systematically obscure the structure and workings of the relationship. Marx's exposition draws on Hegel's logic of illusion, according to which relations between apparently independent determinations can be seen as internally generated relations. This is the measure of Marx's materialism; it is what he means by a definite social relation."[64]

This passage also displays the brilliance of her jurisprudential inflection of the commodity fetish. She underscores the contractual nature of wage labor, which produces a formal equality between labor and capital, that conceals and preserves the concrete social inequality that persists in actuality. One can also see from the quotation another instance of Rose focusing on the objectification of concrete labor, the abstract moment in which labor is transformed into a *thing* that is bought and sold. That moment, then, is the cornerstone for various other deformations of social life.

Later in the essay she connects these other social deformations to recognition theory:

---

62. Postone, "Rethinking Marx's Critical Theory," 41.
63. Rose, *Mourning Becomes the Law*, 67.
64. Ibid., 67–68.

> Now all this requires detailed exposition: I could show how struggle for recognition between lord and bondsman issues in the education of the bondsman through his experience of fear both of the absolute master—death—and of the relative master—the lord. The bondsman is able to overcome both kinds of fear by risking his life and by working, by acknowledging the plasticity of the world and hence the otherness of the lord, of matter, of himself, while the lord only discovers his dependence on the bondsman. The outcome of this is not, however, the triumph of the bondsman (nor the working class in its relation to the bourgeoisie, as has been erroneously extrapolated to Marx) but *the internalization of the struggle* between lord and bondsman in *the status of the legal person*. Individuals, defined abstractly as legal persons, lose their relation to desire, work, and otherness, their own and that of others. Legal persons understand themselves to be confronting 'the world' in unstable attempts to maintain a stoical or skeptical relation to it, when 'the world' has itself been compacted and projected out of the misrecognition of work, desire and engaged otherness. This alienation of 'the world' and subsequent abjection of the self result in the unhappy consciousness.[65]

Notice, first, that Rose takes issue here with the classical Marxist reading. The struggle between capital and labor does not lead to the inevitable triumph of labor, contra Lukács, but to the subjective internalization of legal personhood. The shape this takes is misrecognition—not just of the world, but of the concrete, qualitative dimensions of life: they "lose their relation to desire, work [concrete labor], and otherness, their own and that of others," which is their unhappiness. The fetishism, the misrecognition, is conceived as an illusion arising from the abstract misrepresentation of the concrete (desire, work, otherness). Here we can see the persistence of Rose's critical Marxism. The problem lies in the distribution of labor's products, a distribution that separates them from desire, work, and relation to others. And misrecognition is just another name for the illusions the commodity produces:

> [M]y relation to myself is mediated by what I recognize or refuse to recognize in your relation to yourself; while your self-relation depends on what you recognize of my relation to myself. *We are both equally enraged and invested*, and to fix our relation in domination or dependence is unstable and reversible, to fix it as "the world" is to attempt to avoid these reverses. All dualist

---

65. Ibid., 73.

relations to "the other," to "the world" are attempts to quieten and deny the broken middle, the third term which arises out of misrecognition of desire, of work, or my and of your self-relation mediated by the relation of the other.[66]

This connection between the commodity fetish and misrecognition gives us an important insight into how Rose's later development continues her critical Marxism. The ethical "turn" that appears in *The Broken Middle* is an attempt to articulate a form of resistance to the objectification, the commodification, of desire, work, and otherness. The refusal to mend the middle is a straightforward refusal to cooperate with the commodity's illusions, and it does so through what can be seen in the terms of *Hegel contra Sociology* as a revolutionary standpoint—that is, the standpoint of concrete labor. All of Rose's work from *The Broken Middle* forward can be interpreted as the articulation of this revolutionary standpoint of enunciating desire, labor, love, otherness in a way that is non-reformable, or, what amounts to the same thing, *non-commodifiable, non-objectifiable*. Seen from this vantage, there is no other way to understand what Rose is doing except a critical Marxism, or even a Marxism by another name.

Yet, as important and significant an insight that I think this is, the re-reading of Marx that I am presenting would propose making an even more thoroughgoing turning of the critical screw. My argument is that Rose's mistake, her own misrecognition in this critical moment, lies in not submitting labor itself to the dialectic. She continues at least to construe concrete labor, because it is mistaken for a transhistorical quality of humanity, as a site outside of commodification, outside the abstract deformation. If this site can be leveraged in a way that cannot be re-formed as a commodity, then we have identified a site of revolutionary disruption of the cultural process by which capital is reproduced. But on the rereading of Marx that I have proposed as a necessary supplement, there is no such site within the standpoint of labor, even so-called concrete labor. The commodity is not simply an abstract objectification, or quantification, that alienates it from the concrete, qualitative social process; it is not just the transformation of the social process of labor into a *thing* to be sold and bought. Both the concrete and abstract aspects of the commodity are the effect of a much more fundamental diremption produced and reproduced by labor's role as mediator of our social relations.

Misrecognition looks quite different when labor becomes the object of critique, rather than the standpoint of resistance. First, it means that the comedy of misrecognition cannot be understood as a transcendental aspect of consciousness, it cannot be naturalized. Misrecognition is the social effect

---

66. Rose, *Mourning Becomes the Law*, 74–75

of commodification on consciousness. This also means that we ought to recognize—and I acknowledge that this point is a strong misreading of Rose—that the broken middle itself is the true object of Rose's critical project, not its standpoint. Misrecognition is not comedic because we come to affirm, or fix, misrecognition as a transcendental aspect of all self-consciousness (which is how, for example, Williams's focus on self-dispossession construes it), but because it is the *broken middle* as a concept that makes the social determination of misrecognition knowable as contingent. Misrecognition can only be comedic, rather than tragic, if it can be comprehended, known, as produced by the commodity, and in being known, it can be transformed. As such, the broken middle is not a condition to be affirmed but one to be abolished. This is why we must insist that the ethical orientation of Rose's later project, precisely because it is a response to the double bind produced by the commodity fetish, is not a retreat from objective social critique (as Osborne and Gorman argue), nor is it a practical method for managing the timeless tendency of consciousness to misrecognize ourselves, the world, and one another. Rather, we must understand the ethical dimension of her later project as forcing a confrontation with the reality of commodification and the questions, What are we to do? and How are we to act, within these conditions? She wanted that anxiety of beginning, the equivocation of the middle, and the agon of authorship to be ways of acting that forbade our acts from reproducing the conditions that separated law from ethics. In Gorman's language, this is how Rose sought not just to "exploit the internal disparity between bourgeois society and its ideals" but also to criticize "the present from the standpoint of the future immanent within it." It is interpreting the broken middle as the standpoint of her project that prevents us from recognizing how this immanent future is present in Rose's project.[67]

67. Milbank is better here than Gorman or Williams. Gorman notes that Rose is at her most Adornian at just the point that her speculative account of misrecognition refuses to name a positive alternative beyond the diremption of law and ethics. But John Milbank offers a compelling alternative reading. Milbank sees Rose rejecting Adorno's refusal to give any positive content to alterity. As he puts it, commenting on the concluding sentence of *The Broken Middle*, which reads, "The more the middle is dirempted, the more it becomes sacred in ways that configure its further diremption":

> It is no use reading this sentence (as it is often so read) as if it were merely an ethical, or even a negatively theological, injunction to refrain from construing holy middles, since this will only further the damage of brokenness. For Rose is rather saying that, just because dynamic temporal mediation remains constitutively necessary to any human society . . . and yet under the defining circumstances of modernity is in a sense impossible, the "holy" construal of the middle remains inevitable, though deluded. If the undeceived can, for her, still nonetheless remains realistically hopeful of some relative repair (and

On all of these points, I see great value in Rose's project and want to defend it against any reading, Marxist or religious, that would eliminate its critical Marxist element. However, that does not mean that I believe she succeeded in conceiving a way of thinking and acting that confounds commodification, and my critiques are levied at this question.

This leads me to another point. I have argued, drawing on the work of Moishe Postone, that the problem of commodity fetishism is not about the objectification of concrete labor, but the fact that labor mediates all social relations in capitalist society, that all other forms of relation are subordinated to labor. Rose may not unambiguously affirm the broken middle as the standpoint of critique, but she does unambiguously affirm concrete labor as that standpoint. Inasmuch as she bestows this status on concrete labor, the formation (*Bildung*) in speculative reason cannot do the work she requires it to do. In other words, the comedy of misrecognition that she commends, in which we come to know the world not just in spite of our failures but through them, must itself be another instance of illusion. What she understands as an education for consciousness from the standpoint of concrete labor is itself the very process by which the commodity moves through society and reproduces itself—that is, it is the dynamic movement of capital's self-valorization as the subject-object of modern social life. This is the pathos of Rose's project, and one might even say its tragedy. When she holds out "the struggle to recognize" as the key to a formation of consciousness that cannot itself be re-formed into commodification, objectification, the very process by which she defines that movement—"to know, and still to misknow, and yet to grow"—remains a form of labor ("love's work"), and thus amounts to a description of the destructive innovation, the deterritorization, by which capital reproduces itself.

This different reading of Marx yields a different analysis of law's diremption from ethics. Their separation is neither exhaustively analyzed as a historically contingent expression of bourgeois property right nor as a particular inflection of the metaphysical relation of the ideal and real. Rather,

---

she sometimes appears to speak in such terms) then it is still not clear what historical-ontological grounds she has left open to legitimate even such a meager possibility.

Milbank continues: "The only serious and responsible resistance to this process must be to understand it and to suffer it, and to mourn and so redeem in mere imagination its continued ravages. A counter-community of the genuinely mournful would then seem to be the minimum possibility of actual and fully authentic resistance." Milbank, "On the Paraethical: Gillian Rose and Political Nihilism," 75, 79. But, if such a community is a possibility, it must arise concretely from this mourning, lest it be another surreptitious totalitarianism, a form of arbitrary domination, a form of unfreedom and violence.

the most basic analysis of that separation will comprehend the split between law and ethics as what social relations look like when labor is their medium. Rose's revival of Hegelian speculative reason can subvert the tendency to totality that we see in all those modes of thought that uncritically collude with the objectifying or abstract aspect of the commodity by seeking to mend the middle. But the gesture of keeping the middle open, and seeking to disrupt the objectifying moment from the standpoint of concrete labor—this is simply to celebrate capital's engine of innovation. The triune structure of Rose's speculative reason can break open the unmediated, mutual exclusions that define neo-Kantian forms of thought, but it cannot grasp on its own terms that the totality is not realized primarily through the mending of the middle, but through the act—the labor, that is—that keeps it perpetually open. That is the moment where Hegel's comedy redounds as tragedy, but it is Marx who enables us to know it. In the concluding section, I will further elaborate on the interpretation and critique of Rose that I have developed here to show how it illuminates and lends a greater coherence to the role of political theology in her later project.

The Turn to Theology

It is frightening to consider the diligence with which theologians avoid discussion, not so much of the material implications of their commitments, but of the material determinations of them. Despite the massive influence that we have seen in theology and religious studies of the turn to language and culture in the last thirty years, there has been little consideration of the social, historical, and material determinations of theological concepts and religious practices. The fear, of course, is that talk of such determinations is tantamount to a crude materialist reductionism. But this does not need to be the case. We can speak with coherence about the material conditions that determine theological and religious concepts, as well as the material consequences of those concepts, without presupposing a materialist metaphysics. And yet, it is rare that theologians and religious scholars discuss these implications, at least in terms of their explicit political and economic consequences.[68]

68. Rowan Williams and Kathryn Tanner are not just the exceptions that prove the rule but are not even exceptions. They discuss how we might think about economic activity, for example, in the light of theological thinking and religious practice. But this is not quite what I mean. I am talking instead about the way in which even that way of thinking about theology and religious practice is an iteration of distinct social relations, and its ideas will have specific consequences for those relations. In this respect, theological ideas and reflection on religious practice in general remain abstract.

I have argued that we cannot understand Rose's project except as a critical Marxism, and I hope to have shown that an immanent critique of labor, like that developed in Postone's rereading of Marx, is a necessary supplement to that project. On the one hand, this reading calls into question the fundamental assumptions about the commodity form that lead to Rose's articulation of the broken middle and her theory of *Geist* as the comedic drama of misrecognition. On the other hand, seeing this enables us to carry forward Rose's initial project of critical Marxism in a new key. What Rose gained from reconstructing critical theory on Hegel, rather than neo-Kantianism, can now be supplemented once again with a rereading of Marx. We can see Marx as a speculative thinker in Rose's sense, but one who is able to supply the critique of political economy that Rose's interpretation of the commodity fetish lacked. It is on this basis that we can rehabilitate Rose's ethical aim to act—not from the standpoint of labor with the broken middle as the object of critique, but with labor itself as the object of critique—in such a way that this immanent future becomes an intuition, a concrete actuality for thought, no mere abstract *Sollen*.

But what does such an act look like if the aim is not (as Rose thought) to make concrete labor thinkable, but instead to think a social relation that is not mediated by labor? It is in response to this question that I want to return to my initial remark that my aim in this essay is not just to retrieve Marx within Rose's work but also to argue that this cannot be done apart from her turn to theology and religion. Just as Rose needs a Marxian supplement for her ethics, so does that supplement require theology or religion. I will conclude by offering three brief points in support of that claim.

First, as many thinkers who engage the intersection of Rose's work with critical theory have noted, there is no unequivocal application of her ideas to religion or religion to her ideas. As she noted in *Hegel contra Sociology*, the speculative identity of the modern state (law) and religion (ethics) is the fundamental proposition upon which to base the retrieval of Hegel for social theory. As she states, our concept of the absolute (God) is our understanding of our own freedom. Religion mends the diremption of law and ethics in another, transcendental world, and thereby reinforces the domination and unfreedom in this world. Conversely, the state seeks to impose its concept of law on the social world in order to unify law and ethics in this world, but it does so by suppressing difference and the moment of ethical critique. Human freedom is, then, bound or liberated based on the concept

---

In this respect, theological ideas and reflection on religious practice in general remain abstract, and remain subject to the critique of bourgeois law that Rose made. Williams, "Theology and Economics"; Tanner, *Economy of Grace*.

of the absolute, the unity of law and ethics. The diremption of religion and the state is the index of human domination in the modern world.

Rowan Williams has proposed a distinctive and influential interpretation of the role of Rose's broken middle in theological thought. It serves an important purpose, Williams says, by the critical work it does "between politics and metaphysics." A thought that occupies the broken middle works in that space between religion and politics. If it does its critical work well, then it will produce a speculative recognition of the politics that is within religion, the religion that is in politics, and how the illusions of one to dominate the other can be dispelled and a more constructive relation emerge between them. This means that, thinking from the middle, we cannot claim to possess knowledge of the absolute, except as a positing of our own subjectivity.[69] On the one hand, this reading would support an agnostic reading of Rose in which what matters is not the metaphysical reality of the absolute, or God, but rather, like Schmitt, Benjamin, and Taubes, the political function of religious concepts and the religious function of political concepts. That is, the middle is a space of critical facetiousness. Agamben is perhaps the most thoroughgoing practitioner of this mode of thought. Yet, there is also the equal possibility, which Williams himself follows and commends, of understanding this agnostic reticence as an apophatic gesture of humility and self-dispossession, which opens out onto a distinctive relation to the world, desire, work, the other, and God.

But an important implication of the rereading of Marx that I have proposed as a supplement to Rose is that it enables us to claim much more knowledge of the absolute than either of these interpretations allow. It gives us a basis, for example, to identify the absolute as the unholy trinity of labor, commodity, and capital in their dynamic, perichoretic mutuality. Capital depends on a false agnosticism, a false mysticism, which occludes our recognition of these three are our god. It is far from the case that we cannot know the absolute, but it is very much the case that knowledge of the absolute is obscured by our society's god. This is a unique kind of claim. It is not a positive claim to possess knowledge of the absolute, but it is a positive claim to possess the knowledge that our god is not God. There is a certain apophaticism here, as with Thomas Aquinas: "what God is not, is clearer to us than what God is."[70] And in this way there is also a reiteration of the radical critique of idolatry that animates Judaism, Islam, and Christianity.

---

69. Hegel quoted in Rose, *Hegel contra Sociology*, 92.
70. Thomas Aquinas, *Summa Theologiae* I.1.9.3.

We can point to Herbert McCabe's observation here, that the great insight of the Hebrew people was that God is not a god.[71]

On this point, a critical Marxism can certainly acknowledge that religion and theology are more than mere illusions. Religion and theology have critical resources for undermining the basic mystification of our capitalist social relations. In this instance, critical Marxism and religion can make common cause. But, even acknowledging this commonality, this recognition does not appear to require the kind of turn to theology and religion that Rose made. In fact, it might actually run in the opposite direction: that is, religion or theology could not, on this analysis, succeed in avoiding idolatry without the resources of Marxist analysis. Indeed, at the very least it suggests that a theology with no material interest in overcoming capitalism is a theology that has no actual commitment to having no gods before God. And yet, we cannot say the same about a critical Marxism *per se*, which appears not to need theology in the same way.

This leads me to my second point. The religious and theological rejection of idolatry in Judaism, Islam, and Christianity is not abstract. It is about social orders of living, ways of life, forms of law and moral action, that are consistent with the repudiation of idolatry. Religion and its theological concepts are social affairs, ways of mediating social relations, and none of these religious communities understands its relations to be mediated by labor. Even a critical Marxism cannot claim the same. As Rose stated well in *Hegel contra Sociology*, the trouble with Marxism is that Marxism is a culture, and that is the one thing about which it has no concept.[72] It seems, then, that religion is a constitutive component for any non-reformable revolution to obtain. A critical Marxism must have a critique of political economy and a cultural formation, a *Bildung*, that is capable of disrupting and replacing the social order of labor, commodity, and capital. Apart from such a formation, as Gramsci, MacIntyre, and even Rose herself have insisted, Marxist politics is a peculiar iteration of bourgeois culture, an especially strident form of emotivism.[73] So just in the same way that the religious and theological opposition to idolatry requires, at least in our social conditions, supplementation by Marx, so does Marxism require religion as the cultural formation of social relations that render its opposition to liberal, bourgeois law more than an abstract *Sollen*.

71. McCabe, *God Still Matters*, 59.

72. *Hegel contra Sociology*, 229–35.

73. On this point, it is perhaps helpful to mention the late Mark Fisher's essay, "Exiting the Vampire Castle," *OpenDemocracyUK*, 24 November, 2013, available at https://www.opendemocracy.net/ourkingdom/mark-fisher/exiting-vampire-castle (accessed 22 August, 2017).

Finally, we can also see from this standpoint that Rose's focus on the contradiction of law and ethics, of substance and subjectivity, was misplaced. It was not quite the case that the foundations of this problem were jurisprudential, the internalization of formal, legal personhood. Modernity's ancient problem is how to understand the nature of free human self-determination. As Bernard Lonergan observed in his extended analysis of the *verbum*, the inner word, that the mind produces in coming to understand anything at all, one of the most persistent and long-standing philosophical mistakes is the tendency to confuse action with motion, to mistake the *act* of understanding with the production of knowledge.[74] We have the persistent illusion, as early as Plato, that what it means to be a self, to have a soul, is to have the capacity to *move oneself*. Modern capitalist society may be the first social arrangement in history to place this illusion at the center of its social relations. Motion, production, labor—these are not action, much less are they creativity; they are forms of motion. Actuality makes motion possible; we do not produce it. The problem, then, is not about how we mediate law and ethics, or substance and subjectivity, but what is actual in the relation of substance and subjectivity that is a positive rather than negative determination.

Critical Marxism requires such a social actuality. Christianity, at least, proclaims that this social actuality, which precedes the relation of law and ethics, is *charis*, God's grace. As it is spoken of in the New Testament, that grace is not produced by labor of any kind. It is an actuality, a justice, that God establishes for the world, for the first time, through the faithfulness ("religion") of Jesus of Nazareth, in and through his execution by the powers of the Roman imperium ("state"). This grace is actual as a new social relation, mediated by the person of Jesus of Nazareth. It is true that our present order of social relations is idolatrous, and, in that regard, it requires the Marxist insight. But insofar as the church maintains that grace is the actuality of a new relation of law and ethics, operative as a distinct social relation, then we can speak at least of Christianity as a necessary religious supplement to Marxism.[75] Rose's work suggests that she realized this, and perhaps it is her life itself, and not just the turn to theology and religion in her work, that testifies to that recognition. In the end, despite the elevated importance Rose gave to irony in her work, maybe the religious life is a comic life, a truly revolutionary life, because it is not at all facetious.

---

74. Lonergan, *Verbum*, 204.

75. I speak here of only Christianity not to the exclusion of Judaism and Islam. I suspect that similar claims may be made for the Torah and Qur'an. Those are not arguments that I would presume, as a Christian theologian, to make.

Bibliography

Elson, Diane. *Value: The Representation of Labour in Capitalism.* Brooklyn: Verso, 2015.

Gorman, Tony. "Gillian Rose and the Project of a Critical Marxism." *Radical Philosophy* 105 (2003) 25–36.

Hegel, G. W. F. *Phenomenology of Spirit.* Translated by A. V. Miller. Oxford: Oxford University Press, 1977.

Hsiao, Andrew, and Audrea Lim, eds. *The Verso Book of Dissent: Revolutionary Words from Three Millennia of Rebellion and Resistance.* Edited by Andrew Hsiao and Audrea Lim. New York: Verso, 2016.

Landa, Ishay. *The Apprentice's Sorcerer: Liberal Tradition and Fascism.* Boston: Leiden, 2010.

Larsen, Neil, et al. *Marxism and the Critique of Value.* Chicago: MCM, 2014.

Lonergan, Bernard. *Verbum: Word and Idea in Aquinas.* Edited by Frederick E. Crowe and Robert M. Doran. Toronto: University of Toronto Press, 1997.

Marx, Karl. *Capital: A Critique of Political Economy.* Vol. 1. Translated by Ben Fowkes. New York: Penguin, 1990.

McCabe, Herbert. *God Still Matters.* Edited by Brian Davies. Continuum Icons. London: Continuum, 2002.

Milbank, John. "On the Paraethical: Gillian Rose and Political Nihilism." *Telos* 173 (2015) 69–86.

Murthy, Viren. "Introduction: Reconfiguring Historical Time: Moishe Postone's Interpretation of Marx." In *History and Heteronomy: Critical Essays,* edited by Viren Murthy and Yasuo Kobayashi, 9–30. University of Tokyo Center for Philosophy Booklet 12. Tokyo: UTCP, 2009.

Osborne, Peter. "Gillian Rose and Marxism." *Telos* 173 (2015) 55–67.

———. "Hegelian Phenomenology and the Critique of Reason and Society." *Radical Philosophy* 32 (1980) 8–15.

Postone, Moishe. "Anti-Semitism and National Socialism." *New German Critique* 19, Special Issue 1: Germans and Jews (1980) 97–115.

———. "Critical Theory and the Twentieth Century." In *History and Heteronomy: Critical Essays,* edited by Viren Murthy and Yasuo Kobayashi, 49–61. University of Tokyo Center for Philosophy Booklet 12. Tokyo: UTCP, 2009.

———. "Labor and the Logic of Abstraction: An Interview." *South Atlantic Quarterly* 108 (2009) 305–30.

———. "Rethinking Marx (in a Post-Marxist World) (1)." Obeco-online.org. Accessed January 3, 2018. http://www.obeco-online.org/mpt.htm.

———. "Rethinking Marx's Critical Theory." In *History and Heteronomy: Critical Essays,* edited by Viren Murthy and Yasuo Kobayashi, 31–47. University of Tokyo Center for Philosophy Booklet 12. Tokyo: UTCP, 2009.

———. "The Subject and Social Theory: Marx and Lukacs on Hegel." In *History and Heteronomy: Critical Essays,* edited by Viren Murthy and Yasuo Kobayashi, 63–83. University of Tokyo Center for Philosophy Booklet 12. Tokyo: UTCP, 2009.

———. *Time, Labor, and Social Domination: A Reinterpretation of Marx's Critical Theory.* Cambridge: Cambridge University Press, 1993.

Rockmore, Tom. *Fichte, Marx and the German Philosophical Tradition.* Carbondale, IL: Southern Illinois University Press, 1980.

Rose, Gillian. "The Battle over Walter Benjamin." 1979, audio lecture, The Frankfurt School lectures, University of Sussex Library, 4162, class R8059.
———. *The Broken Middle: Out of Our Ancient Society*. Oxford: Blackwell, 1992.
———. "The Dialectic of Enlightenment." 1979, audio lecture, The Frankfurt School lectures, University of Sussex Library, 4163, R8060.
———. "The Dispute over Marx and Weber." 1987, audio recording, Sociological Theory and Methodology multi-lecturer series, University of Sussex Library, 7702.
———. "Does Marx Have a Method?" 1987, audio recording, Sociological Theory and Methodology multi-lecturer series, University of Sussex Library, 7703.
———. "The Greatness and Decline of Expressionism: Ernst Bloch." 1979, audio lecture, The Frankfurt School lectures, University of Sussex Library, 4161, class R8058.
———. *Hegel contra Sociology*. Radical Thinkers. Brooklyn: Verso, 2009.
———. "Introduction to Critical Theory." 1986, audio recording, Sociological Theory and Methodology multi-lecturer series, University of Sussex Library, 7658.
———. "Marxist Modernism." 1979, audio lecture, The Frankfurt School lectures, University of Sussex Library, 4159, class R8056.
———. *The Melancholy Science*. Radical Thinkers. Brooklyn: Verso, 2014.
———. *Mourning Becomes the Law: Philosophy and Representation*. Cambridge: Cambridge University Press, 1996.
———. "The Politics of Realism: Georg Lukács." 1979, audio lecture, The Frankfurt School lectures, University of Sussex Library, 4160, class R8057.
———. "The Search For Style: Adorno, Kafka or Mann?" 1979, audio lecture, The Frankfurt School lectures, University of Sussex Library, 4164, R8061.
———. "Simmel, Lukacs, and German Critical Theory." 1982, audio recording, Sociological Theory and Methodology multi-lecturer series, University of Sussex Library, unnumbered.
———. "The Unity of Sociological Thinking." 1986, audio recording, Sociological Theory and Methodology multi-lecturer series, University of Sussex Library, 7812.
Shanks, Andrew. *Against Innocence: An Introduction to Gillian Rose*. London: SCM Press, 2008.
Solomon, Robert C. *In the Spirit of Hegel*. Oxford: Oxford University Press, 1985.
Tanner, Kathryn. *Economy of Grace*. Minneapolis: Fortress, 2005.
Tubbs, Nigel. "Gillian Rose and Education." *Telos* 173 (2015) 125–43.
Williams, Rowan. "Between Politics and Philosophy: Reflections in the Wake of Gillian Rose." *Modern Theology* 11, no. 1 (1995) 3–22.
———. "The Sadness of the King: Gillian Rose, Hegel, and the Pathos of Reason." *Telos* 173 (2015) 21–36.
———. "Theology and Economics: Two Different Worlds?" *Anglican Theological World* 92, no. 4 (607–15).

Chapter 9

Law All the Way Down
Gillian Rose and Robert Cover as Jewish Philosophers

Vincent Lloyd

Critical theorists are suspicious of the way the world seems to be. They are also suspicious of the ways we ordinarily talk about the world, language that confirms the way the world appears. The world is actually quite different, critical theorists assert. The truth has been concealed—for example, by ideology, the ideas of the wealthy and powerful that shape how we perceive and describe the world and ourselves. As opposed to ordinarily language philosophers who refuse as nonsensical investigation beyond or beneath language, critical theorists take a suspicious stance. It is a stance that resonates with theology, and particularly with Christian theology. Beneath the deceptions of the world is something else, something more truthful, more loving, more beautiful—something that can be apprehended with the right practices or training or commitment. That a close, unacknowledged connection exists between critical theory and Christian theology was one of the most significant insights of Gillian Rose. As a Jew who, like many Jews, spent her life wrestling with her religious and ethnic identity, Rose was suspicious of the crypto-Christianity she found in French and German thought, yet she was also thoroughly formed by her early engagement with the Frankfurt School. In a sense, Rose first embraced her Jewish identity by thematizing the crypto-Christianity of critical theory, but she also, even more significantly, undertook a distinctively Jewish intellectual project. Ordinary language philosophy, in which she was grudgingly trained as an Oxford undergraduate, offered no solution; she would have to find her own way forward.

At the same time, across the Atlantic, another brilliant and idiosyncratic intellectual was struggling to bring his Jewish commitments into his scholarship. Robert Cover was a law professor at Yale who had never been satisfied with the well-worn debates about the relationship between law and morals. Neither committed to natural law nor to positive law jurisprudence, Cover sought a way to reframe how law is understood. A new wave of scholars was stripping law of its privilege, examining law as one of many aspects of culture. Cover was intrigued but wary. For him, the physical violence that law could inflict ought never to be forgotten, and too often scholars approaching law through culture forget it. Careful examination of Jewish sources provided Cover a way forward, helping him to identify the defects of regnant views of law and pointing him toward an alternative. Like Rose, Cover undertook a distinctively Jewish intellectual project. Like Rose, Cover's fascinating, frustrating, and enormously powerful insights have too often been ignored.

My claim in this chapter is that Rose and Cover's thought is closely related. Reading them together can correct defects and excesses in each and can display a promising and as yet little developed approach to Jewish thought and philosophy. In short, both Rose and Cover take law as foundational. For them, law is not confined to the courtroom or the synagogue; it is constitutive of our worlds and ourselves. Formal law, as found in a law book or sacred text, is only a special case of the normative fabric out of which all is woven. There is an oft-repeated, gnomic proverb about the person who believes that the world rests on the back of a tiger, the tiger resting on the back of an elephant, and the elephant resting on the back of a turtle. When this person is asked what the turtle rests on, she responds, "It's turtles all the way down." For Rose and Cover, it is law all the way down. This is an insight each takes from their Judaism—just as love is the core message of Christianity, for them law is the core message of Judaism—and it is an insight that each applies to the world writ large, offering it in an idiom designed to appeal to those without Jewish commitments. In a sense, Rose and Cover are continuing the project of critical theory, rejecting tigers for turtles, appearances for law. But law, as they understand it, is essentially contestable and always contested. We are always arguing about what ought to be done, according to law or, more broadly, according to social norms. This activity is not secondary or derivative, Rose and Cover argue; it is essential. We go wrong when we obscure normative questions—for instance, by taking philosophy to be the activity that uncovers Being (Heidegger) or différance (Derrida) or the virtual (Deleuze). This, Rose argues, is crypto-Christian, and leads astray. The Jewish contribution to philosophy is to replace quest with argument, to replace dwelling in a heavenly city with the challenges of life in a rambunctious, judgmental earthly city.

Jewish Lives

Both Gillian Rose and Robert Cover died young, the former at forty-eight, in 1995, and the latter at forty-two, in 1986. Both began writing about Judaism late in their relatively short careers, though both had spent some of their lives immersed in Jewish families and communities. While Rose was trained as a sociologist she became best known for her writings on Continental philosophy and for her memoir; while Cover's early work was as a legal historian he became best known for his writings on jurisprudence. Rose was always pulled toward abstraction, and her best insights often appear as nuggets hidden in dense engagement with philosophers. Cover's writing is in some ways just the opposite. He discusses concrete legal cases and historical events, but he gleans from them insights that are far from obvious, though he often expresses these insights cryptically. Before turning to a critical dialogue between the two, let us briefly review the distinctiveness of their two lives, each devoted to justice in quite different ways.

As a teenager, Cover spent the summer preparing educational materials at a Brookline synagogue and studying Talmud.[1] The rabbi reports that, by the end of the summer, Cover had become the teacher and the rabbi had become the student. After undergraduate studies at Princeton, Cover joined the Student Nonviolent Coordinating Committee, organizing with black communities in rural Georgia. He was jailed for three weeks, he was beaten, and he went on hunger strike. Before attending law school at Columbia, Cover taught at the school of the Princeton Jewish Center and at the Jewish Theological Seminary's Camp Ramah in the Poconos. In his law school application, Cover professed to have no "extraordinary" academic record, but scholarship was not his primary interest. "I am far more interested in the uses to which knowledge can be put than in the pursuit of knowledge itself," he wrote.[2] Throughout his academic career, Cover was known as an activist: speaking through a megaphone at a rally for imprisoned black radicals, building support for South African divestment, walking the picket lines

---

1. This biographical information comes from "Tributes to Robert M. Cover."
2. Ibid., 1704.

with service workers, and advocating for the homeless. Guido Calabresi, Cover's friend and former colleague, recalled of Cover, "He was deeply devoted to his heritage. And yet he never let its great traditions exclude others, but made of them a light for all people, and a searing criticism of injustice everywhere, within as well as without."[3] Cover kept kosher, attended synagogue regularly, and spent the Sabbath studying Talmud with friends. Yet Judaism initially played no role in his published scholarship. Cover introduces his first book, *Justice Accused*, as motivated by the dilemmas faced by judges confronted with the cases of draft resisters.[4] Instead of tackling issues surrounding the Vietnam War directly, Cover turned to a previous grave injustice, the Fugitive Slave Act, and tracked how judges responded to what many at the time acknowledged was an immoral but legal practice. It was not until the article for which Cover is best known, "Nomos and Narrative" (1983), that he began reflecting on lessons of the Jewish tradition for the law. When he died, Cover was working on the translation of a sixteenth-century Jewish legal text that explored yet another dimension of the complex connection between law and justice.

Rose's relationship with Judaism was significantly more conflicted. Her grandparents were religious but her parents' Jewishness was, as she describes it, only cultural. This was "rather liberating" since "it meant that I could explore what it meant to be a Jew religiously" without the weight of parental compulsion.[5] She thought little of Judaism during her education—analytic philosophy at Oxford, critical theory in New York, and a sociology doctorate at Oxford. Unlike Cover, and unlike her younger sister, the prominent public intellectual Jacqueline, Rose never embraced the role of activist despite her persistent intellectual concern with justice. Her career took place largely within the academy, first at the University of Sussex, then at the University of Warwick. Rose published books on Adorno, Hegel, and the legacy of neo-Kantianism, but it was in the early 1990s that her attention shifted. In five books finished in five years, Rose elaborated on the crypto-Christianity of critical theory and explored the extent to which this crypto-Christianity infected Judaism itself. She did this through essays (collected as *Judaism and Modernity* and *Mourning Becomes the Law*), through the long, opaque *The Broken Middle*, and through a pair of memoirs that mixed personal experience, religious reflection, and philosophical inquiry (*Love's Work* and *Paradiso*). Rose never presented herself as a Jewish thinker. She worried that such labels overdetermine. Judaism, for her, was formative but

3. Ibid., 1700.
4. Cover, *Justice Accused*, xi.
5. Lloyd, ed., "Interview with Gillian Rose," 211.

not determinative: it could be negotiated, judged, and reframed just like all other aspects of the world that she encountered. Writing and, more generally, living entail, at their best, the negotiation of identity: naming, describing, judging, and naming again. At the start of *Judaism and Modernity*, Rose states, "If I knew who or what I were, I would not write; I wrote out of those moments of anguish which are nameless and I am able to write only where the tradition can offer me a discipline, a means, to articulate and explore that anguish."[6]

On the one hand, Judaism does not have a privileged position for Rose. It is one of the identities she negotiates. On the other hand, it was through her return to Judaism that Rose was able to formulate this very understanding of identity. Practically, this return to Judaism meant studying Hebrew, visiting Israel, serving on a Holocaust commission, and immersing herself in Jewish texts. Theoretically, it meant a new approach to law. Her return was made possible when she was told that Judaism does not require belief, it only requires following the law. Rose concludes that Judaism had seemed so unappealing because the Judaism she encountered in philosophy rejected the centrality of law. Two motives for this rejection complemented each other: the desire to avoid the Christian charge of legalism and the desire for Judaism to offer an alternative to the rationalism of modernity.[7] In her early work on Hegel, Rose had already explored how law might be embraced without crude legalism; this was the starting point for Rose's engagement with Jewish thought. She brought a flexible, expansive conception of law to her engagement with twentieth-century Jewish texts, charging them with rejecting the distinctiveness of Judaism altogether and unwittingly accepting a Christian framework that would define Judaism as perpetually "other." Yet it was also through this engagement with Jewish texts that her concept of law was refined; it became a part of her general philosophical stance as well as part of her own self-understanding. Negotiating identity is like negotiating law. It requires determining the meaning of concepts, determining when they are to be applied, contesting the facts of given circumstances and their salience, and ultimately making judgments. Unlike Cover, Rose did not begin with a conception of Judaism based on certain authoritative texts, but, like Cover, she ended with a conception of the world shaped by her understanding of Jewish thought.

6. Rose, *Judaism and Modernity*, ix.

7. Rose saw a parallel with the way some feminists embraced women as the "other" of the rational, modern world. Ibid., 3.

Halacha beyond Halacha

Before turning to the work of Rose and Cover itself to explore the nuances of their understandings of law, how each is distinctive, and how they complement each other, I will summarize their shared view in broad strokes. The vision of law that both Rose and Cover embrace is, first and foremost, difficult. Law, on their view, is not the sort of thing that can be codified in a book. Or rather, if it is codified, it is codified in multiple places, and those codes always underdetermine the meaning of law. That there is law is certain—there is something that ought to be done and sanction if it is not done—but it is always opaque. In an important sense, the existence of law is the primary article of faith: even though no human can know it, even though it will be eternally contested, law exists. Put another way, there are facts about what law is. Against those who would reduce law to expressions of self-interest or class interest, Cover and Rose believe that there is such a thing as law undistorted by interest—for law goes all the way down. They do not believe that we can access undistorted law, but the work of identifying and sorting through distortions that they commend is motivated by the belief that there is law to be known. It is important here to remember that Rose and Cover use law in a very broad sense. Law means normativity, what ought to be done. Note how their position is distinct from that of the virtue ethicist. Rose and Cover agree that we are formed by community, and community gives us our sense of what ought to be done. However, they reject the notion that proper formation in a community will lead naturally to right action.[8] Because normativity remains opaque, even to the oldest and wisest in a community, there will always be contest over what ought to be done. Indeed, such contest marks the vibrancy of a community, just as it marks the vibrancy of an individual when such deliberation and judgment occurs in one's own mind. Even more strongly, Rose and Cover take law to be constitutive of community as it is of individuals: it is law all the way down.

What precisely does Rose mean by law, a term that appears throughout her writings but never receives a full exposition? Rose is frustrated with her contemporaries, really with the past two centuries of philosophy, because it has claimed to speak about law but has overlooked the foundational nature of law. The introduction to Rose's *Dialectic of Nihilism* (1984) is titled "Legalism without Law," naming this problem. Both Neo-Kantian and recent French philosophy, Rose suggests, take the form of natural law jurisprudence. There are laws and social norms in the world but these are ultimately arbitrary, subject to critique and reform based on a deeper (or higher) law.

---

8. For a particularly compelling statement of this view, see McDowell, "Virtue and Reason."

For French philosophy—"postmodernists" including Foucault, Derrida, and Deleuze—the deeper or higher law has no content other than its disruptive potential. It does no more than demonstrate the arbitrariness of the order of the day. In other words, Rose charges that contemporary French philosophers identify injustice but have no vision of justice, and even the view they put forward of injustice tends to be totalizing, encompassing all of the arbitrary world rather than allowing for the discernment of specific instances of injustice that would then allow these injustices to be addressed. Contemporary French philosophers' shared debt to Heidegger is one of the problems. Rose characterizes Heidegger as offering "Yahweh without Torah," revelation of that which is otherworldly but which does not offer guidance for addressing specific injustices effectuated by worldly law.[9] This structure will repeat itself from Bergson through Derrida, Rose charges.

Dialectic of Nihilism is primarily critical, a critique of legalism. She concludes the book with a call to jurisprudence, but she will struggle to write constructively about law in her subsequent philosophical work, resulting in limited success.[10] It is only in her posthumously published *Paradiso* that she realizes that it is through memoir that she can most fully engage with law because she asserts that law means "the workings of the world."[11] In other words, law is basic, and it is (or ought to be) the primary interest of philosophers—philosophy, at its best, is jurisprudence and jurisprudence, at its best, is not confined to the courtroom but speaks to life in the world more broadly.[12] Rose hints at this in her philosophical work when she points to Hegel as offering the best model for understanding law. On Rose's reading of Hegel, we come to be subjects "in the encounter with law-giving and law-testing Reason."[13] This is simply a technical way of describing the "workings of the world." As we live in the world, we have views about how the world ought to behave. Sometimes, we encounter new phenomena, notice regularity, and develop a new "law" to explain what is to happen in certain circumstances. Sometimes, we encounter a phenomenon that does not follow the law we expect it to follow, causing us to revise our understanding of law. Note how this is precisely the same process through which law is discerned in a common law legal system (i.e., a system where law is exclusively

---

9. Rose, *Dialectic of Nihilism*, 80.

10. "By drawing out the legal arguments and the legal history at the heart of post-metaphysical reason, an attempt has been made to draw us back into the antinomy of culture, into the tradition which holds us, and, so, to open it again—in this aporetic way—under the title, if there must be one, of jurisprudential wisdom." Ibid., 212.

11. Rose, *Paradiso*, 19.

12. This point is developed in Lloyd, *Law and Transcendence*.

13. Rose, *Dialectic of Nihilism*, 6.

discerned from precedent, opposed to a civil law system where law is given in statutes).[14] Rose is casting us all in the role of judges as we navigate the world—as we live in a world of law. "The drama which Hegel develops as a new philosophical modus," Rose writes, "is the drama of the law itself."[15]

When Rose is invited to Jerusalem to discuss the meaning of Jewish philosophy, she plays the contrarian. Given two choices, that Jewish law contains within it all that is needed for ethical action and that Jewish law needs to be supplemented by a separate, independently derived ethics, she chooses neither.[16] The choice, Rose argues, is a product of modernity, when law and ethics are split. There is no way of avoiding this split; it must be acknowledged and grappled with even though it is ultimately artificial. The split between law and ethics conceals the normativity underlying both; they are tigers and elephants, we might say, standing on top of the turtles of law. There is no way of accessing those turtles except through the tigers and elephants; to imagine otherwise results in distortion. Understanding the world as it is, including history and social structures, must precede understanding what is most fundamental: law in the broad sense, that is, normativity. As Rose elusively puts it, "there may be law beyond Halacha and only then 'an ethics.'"[17] The contemporary debate about the relationship between halacha and ethics presupposed the Kantian split between an autonomous realm of morality and a heteronomous realm of law; the historical specificity of this split must be acknowledged in order to reach law beyond halacha. Rose argues that the misguided question about ethics and halacha is not a Jewish problem but a modern problem, a problem effecting all religious traditions and philosophical positions in modernity; of this Kant is exemplary. Rose offers no solution, or rather, her solution is to acknowledge the problem, thereby allowing it to be addressed directly—in other words, allowing us to approach more closely that which the ethics versus law split conceals: law in the broad sense, in the sense that goes all the way down.

Another theoretical concept that is centrally important to Rose yet which she never clearly defines is the middle. It was in the title of her major mature work, *The Broken Middle*, and it is a recurring character in her essays on Judaism. The little that is clear about Rose's view of the middle is that the middle is broken, and it ought not to be repaired. She is consistently critical of attempts to "mend" the middle or to sanctify it. What Rose seems

14. Brandom also suggests this way of reading Hegel on analogy with the common law in "Some Pragmatist Themes in Hegel's Idealism."

15. Rose, *Dialectic of Nihilism*, 6.

16. The occasion for this discussion is reflection on the debate between Eugene Borowitz and Aharon Lichtenstein.

17. Rose, *Judaism and Modernity*, 26.

to mean by the middle is the space lost by the differentiation characteristic of modernity, a differentiation both of the social world (for example, political institutions from religious institutions) and of the conceptual sphere (for example, political concepts from religious concepts). Just as modernity produces such differentiation, so too does it produce the desire for reconciliation.[18] Reconciliation offers promises it cannot deliver for it assumes the naturalness of the division that must be reconciled. Put in specifically Jewish terms, it assumes that halacha and ethics are genuinely two distinct domains in need of reconciliation. Efforts to "mend" the middle, in Rose's terminology, are attempts at reconciliation, and they are to be avoided. The middle is irreparably broken. What this means in terms of Rose's account of law is that law will never perfectly match the customs of a community. This was the Athenian ideal, but Athens is no more.[19] Concepts and institutions create irreconcilable sets of norms, for example ethical norms and formal laws that at times conflict. Such concepts and institutions function as tigers and elephants, all standing on top of the turtles of normativity and making it possible for us to access this foundational normativity only through them. The concepts and institutions of the modern world distort, and our work, the work of critical theory (and of life), is to discern those distortions and so to make visible what lays beneath—law in the broadest sense. This is the work of the wise judge, hearing the arguments and examining the evidence rather than mechanically applying a rule. Indeed, Rose writes that the middle *is* law.[20]

Rose offers another way of putting this point: because of the diversity of people living together (another feature of modernity), concepts and institutions must be advanced that allow for coexistence. The concept of human reason is one that serves this purpose, and political institutions serve

---

18. Although Rose is particularly focused on modernity, with Kant and Hegel forming the protagonists in her conceptual story, she also traces the beginnings of such differentiations to Roman law, particularly the emergence of the category of the person and prose writing. See Rose, *Hegel contra Sociology*, 138. Indeed, following Hegel, Rose seems to suggest that the middle is broken after its heyday in Athens.

19. Ibid., 89: "In an ethical community law would not be set apart from the totality of social institutions . . . . In a simple, just, ethical community real recognition would be enshrined in custom, *Sitte*. Hence ethical life, *Sittlichkeit*, would be natural, the concept and intuition equal. . . . This life would consist of mutual recognition in all social institutions." See also ibid., 132: "Greek society is not perfectly just, but its injustice is recognized, and hence transparent and visible."

20. "The law, therefore, is not the superior term which suppresses the local and contingent, nor is it the symbolic which catches every child in the closed circuit of its patriarchal embrace. The law is the falling towards or away from mutual recognition, the triune relationship, the middle, formed or deformed by reciprocal self-relations." Rose, *Mourning Becomes the Law*, 75.

this purpose as well. In this context, Rose's point about the broken middle means acknowledging that all such unifying concepts and institutions ultimately get things wrong; they do not fit perfectly. Too often, this is forgotten and middles are sanctified: we imagine that a certain political process, for example, can get things right, if only we understand and execute it properly. In addition to concealing the misrepresentation of the diverse communities to which they speak, such claims set up strong, unjustified boundaries between the community subject to the unifying mechanism and all other communities—those that are charged as being "irrational," for example, or "theocratic." By urging an embrace of a broken middle, Rose is urging a rejection of self-confidence in our own community, in the view that the way we do things is the way things ought to be done. Rose is arguing that we badly misunderstand the way we do things, our law in the broad sense, and addressing these confusions should be our first priority. Indeed, attending to the broken middle means attending to injustice. Rose interprets Nicolas Poussin's painting *Landscape with the Ashes of Phocion*, featured on the cover of *Mourning Becomes the Law*, as representing the tension between the rational order, represented by stately background buildings, and ethical imperative, represented by Phocion's widow gathering his ashes. The painting does not privilege the widow over the rational order, Rose argues. Rather, it displays the unavoidable conflict between the two that results in particular injustices. By understanding the features of this separation between law and ethics and the necessary harm that it causes, we are motivated to address those specific injustices. We are not distracted by dreams of a heavenly city where law and ethics are one.[21]

Like Rose, Cover opposes the model of law that he endorses to a commitment to autonomy pervasive in the West, and particularly in Western legal thought. Starting with autonomy puts the self before the law: it imagines a self who approaches the law.[22] In an essay entitled "Obligation: A Jewish Jurisprudence of the Social Order," Cover begins to develop an alternative, taking Moses's reception of the law at Sinai as paradigmatic. The law is not chosen but given; nonetheless it obliges. "All law was given at Sinai and therefore all law is related back to the ultimate heteronomous event in which we were chosen—passive voice" (240).[23] First comes the law, what ought to be done, then comes those who do it. Identity is constituted by the law: an in-

21. Ibid., 26.

22. This imagery evokes Kafka's parable "Before the Law." Butler draws similar implications from this parable and in her early work endorses a view of law or norms all the way down. See her *Gender Trouble*.

23. Parenthetical references to Cover's writings are to *Narrative, Violence, and the Law*.

dividual is, most essentially, one who follows the law. This is Cover's reading of the Jewish tradition that, he suggests, poses the most promising alternative to the Western fetishization of autonomy. To dramatize this distinction, Cover recalls a Talmudic dispute about whether it is better to follow the law out of love or out of obligation. The blind are excused from certain Jewish duties, and a blind rabbi feels proud of himself for performing these duties nonetheless, out of love, as supererogation. On Cover's reading, the Talmudic text concludes that such supererogation, which implies autonomy, individual choice to fulfill duty, is actually inferior to obligatory fulfilment of duty, in which one's will is identified as completely as possible with law.[24]

Cover begins the publication for which he is most known, "Nomos and Narrative," by applying this Jewish focus on obligation to law, and to the world more broadly. "We inhabit a *nomos*—a normative universe" (95). Life in the world consists of judging right and wrong, what ought or ought not to be done, what deserves reprimand and what deserves praise. "To inhabit a *nomos* is to know how to *live* in it"—which means not only following the law but knowing what the law is (97). The more we understand the world properly, the more we follow the law properly. There is no direct access to law in this broad sense; that is why so much of life consists in discussing and adjudicating normative questions. The most common way to access *nomos* is not through rulebooks but through stories and through the interpretation of stories. Some of these stories are treated as more authoritative than others and some interpretations are more authoritative than others, but they all provide access in some way to what ought to be done, to the normative substance of our world. Reason and emotion do not supervene on the self; they supervene on law. As Cover puts it, law in the expansive sense that he develops "enables us to submit, rejoice, struggle, pervert, mock, disgrace, humiliate, or dignify" (100). All of these actions and emotions can be derived from our relationship to the normative order, to law. Indeed, they cannot be understood otherwise. It would be impossible to understand disgrace without understanding how one ought to act, for example. The only way to live outside of the normative order, Cover suggests, is to be insane. Only the actions of the mad have no relationship to what one ought or ought not to do. Even especially bad and especially good people are extraordinary in relationship to the normative order. They may, for instance, inhabit or interpret the normative order so creatively that they cause new ways of living to come into being.

24. Cover offers a quite naturalistic explanation for the Jewish focus on obligation over autonomy (242). Given Jews' minority status and so their limited access to means of coercion, orderliness was guaranteed by sanctifying law-following rather than by reprimanding law-breaking.

Cover recognizes the affinity between such a view and Christian views of community (he does not mention the affinity with an image of Athens), but Cover adds features to make his understanding of law distinctively Jewish.[25] Law may be portrayed inhering in a community as described above, but this is only an ideal, imagined as a heuristic. There is never any agreement on the meaning of law or on who is subject to what law. From our perspective, there is only contest, argument; it is from an imagined God's eye perspective that there is *nomos* constituting a world. Cover suggests that the opacity of law is productive, in his terminology "jurisgenerative." Disagreement over the meaning of law leads to new law. From one community arguing over the meaning of a story that contains the law comes two communities, each with a different interpretation of that story. Because each of the two communities now internally shares a way of interpreting the authoritative story, new norms arise for each community based on that interpretation. What was once a hermeneutical debate now gives rise to new social practices.

On Cover's view, formal law, that is, law in the narrow sense that is its ordinary meaning, arises because of the proliferation of *nomoi*. Because of the opacity of law, multiple communities arise with different laws, taking different texts and interpretations as authoritative. These multiple communities need a way to interact with each other now that they lack shared authorities; for this the myth of autonomy and the myth of universal law are born. Cover labels this *nomos*-neutral way of understanding law "imperial." It promises objectivity and universality, offering a way to bring peace to a world of potentially intractable conflict. Formal law presents itself as superior to the law of local, tight-knit communities, but Cover rejects this self-presentation. Law is law, he argues, whether it is constitutive of the Amish or of America. Like Rose, Cover deflates the pretensions of formal, modern, institutionalized law, turning instead to a more expansive and more fundamental understanding of law. Law is a label attributed to certain aspects of the normative fabric in order to emphasize their seriousness— and to advance certain interests, Cover suggests. Using the word law, he writes, "is a move, the staking out of a position in the complex social game of legitimation" (175). It is not a decisive move; in fact, it is quite precarious.

25. For Christian views that powerfully develop along these lines, see Pickstock, *After Writing*; Cavanaugh, *Theopolitical Imagination*. Cover's view also strongly resonates with the view of Hegelian mutual recognition described by Rose. For instance, he writes of the world where *nomos* is rightly recognized, "Interpersonal commitments are characterized by reciprocal acknowledgment, the recognition that individuals have particular needs and strong obligations to render person-specific responses" (106). On this Hegelian norm-following alternative to autonomy, see also Brandom, "Freedom and Constraint by Norms."

Because in reality formal law is continuous with all other law, and all law is accessed through story and interpretation, the meaning of formal law can shift dramatically when different stories or interpretations are privileged. The meaning of a key word or the relative significance of phrases in a legal text can be transformed when, for example, a new novel is published that captures a community's imagination and helps to interpret, and shape, its normative world. Far from being a rigid set of rules, formal law is caught up in a struggle of texts and authorities that pervades a culture.

Where Rose explores the implications of this move for halacha and ethics, Cover explores the implications for American constitutional law. "Nomos and Narrative" is ostensibly a reflection on a Supreme Court case involving Bob Jones University, a conservative Christian institution that prohibited interracial dating.[26] The case brought to the fore the conflict between two types of law, the law taken as authoritative by the university administrators and the law taken as authoritative by the US Supreme Court. Like Rose, Cover does not so much provide a resolution to this conflict as he does reframe it with his expansive understanding of law. As part of this response, Cover poses a very distinctive account of the role of courts. Rather than applying the law to a set of facts, Cover argues that courts are "jurispathic," by which he means they impose order on law. There is an excess of law, in Cover's view: a single individual feels the pull of laws of multiple communities—say, Jewish, American, New York, white, and so on.[27] All of these laws, together, are constitutive of the world. When one acknowledges that so many laws exist, it becomes a monumental task to determine what ought to be done. This is the genuine business of a court: to determine, at a given place and time, which law has force. Cover notes that the founding narrative of law courts, Aeschylus's *Oresteia*, describes Athena instituting the first court because of a conflict between multiple laws, between Apollo's law and the Furies' law. This is the perspective that is necessary to bring to the Bob Jones University case, Cover argues. The Court is not merely applying the Constitution. It provides a forum for the competition between multiple laws, and it ultimately determines which of these laws holds sway.

Reading Rose and Cover together begins to fill out a picture of a philosophical position that takes law as foundational. These two scholars share

---

26. The clear parallels with Jewish communities forbidding intermarriage go undiscussed in the essay.

27. Even within the realm of law in the narrow sense, Cover finds excess in jurisdictional redundancy (that a given case could be tried, for example, in either federal or state court, or the courts of two different states). Cover develops an argument for the useful features of this excess of law in "The Uses of Jurisdictional Redundancy: Interest, Ideology, and Innovation" in *Narrative, Violence, and the Law*, 51–93.

the view that law goes all the way down. Law is not chosen by or enforced on an individual; law in the broad sense constitutes individuals. Becoming an adult is becoming aware of law: knowing what is to be done in which circumstances. Rose approaches law from the perspective of the individual, ultimately from her own perspective, explicating law as she explicates her own life in the world. For her, the individual becomes a judge. Cover approaches law from the perspective of a judge in the more conventional sense. Like Rose's judge, Cover's judge must be fluent in social practices and capable of discerning norms. Like Rose's judge, Cover's judge is incapable of perfectly grasping law; law is always opaque for both Rose and Cover. While Rose acknowledges the differentiation of the social world and the diversity of individuals and communities that are so central to modernity, these play a secondary role in her account of law. Community affiliations all contribute to constituting the individual, and they are all navigated by the individual. The individual must decide which have jurisdiction when and where. In contrast, for Cover, whose own private self rarely enters his work, to be a judge is to inhabit a role. The judge brackets the extent to which his or her self is constituted by this or that aspect of law. Instead, the judge looks out on the world of multiple and conflicting law from above, as it were. From that perspective, the judge must sort out the many layers of law in a way that is actionable in the world. To return to the metaphor, the judge must explain which turtle is on top of which. Doing this requires, as the use of metaphor suggests, telling a story, for narrative is the medium through which we relate to the normative fabric of our world. Rose also seems to come to this conclusion by her last works where she engages with law through autobiography, but in her theoretical reflections narrative is not a central category.[28]

It is not necessary to fault either Rose or Cover for missing or underdeveloping some aspect of her or his position. Given the division between public and private realms that comes with modernity, it is necessary to envision both private and public ways of interacting with law, both private and public ways of judging. What is worrying in both Rose and Cover is that they at times seem to foreclose the possibility of public or private judging, respectively. Cover's account of the judge implicitly advances the public judge as a paradigm for navigating the normative world, but this public judge is disembodied, and Cover ignores questions of how the judge herself is constituted by the law she judges. Rose's private judge worryingly collapses ethics and politics, portraying the pull of social norms as but one

---

28. To some extent *The Broken Middle* is exceptional in this regard, with its attention to the literariness of the works of Kierkegaard, Kafka, and others.

element of law partially constitutive of, but always critically interrogated by, the subject. Rose suggests that specific injustices ought to be addressed by a community—as she believes the Poussin painting illustrates—but there is no place in her account of law for the political calculus necessary to mobilize a community to address injustices. Such calculus requires bracketing one's own ambivalent investment in various communities and their laws in order to look at the law from above, as it were, just as Cover recommends. At the end of the day, it is no surprise that Rose was a memoirist and Cover an activist. Both are vocations called for from a perspective that understands law as going all the way down.

Violence, Faith, and Hope

If critical theory unveils that which lies beneath or behind the ordinary, critical theory becomes crypto-Christian when what is unveiled has no content other than its transcendence. This is what Rose charges about her contemporaries in France and their master, Heidegger. They each embrace the same structure—fundamentally a structure of fantasy, with the object of fantasy always hollow—but give the transcendent a different name.[29] Fantasy is violent: the object of fantasy is so entrancing that it clouds judgment in the world. When the object of fantasy has no content and so no effect other than relativizing worldly law and norms, the result is what Rose describes as melancholy, a loss of imagined fullness that is forever mourned. This melancholic stance results in further violence because the melancholic's perception of the world is dulled and her concern for worldly injustice diminishes. Critical theory that identifies law as that which lies beneath or behind the ordinary refuses such fantasy. Law, in the sense developed by Rose and Cover, is not detached from the world or in any way transcendent. Rather, law is accountable to the world. It is the normative substance of the world, discernible by examining precedent and using practical wisdom. Ideology does not obscure a secret like Being or différance; it obscures the most ordinary activity of all, doing what one does, what one ought to do.[30] The world is filled with norms, and every day each of us navigates a world of norms—even though the ideas of the powers that be would blind us to our own mundane activity. Rose and Cover propose to take us back to the world

---

29. A similar point has been made in more recent years by Slavoj Žižek who explicitly embraces the psychoanalytic language of fantasy.

30. This distinction is developed as that between the "ordinary," to which law is accountable, and the "obvious," which obscures law, in Lloyd, *The Problem with Grace*.

with which we are already familiar, not to take us on some flight of fancy through practices that access a world of the extraordinary.

Central to the stories that both Rose and Cover tell is the violence of law. This is distinct from the violence of those who would transcend law. Violence is essential to normativity: implicit in the claim that something ought to be done is the claim that sanction will follow if it is not done. Moreover, for both Rose and Cover, for different reasons, law is opaque to us. This means that even our best efforts to follow the law always go wrong. Sanction will inevitably follow. The more invested we are in those forces that obscure our view of law—that is, ideology—the more penalties we will face. Ironically, one of the ruses of ideology is to present law as a straightforward set of rules to follow in order to avoid sanction. Rose and Cover insist that all such law codes are simulacral and actually lead to more violence as they conceal the reality of law.[31] By emphasizing law's violence, Rose and Cover are also leveling a powerful criticism against those who are too eager to embrace narrative or discourse as fundamental, for such views often obscure the violence that is thread throughout life in the world, when life in the world is understood as fundamentally a life of law. What those who embrace either codified law or pure narrative lack is a sense of the religious—what Rose names faith and what Cover names hope. When the extent that violence permeates the world is acknowledged, faith or hope becomes essential.

Rose illustrates the violence accompanying law through retelling the story of Camelot. King Arthur imagines Camelot as a place where violence will come to an end. This will be achieved through sound judgment: King Arthur himself will be an even-handed judge, bringing an end to feuds. The law in Camelot would be "knowable and reliable," and this ideal attracted some of the best knights in the land, including the particularly idealistic Launcelot who befriends the king.[32] Harmony in the kingdom does not last long. Launcelot falls in love with King Arthur's wife, Guinevere. According to the law of the land, Launcelot ought to be banished and Guinevere ought to be killed, but this would be devastating for King Arthur. It would also be devastating for the king to make an exception to the law, for he is deeply invested in the just application of Camelot's law. This dilemma illustrates for Rose the violence that always accompanies law. If the law is followed, a friend and a wife will be lost, and yet it is equally clear that following the law

---

31. Rose writes, "The boundary stake of abstract legality not only pierces the individual soul but renders invisible the actuality of others, their work, desire and otherness, as well as oneself as other, and it is this anguish which makes phantasy projections of community, secured by an idealised outer boundary of religion, nation, so compelling." *Mourning Becomes the Law*, 98.

32. Ibid., 122.

is essential; ultimately, King Arthur does decide to follow the law. The king is sad, and Rose urges that the sadness brought about by the violence of law must be acknowledged. Indeed, Rose draws a very strong conclusion from the king's sadness: "Philosophy, ancient and modern, is born out of this condition of sadness."[33] By this Rose means that philosophy, at its best, grapples with the realization that no code of laws can fit the world properly, yet it remains necessary to posit such law codes. Philosophy at its worst is the activity of legitimating particular law codes, lending authority to the claim that they capture the normative world perfectly; or, equally bad, philosophy takes its task to be extolling that which rejects or refuses law (the recent fad of affect theory comes to mind). In a sense, Rose is arguing that philosophy ought to be the critique of ideology, for ideology advances a form of a law code (*these* are the concepts that explain the world) in a way that obscures the complexities of the world. King Arthur, after all, is a king: he imagines himself to be creating a fair and impartial legal system, but he remains the sovereign, and the ways that this legal system advances his own interests presumably remain obscure to him.

Philosophy responds to violence at an intellectual level, but what responds to violence at a practical level? Rose offers two related answers: mourning and faith. Violence is always present, but if it is not acknowledged then it festers. It affects our lives but its presence is repressed. This is melancholy: an attachment to a vision of peace that has been lost. The proper response to violence, Rose argues, is to mourn the peace lost—the vision of Camelot, or of love and friendship. Mourning is an acknowledgment that the world cannot be systematized, that no code of laws fits the world perfectly. Most importantly, mourning ends. It acknowledges a specific loss and indicates the work required to make sense of that loss, and so to go on living. As Rose writes, "Completed mourning acknowledges the creative involvement of action in the configurations of power and law: it does not find itself unequivocally in a closed circuit which exclusively confers logic and power."[34] In other words, because our engagement with law is dynamic and constitutive (law of us and we of the law), our view of law is often in need of correction. We are right to be sad that we did not understand law rightly, but we must not let this distract us from our next attempt to get law right. Not understanding law rightly can have quite concrete consequences, including physical pain and suffering. Rose urges us to "fail towards" law.[35] In the

---

33. Ibid., 124.

34. Ibid., 12.

35. Rose, *The Broken Middle*, 59 and elsewhere. Note how Rose differs from Samuel Beckett's suggestion that we "fail better." In a sense, Beckett identifies law with goodness; Rose does not.

process, to cite the title of Rose's most accessible scholarly book, mourning becomes the law. By this Rose explains the significance of law as she understands it, involving less code than a mixture of reason and affect that can never be pinned down. As she writes, "mourning returns the soul to the city, renewed and reinvigorated for participation, ready to take on the difficulties and injustices of the existing city."[36] Where repressing the violence of law leads to nostalgia or fantasy, an image of perfect law (and so a perfect world and perfect self) animating life, acknowledging and mourning this violence means worldly engagement, including right perception of concrete injustice and so right action in response to injustice.

Paired with mourning, for Rose, is faith. Melancholy means a lack of faith: an unwillingness to continue serious engagement with the world. Faith means perseverance in the face of obstacles, in the face of things going wrong, and this is exactly what Rose commends. Put another way, faith means acknowledging that we are constituted by law and that we constitute law. Rather than searching for a law tablet or imagining a heavenly city, we must examine evidence, study precedent, and assemble a theory about the meaning of law. To do this, we must start by setting aside what we think we know; this, clearly, requires faith. In her clearest definition of faith, Rose describes faith as "the capacity of being in uncertainties, mysteries, doubts" and, at the same time, "the enlarging of . . . reason in the domain of praxis, of practical reason."[37] Faith is not just doing what one has been enculturated to do, applying the concepts that one has been taught. Faith means the ability to bracket those presuppositions and to carefully weigh the evidence knowing that this might force a change in one's presuppositions—in other words, to genuinely judge.

This might seem like a secular faith, a penumbral meaning of the word faith that has little to do with religion.[38] But perhaps this sense of faith is only secular as opposed to Christianity. Perhaps it is an essentially Jewish understanding of faith. Indeed, Rose herself thinks so. She writes that her own embrace of Judaism came when she was told, at a dinner party, "An Orthodox Jew doesn't have to worry about whether he believes in God or not. As long as he observes the law."[39] However, after she returned to the Jewish community, Rose discovered that Jewish thinkers themselves often embraced a problematic notion of law, a notion largely derived from Christian and modern caricatures of Judaism as their "other." The result has been

---

36. Rose, *Mourning Becomes the Law*, 36.
37. Rose, *Paradiso*, 31.
38. As argued in Lloyd, "The Secular Faith of Gillian Rose."
39. Rose, *Love's Work: A Reckoning with Life*, 23–24.

that Judaism embraces law but disclaims violence.[40] Ironically, it is Judaism that has embraced a secular faith.

Rose commends faith but has little patience for hope.[41] Hope suggests another form of melancholia, projecting a perfect, lost object into the future rather than into the past. In contrast, Cover embraces hope as integral to law and as closely connected with law's violence. This violence is much more literal for Cover than it is for Rose, but Cover agrees that it is too often forgotten. On Cover's account, it is essential to remember that the simple words of a judge directly result in the punishment of criminal defendants. Cover draws on Elaine Scarry's account of torture to highlight this connection. As Cover characterizes it, "the torturer's interrogation is designed to demonstrate the end of the normative world of the victim—the end of what the victim values, the end of the bonds that constitute the community in which the values are grounded" (205). When a torturer asks his or her victim to betray friends and family members the intent is less to gain information than it is to thoroughly demolish any remnants of the victim's normative world. For Cover, the scene of torture provides a model for law writ large. If law as we normally experience it is fundamentally ambiguous and contested, there are moments when it must become crystal clear. In those moments, law does violence at the level of meaning (only one meaning prevails, that proclaimed by the judge) and at the level of bodies (the physical coercion of torture or prison). Meaning and bodies are inextricably linked, and the law works on both, Cover argues. But Cover also reminds his readers that there is no special privilege to the law spoken by a judge in a courtroom or the normative order created in a torture chamber. If violence is seen as necessarily connected with law, every instance of violence affirms some normative order—that of a parent or teacher or nation or mafia don. These figures make the connection between proclamations of law and violence particularly clear, but Cover's point extends to suggest that any interpretation of law, whether explicitly proclaimed or implicitly assumed, involves some level of violence. Normative worlds are competing, their jurisdiction contested, as we all act as judges. Rose focuses on lower level judges, as it were, on the way we all act as judges and so all participate in violence. Cover focuses on the most explicit proclamations of law, with particular attention to the paradigmatic case of the official judge. Cover famously began one of his last public lectures by stating, "Warren Burger is a violent man."[42]

40. See especially Lloyd, ed., "Interview with Gillian Rose," 209.

41. The exception is in her very last writing, *Paradiso*, where Rose is heavily flirting with Christianity.

42. "Tributes to Robert M. Cover," 1720.

In one sense, Cover would seem to locate argument as the opposite of violence.[43] Debating what ought to be done means that the law is in flux, underdetermined. This is precisely the opposite of the moment when a judge proclaims a ruling and a defendant is taken away in chains. Then, the law is crystal clear. Yet such debate is not really the opposite of violence; it is another domain of violence. Indeed, Cover suggests that violence is so insidious because the conversations in a law school classroom or a barbershop about what ought to be done seem so innocuous. They are not innocuous, Cover charges; they are part of the "field of pain and death," which is normativity (203). Indeed, Cover notes how the American legal system portrays the judge as interpreter of law, authorizing rather than carrying out a punishment, creating a psychic cushion between the judge and the violence imposed on the body of a criminal defendant. Moreover, words such as "blame" and "punishment" allow for seemingly abstract theoretical reflection that conceals the brute force involved in the act of judgment. Such terminology "justifies the judge to herself and to others with respect to her role in the acts of violence" (212). What is most violent, Cover seems to be suggesting, is the act of judgment and the theorization of judgment. Like Rose, Cover takes issue with the formal articulation of the law, where theorizing the law is a second-order articulation, proclaiming a law for the law. While both Rose and Cover point to the violence of such articulations, Rose is much more explicit than Cover about what an alternative might be. Where Rose takes Heidegger and his French followers to exemplify false consciousness about law's violence, Cover takes aim at those who would endorse a world of narrative. Saying that the world is narrative all the way down, with law as one genre, loses focus of the fundamentally violent nature of the world, and of acts of interpretation. When we think of narrative we do not think of suffering and bodies in pain; we do, or at least we should, when we think of law.

Cover evocatively describes law as a bridge to the future. It is in law that hope resides. What Cover means by this is rather obscure. He writes cryptically, "Law is neither to be wholly identified with the understanding of the present state of affairs nor with the imagined alternatives. It is the bridge—the committed social behavior which constitutes the way a group of people will attempt to get from here to there" (176).[44] If law goes all the way down, constituting our worlds and our selves, it would seem to relate

---

43. Owen Fiss recounts, "Like Hannah Arendt and Michael Walzer and the other great theoreticians of participatory democracy, Bob took a rare and unusual pleasure in disagreement, not because he was cantankerous—quite the opposite—but because he recognized plurality as the essential feature of the human condition." Ibid.

44. Italics removed.

to the present rather than the future. Cover opposes his vision of law, as a bridge, to apocalypticism. He describes apocalypticism as antinomian: a vision of a future where all law is overturned, for instance by the return of the Messiah or a revolution. Law provides an engine of change that also assures continuity. Interpreting law anew changes a community: law changes as it is interpreted differently. The current world involves varied and opaque law. Though constituted by law, the world is not transparent to us. Our hope is that the world may become more transparent to us—in a sense, that we may come to better know who we are. Cover's hope is relative, that it may become *more* transparent, not perfectly transparent. As we engage in the work of interpretation now, we move toward this better future. Dramatic transformation is still possible in a world of law. In Cover's view, "Every legal order must conceive of itself in one way or another as emerging out of that which is itself unlawful" (118). For example, Moses brings law tablets to the people of Israel, instituting a robust body of Jewish law. Repeatedly in the Bible, as Cover reads it, there are reminders of law's extra-legal provenance, most famously the sacrifice of Isaac. By pointing to these examples, Cover does not mean to suggest that there is something outside law. Rather, he demonstrates how dramatically law can transform when it is taken as foundationless—that is, when law goes all the way down.

Cover illustrates this point through a close study of the renewal of semikhah in the sixteenth century. A lineage of divinely ordained judges, charged with special responsibilities, had been part of the Jewish community since Moses, but the lineage broke in the first centuries of the Common Era. The Jewish legal system adapted, creating ways for non-ordained judges to carry out the tasks prescribed for ordained judges. In 1538, Jacob Berab convened a group of respected scholars at Safed who, he claimed, would renew the ordination. Renewing the lineage of ordained priests was believed to be a prerequisite for the return of the Messiah. Cover describes the attempted renewal of semikhah as a risky move, indicating deep dissatisfaction with the world as it is but also indicating deep commitment to law. The attempt to renew semikhah demonstrates, on Cover's view, how a practice that from most perspectives would seem obviously extralegal can serve as a pivot on which to radically transform law—or at least to attempt this. Cover notes that Berab's failure led to the rise of individualistic mysticism that was fundamentally antinomian: Safed became a seat of Lurianic Kabbalah. Rose would read this story as faith turned to faithlessness; Cover reads it as hope disappointed. The restoration of semikhah was motivated by messianic hope, not commitment to careful navigation of the law, although it was not antinomian.

Cover, unlike Rose, points to a way that hope can be expressed in law, a way that hope and faith can work together in the pursuit of justice. Faith and hope are combined in the figure of the martyr, Cover suggests. Martyrs dramatize the conflict of laws and force the dominant law to express itself explicitly, in a most violent form. Martyrs are not antinomian, on Cover's reading. They are extremely faithful to a law that just happens to be out of favor, God's law, but they are hopeful that it will again come into favor, in part by their faith. They recognize that law creates the horizon of possibility for the future, and they believe that no future is better than the future possible under the false, worldly law that prevails today. "Their triumph . . . is the imagined triumph of the normative universe—of Torah, Nomos—over the material world of death and pain" (207).

Like Rose, Cover argues that justice is advanced when we do not shy away from the violence of law. He writes, "As long as death and pain are part of our political world, it is essential that they be at the center of the law. The alternative is truly unacceptable—that they be within our polity but outside the discipline of the *collective* decision rules and the individual efforts to achieve outcomes through those rules" (236). For Cover the world may be law all the way down, but formal law has a special role to play. It allows for the violence of the world to be carefully examined and for the contest over that violence to be public. Formal law here means a venue in which certain elements of law in the broad sense are named, described, and judged (he has in mind an American-style adversarial context). Rose suggests philosophy and, more generally, writing as means of making the law explicit. Cover would rightly worry that these practices are insufficiently public and are insufficiently guided by clear norms (what H. L. A. Hart calls secondary rules, rules for identifying law).[45] On Cover's view, both philosophy and memoir might talk about violence, but in doing so they may at the same time conceal violence. Abstraction and narrative increase the distance from suffering and death.

The model that Cover commends is one he finds in a story from the Talmud and, in a slightly different version, in Josephus. A king's servant is accused of a crime. The king is summoned to court and wows the judges and spectators with his power. Only one judge has the courage to address the king and remind him that he is accountable not to other humans but to God and so to the law. Then everyone is killed. The lesson extracted from this story in the Talmud is that the king is neither to judge nor to be judged. In contrast, Cover identifies with the sole judge who was willing to risk everything and address the king. What if other judges had followed his lead?

---

45. Hart, *The Concept of Law*.

That was the judge's hope, Cover argues, and just because the hope was not fulfilled does not mean it was wrong. Cover uses the story to position the judge in opposition to power and particularly to the power of a state. That power will try to overawe judges, but the judge must have faith and hope. To act as a judge without official sanction, whether it be in the face of the king or in the renewal of semikhah, is both risky and commendable, and represents a deep investment in understanding the law. "Integrity," Cover writes, "is the act of maintaining the vision that it is only that which redeems which is law" (201).

Rose, of course, also commends risk: setting aside presuppositions when judging a case. But Cover introduces a crucial addition to Rose's account when he places confrontations with power at the center of right judgment. Where Rose's paradigm of faith is found in the practice of love, with its risk of disappointment and its challenges to the self, Cover's paradigm of faith is found in the figure of the judge as martyr confronting a king. Cover's paradigm both emphasizes how much is at stake in engaging law (life itself) and how much law is infused with the interests of the powerful. Where Rose suggests a community of individuals each struggling to discern who they and their fellows are, individually and collectively, through careful attention to law, Cover suggests a community bewitched by the law of the powerful, shaped by the interests of the powerful. For Cover, proper engagement with law requires hope together with faith because a fulfilling life, or even mere survival, is unlikely in the current legal regime, colored as it is by ideology. Having faith in law does not get you very far if that law, beyond the law of the world, is not recognized by those in power.

Afterword: Jewish Law

Rose and Cover take a Jewish insight, about the centrality of law, and use it to stake out philosophical territory. For them, law goes all the way down not just for Jews but for everyone. In a way, Cover's interest in minority communities defined by their adherence to law cannot but be read as an interest in Jewish communities. However, Cover's position is inconclusive. He neither argues that the norms of minority communities should be unequivocally respected by the state nor that minority communities should unequivocally respect state norms. Perhaps Cover's response is even more Jewish than the problem: there must be never-ending, lively debate about the points of conflict, and this tension will involve interminable suffering that must be owned. While Rose wrote a book about Judaism, her interest there is to apply the same understanding of law that she is committed to in general to Jewish texts, combating the insularity and confusion she encounters in the Jewish community. Rose would fully endorse Cover's prescription for critical debate and acknowledgment of violence. Because she is focused on the individual navigating law and not on the laws of communities, Rose has relatively little to say about intergroup conflict. Her interest is in the pull that multiple groups have on an individual, on how those affiliations can be continuously suspended and reimagined. Indeed, Rose writes of her suspicion of "communitarian empowerment of 'ethnic' or gender pluralities" because naming such groups problematically fixes identity.[46] What she seems to mean is that particular care is needed to avoid such communities stilling the dynamic negotiation of concepts and experiences that makes for a vibrant life and for a vibrant social world. In particular, states should be especially cautious about granting rights to such groups and political engagement should not be motivated by advancing group interest. "Politics does not happen when you act on behalf of your own damaged good, but when you act, without guarantees, for the good of all—that is to take the risk of the universal interest."[47] This point remains underdeveloped in Rose's work. It seems that by the "universal," she does not mean something like all human beings; rather, she means something like a universal sense of justice. On this reading, she would not be endorsing any specific political forms. Political engagement would start with the political practices and institutions that exist and would mobilize around the injustices that they affect.

Recently Judith Butler has re-read a canon of modern Jewish thought and identified relationality as a shared principle underlying diverse philosophical projects.[48] She take relationality as found in the Jewish tradition to offer a message for philosophy and critical thought as a whole: indeed, she endorses and advances the view that relationality is constitutive of everyone's world. Butler argues that understanding relationality in this way destabilizes sovereignty, of state and self, encouraging new personal and political practices to develop that would otherwise be foreclosed. Cover and Rose share Butler's critical instinct, and they share her method of recovering a Jewish insight to fuel critique. They also share her conclusion that sovereignty of self and state is unsustainable, but for Cover and Rose this conclusion follows from a more foundational commitment. They see the world constituted by law, and they see violence inherent in this law. Claims to sovereignty do violence, but relationality offers no relief. Rose reminds us

46. Rose, *Mourning Becomes the Law*, 5.
47. Ibid., 62.
48. Butler, *Parting Ways*. As mentioned above, this is in contrast to Butler's earlier work where social norms were taken as foundational.

that the critical interrogation of law is necessary to address specific injustices without leading to still more injustice. Cover reminds us that a commitment to our convictions, to our sense of justice through law, often requires facing down the powers that be and risking our bodies and lives in the hope that the world will finally come to know a just law.

Bibliography

Brandom, Robert. "Freedom and Constraint by Norms." *American Philosophical Quarterly* 16, no. 3 (1979) 187–96.

———. "Some Pragmatist Themes in Hegel's Idealism: Negotiation and Administration in Hegel's Account of the Structure and Content of Conceptual Norms." *European Journal of Philosophy* 7, no. 2 (1999) 164–89.

Butler, Judith. *Gender Trouble: Feminism and the Subversion of Identity*. New York: Routledge, 1990.

———. *Parting Ways: Jewishness and the Critique of Zionism*. New York: Columbia University Press, 2012.

Cavanaugh, William T. *Theopolitical Imagination*. London: T & T Clark, 2002.

Cover, Robert M. *Justice Accused: Antislavery and the Judicial Process*. New Haven: Yale University Press, 1975.

———. *Narrative, Violence, and the Law: The Essays of Robert Cover*. Edited by Martha Minow, Michael Ryan, and Austin Sarat. Ann Arbor: University of Michigan Press, 1995.

Hart, H. L. A. *The Concept of Law*. Oxford: Clarendon, 1961.

Lloyd, Vincent W. *Law and Transcendence: On the Unfinished Project of Gillian Rose*. Houndmills, UK: Palgrave, 2009.

———. *The Problem with Grace: Reconfiguring Political Theology*. Stanford, CA: Stanford University Press, 2011.

———. "The Secular Faith of Gillian Rose." *Journal of Religious Ethics* 36, no. 4 (2008) 683–705.

Lloyd, Vincent W., ed. "Interview with Gillian Rose." *Theory, Culture, and Society* 25, nos. 7–8 (2008) 203–20.

McDowell, John. "Virtue and Reason." *Monist* 62, no. 3 (1979) 331–50.

Pickstock, Catherine. *After Writing: On the Liturgical Consummation of Philosophy*. Challenges in Contemporary Theology. Oxford: Blackwell, 1998.

Rose, Gillian. *The Broken Middle: Out of Our Ancient Society*. Oxford: Blackwell, 1992.

———. *Dialectic of Nihilism: Post-Structuralism and Law*. Oxford: Blackwell, 1984.

———. *Hegel contra Sociology*. London: Athlone, 1981.

———. *Judaism and Modernity: Philosophical Essays*. Oxford: Blackwell, 1993.

———. *Love's Work: A Reckoning with Life*. London: Chatto & Windus, 1995.

———. *Mourning Becomes the Law: Philosophy and Representation*. Cambridge: Cambridge University Press, 1996.

———. *Paradiso*. London: Menard, 1999.

"Tributes to Robert M. Cover." *Yale Law Journal* 96, no. 8 (1987) 1699–724.

Index

Abraham, 81–82
absolute, 16, 84, 113, 120–21, 127–28, 197
activity, 105
Adorno, Theodor, 10, 11, 55, 111, 112, 115–16, 118, 120–21, 122, 123, 127–29, 131, 145, 179, 187, 193n67
Agamben, Giorgio, 5
Antigone, 10, 12, 36, 77
Anywheres, 30, 44
apocalypticism, 222
aporia, 32, 54, 88, 113
Arendt, Hannah, 23
art, 136
Aristotle, 114, 163n43
Athens, Old, 9, 10, 31, 32, 33, 40
Auschwitz, 33–34
autonomy, 49, 50, 211, 212

Baldwin, James, 49
Barrington-Ward, Simon, 37
Benigni, Roberto, 78–79
bodies, 152–53, 154–55, 167, 171–72
bourgeois, 6–7, 69, 73, 136, 157, 162–64, 166, 168, 177, 183
Braudel, Fernand, 177
Brexit, 18, 19, 30
broken middle. *See* middle, the
Broken Middle, The (Rose), 4, 5, 6, 12, 17, 36, 38–39, 71, 79–80, 83, 177, 178, 192, 209
Butler, Judith, 225

Camelot, 217–18

capability, 94–95, 104
capital, 143–44, 161, 177, 183–84, 189–90
Christianity, 77, 168, 169, 171, 199, 202
Christology, 83–84
church and state. *See* religion: and state
city
    fourth, 33–34, 36
    ideal, 41
    judgment, 39
    material practices, 40
    and Milbank, 138–39
    and philosophy, 29–30
    religion, 44
    third, 19, 23–24, 31, 32–33, 34–35, 36
    See also Athens, Old; Auschwitz; Jerusalem, New
comedy, 19–20, 37, 67, 72, 76–79, 82–83, 85, 124
commodity, 156–60, 184–88
communitarianism, 40, 41, 43
concept, 136, 210
conscience, 147
consciousness, 49, 117
constant, 132
cosmopolitanism, 31
courts, 214
Cover, Robert, 22, 23, 203–5, 207, 211–13, 214–15, 216–17, 220, 221–26
critical theory, 2, 177, 180–84, 202, 216

cross, 170–71

Davis, Joshua, 22
Das Kapital (Marx), 161, 164, 167–68
Derrida, Jacques, 176
desire, 71–72, 73
despair, 96
Dialectic of Nihilism, 11, 12, 181, 207, 208
difficulty, 87, 88, 89–95
diremption, 11–13, 14, 18, 29
Disley, Liz, 52, 54
disrespect, 50
Drichel, Simone, 95
dualism, 80, 88, 138

economics, 35, 145
education, 20, 37–38, 118, 121, 123, 124, 158–59
Enlightenment, the, 90, 91
equivocality, 1, 3, 8, 177
Espinas, Georges, 149–50
ethics, 15, 16, 35, 81–82, 112, 127–29, 131, 139, 209, 210n19
euphoria, 90
Europe, 152–54
exclusive thought, 12–13

failure, 99–100
faith, 94, 219
fantasy, 216
feminism, 97n70
Feuerbach, Ludwig, 18, 127, 168
Fichte, Johann Gottlieb, 117, 144, 169
film, 83
formation, 37–38
Foster, Roger, 52n21
Frankfurt School, 6, 19, 55, 58n49, 176, 182, 202
freedom, 70, 77, 110, 158, 162–64, 196–97

gap, 32
German Idealism, 54
Girard, Rene, 19, 20, 67, 71–73, 79, 80, 81, 82, 83, 84–85

God, 16–17, 70, 74, 77, 80, 83–84, 110, 134–35, 146, 148, 171–72, 197–98
Goodhart, David, 30, 42, 43, 44, 45
Gorman, Tony, 6–7, 22, 111–12, 144, 180, 183, 187
grace, 102, 103, 199
grief, 56

Habermas, Jürgen, 61
halacha, 209
Harnack, Adolf von, 18
Hegel, Georg Wilhelm Friedrich
  absolute, 111, 112, 118, 120–21, 122, 123, 127–29, 131
  appropriation, 55
  art, 76, 81, 143
  Aufhebung, 119–20
  comedy, 19–20, 37, 76–78, 82–83, 85
  consciousness, 115
  economics, 145
  education, 158–59
  epic, 76–77
  ethics, 127–29, 131
  explicitness, 63
  forgiveness, 61
  freedom, 70, 77, 158, 163
  Geist, 190
  God, 146
  intellectual intuition, 117
  interpretations, 126
  and Kant, 68, 69–70, 82, 114, 143, 147–49, 155
  kenosis, 83–84
  labor, 159
  and Marx, 126–27, 144, 145, 156–57, 159–61, 162–63, 164, 168
  Natural Law, 68
  phenomenology, 130
  Phenomenology of Spirit, 50, 51, 75, 155–56
  Philosophy of Right, 163
  politics, 127, 129–30
  propositions, 121–22
  reason, 71
  recognition, 50, 51, 53, 55, 75, 92, 93, 105, 116–17, 118, 120, 121

reflection, 63
religion, 14–16, 51
  religion and state, 14–15, 17, 74, 109, 110, 122
  and Rose, 2, 3, 14, 17, 19–20, 21, 38, 40, 55, 67, 68, 70–71, 74, 75, 87–88, 92, 110, 113, 115, 116–17, 126–30, 132, 133, 135–36, 140, 144, 165, 166–67, 168, 182, 187, 208–9
  and Rowan Williams, 135
  Science of Logic, 119
  speculative, 8, 9, 10–11, 14–15, 74, 127, 181, 182
  sublation, 119–20
  Subject, 155, 159, 161
  sublime, 143–44, 147–49, 155
  substance, absolute, 143–44, 146–47, 155–56
  theology, 133, 135, 139–40, 141
  third city, 34
Hegel contra Sociology (Rose), 6, 14, 17, 18, 35, 71, 74, 109, 111–12, 114, 124, 126, 176, 177, 178, 181, 185
Heidegger, Martin, 130n12, 208, 216
Hill, Geoffrey, 103
Hobbes, Thomas, 68
Hoelzl, Michael, 61
Holocaust, 83
Home (Robinson), 58–61
Honneth, Axel, 50–51, 58, 61, 62, 63
hope, 220, 221–24
Howes, Rebekah, 20–21
humanity, 98
Hyman, Gavin, 21

identity formation, 49
idolatry, 198
imperfection, 101
infinite, 169
in-itself, 114–15, 116
intuition, 117, 136

Jeremiah, 35
Jerusalem, New, 9–10, 31, 32, 33, 40, 41
Johnson, Daniel, 34, 35

joy, 89, 95
Judaism, 22, 33, 202–3, 205–6, 209, 212, 219–20, 224–25
Judaism and Modernity (Rose), 30, 206
judge, 215–16, 221, 224
justice, 36, 49, 223

Kant, Immanuel, 11, 68, 69–70, 82, 109, 114–15, 117, 120, 122, 143, 144, 147–49, 155, 159, 165, 169, 209. *See also* neo-Kantianism
Keats, John, 94–95
Kierkegaard, Soren, 34, 67, 77, 80, 81–82, 101, 176
knowledge, 88, 90–91, 94
Kochi, Tarik, 93, 105
Kolakowski, Leszek, 54
Kortian, Garbis, 55n37
Kojève, Alexandre, 50

labor, 159, 162, 180, 186–87, 188–95
Landes, David, 150–51, 154
language, 134–35
Latz, Andrew Brower, 19
laughter, 72, 73, 79, 85
La Vita Bella, 78–79
law, 12, 13–14, 16, 22–23, 68–69, 79–80, 186, 203, 206, 207, 208–9, 211–15, 217–19, 220, 221–23, 224, 225–26
Law, Stephen, 76, 78
legality, 70
Le Goff, Jacaues, 150
Levinas, Emmanuel, 11, 12, 23
liberalism, 42
liberation theology, 4
Lloyd, Vincent, 5, 22–23, 99, 113, 140, 141
logic of the excluded middle, 115–16
Loick, Daniel, 61
Lonergan, Bernard, 199
loss, 101
Lough, Joseph, 21–22
love, 53, 99
Love's Work (Rose), 32, 37, 96, 101
Lukács, Georg von, 111, 144, 181–82, 184–85, 187, 188–95

Index

Luxemburg, Rosa, 23

MacIntyre, Alasdair, 40
Major, John, 5
Margarets, 100
Marple, Miss, 101–2, 176
Marx, Karl, 21, 22, 126–27, 144, 145–46, 156–57, 159–61, 162–63, 164, 167–68, 176, 177, 178–79, 180, 182, 185, 186–87, 188, 189, 190, 196
Marxism, 5, 6–8, 22, 111, 122, 145, 176, 179, 180, 181, 182, 183–84, 191, 194, 196, 198, 199
McCabe, Herbert, 198
mediation, 12, 57–58, 138–39
melancholy, 219, 220
metaphysics, 8, 31, 40, 45
method, 6–7
middle, the, 8–9, 10, 12, 45, 79–80, 113, 140–41, 184, 197, 209–10, 211
Milbank, John, 8, 12, 33, 55n36, 73, 80, 82, 137–38, 139, 140–41, 193n67
mimetic theory, 72, 73, 82
misrecognition. *See under* recognition
modernity, 9–10, 11–12, 110, 210
monastics, 150–51
morality, 70
mourning, 37, 56–57, 218–19
Mourning Becomes the Law (Rose), 31, 33, 34, 56
Murdoch, Irish, 64

narrative, 215, 217, 221
nation, 29
natural law, 68–70, 73
Naziism, 34
neo-Kantianism, 10, 19, 68, 109, 114, 120, 122, 124, 181
neoliberalism, 5–6
New Ethics, 33
nihilism, 12
"Nomos and Narrative" (Cover), 212, 214
novels, 58

Osborne, Peter, 6, 7, 13, 17, 21, 22, 112, 129, 130–32, 133, 144, 176, 178, 180–81, 183
Other, the, 31, 43

Paradiso (Rose), 89, 93, 96, 99–100, 101, 102, 208
particulars, 157–58
pathlessness, 92–93, 94
Paul, Apostle, 146–47, 170–71
phenomenology, 6–7, 22, 111
philosophy, 29, 31, 45, 55n37, 56–57, 68, 88, 89, 90, 114, 133–34, 153, 204, 218, 223
philosophy, French, 208–9
Phocion, 36
Pirenne, Henri, 149–50
politics
    and the city, 39
    ecclesial, 38
    and Hegel, 127, 129–30
    identity, 40–41, 43
    and metaphysics, 45
    political theology, 4–6, 7, 12, 18, 48–49, 110
    recognition, 61
    and religion, 18, 44, 111
    rights, 61
    secular, 38
populism, 30
postmodernism, 12, 91, 209
Postone, Moishe, 145, 151–52, 182n25, 188–95
Pound, Marcus, 19
Poussin, Nicolas, 211
praxis, 38, 89
property, 73, 119, 128, 136–37, 162–64, 166–67

Radical Orthodoxy, 37n18
reason
    autonomy, 54
    binaries, 8
    comic, 75
    Enlightenement, 90–91
    and Hegel, 71
    politics, 36–37
    postmodern, 91–92

practical, 70, 117
relational, 95, 103–4
repentance, 37
Rose, 90
self-limiting, 54, 55
speculative, 8, 9, 10–11, 13, 14–15, 38, 74, 127, 181, 182, 195
recognition
 appropriation, 48, 55, 56, 57
 civil society, 49–50, 51, 61, 62
 conflict, 51, 52
 cooperative, 48, 58, 61, 62, 62, 63, 64, 65
 family, 49, 61–62
 forgiveness, 53
 Hegel, 50, 51, 53, 55, 75, 92, 93, 105, 116–17, 118, 120, 121
 hyperrationalist, 52
 love, 53
 mediation, 57–58
 misrecognition, 13, 75, 96, 111, 116–17, 118, 119, 120, 123, 192–93
 mutual, 14, 62, 93
 political rights, 61
 reconciliation, 51
 reflection, 63
 relation, 98
 religion, 51, 52
 Rose, 13, 54, 56, 87, 90, 92–93, 97, 99, 105, 117
 self-relation, 57
 struggle, 50
 theology, 64–65
 theory, 19, 47–48, 49, 50, 51, 52, 63–64, 190–91
 triune, 117–18
recollection, 121
relation, 2–3, 19, 57, 79–80, 95, 98–99, 103–4, 225
religion
 and art, 136
 and Hegel, 14–16, 51
 Marxism, 198
 and politics, 18, 44, 111
 recognition, 51, 52
 and state, 14–17, 18, 50, 74, 109, 110, 113, 121, 122, 123, 196–97

See also theology
Robinson, David, 37n19
Robinson, Marilynne, 19, 58, 59, 61, 65
Rome, 146, 167, 185–86, 210n18
Rousseau, Jean Jacques, 29
Rowlands, Anna, 18–19

sacrifice, 71–72, 82
safe spaces, 42–43
Sartre, Jean-Paul, 50
scapegoat, 71–72
Scarry, Elaine, 220
Schelling, Friedrich Wilhelm Joseph von, 117
Schick, Kate, 20, 31–32, 52–53, 54, 113
Schmitt, Carl, 4–5
self-consciousness, 49
semikhah, 222
severe style, 81
Shanks, Andrews, 36, 80, 113, 138
singular, 35, 36, 45
Sittlichkeit, 37
social life, 2
social pathologies, 49
social theory, 10, 67, 68–73, 181
solidarity, 62
Somewheres, 30, 42, 44
sublime, 143–44, 147–49, 155, 156–60

Tanner, Kathryn, 195n68
Taylor, Mark C., 12, 33
Thatcher, Margaret, 5
theology, 37–38, 53, 54–55, 64–65, 133, 134, 135, 139–40, 141, 178n12, 195. *See also* religion
Thomas Aquinas, 154
tickling, 72, 73
time, 150–52, 154, 164
totality, 57n46, 144
tragedy, 67, 72, 78–79, 82–83, 85
transcendental account, 114
tree, 102–3, 104
Trump, Donald, 18, 19, 30
truth, 3, 119
Tubbs, Nigel, 111, 118–20, 121, 124

value, 163–64, 188–95
Van Pelt, Robert Jan, 34
Varnhagen, Rahel, 23, 24
violence, 23, 71–72, 73, 91n25, 137–38, 149, 216, 217, 218, 220, 221, 223, 224, 225–26
Vormärz (Marx), 162
vulnerability, 95, 97, 98–99, 105

Weber, Max, 144, 153n27
Weil, Simone, 102–3, 104
Williams, Rowan, 7, 8, 13, 19, 21, 37–39, 45, 83, 131–33, 134–35, 137, 139–41, 178, 184n33, 195n68, 197
Wittgenstein, Ludwig, 21, 133–34, 139–40
work, of Rose, 5, 112–13
working through, 56–57

Yovel, Yirmiyahu, 119

Žižek, Slavoj, 18, 20, 67, 74, 75, 84–85, 130n12

www.ingramcontent.com/pod-product-compliance
Lightning Source LLC
Chambersburg PA
CBHW020407230426
43664CB00009B/1224